To Steve,

Thank you for your encouragement!

SARAH

ONE CHILD

Do We Have a Right to More?

Sarah Conly

OXFORD
UNIVERSITY PRESS

Oxford University Press is a department of the University of
Oxford. It furthers the University's objective of excellence in research,
scholarship, and education by publishing worldwide.
Oxford is a registered trade mark of Oxford University Press in the UK and in certain
other countries

Published in the United States of America by Oxford University Press
198 Madison Avenue, New York, NY 10016, United States of America

© Oxford University Press 2016

Library of Congress Cataloging-in-Publication Data
Conly, Sarah.
One child : do we have a right to more? / Sarah Conly.
pages cm
Includes index.
ISBN 978–0–19–020343–6 (cloth : alk. paper) 1. Family size—Moral and ethical
aspects. 2. Population—Environmental aspects. 3. Conservation of natural
resources. I. Title.
HQ760.C65 2016
304.6'3—dc23
2015005671

1 3 5 7 9 8 6 4 2
Printed in the United States of America
on acid-free paper

If the earth must lose that great portion of its pleasantness which it owes to things that the unlimited increase of wealth and population would extirpate from it, for the mere purpose of enabling it to support a larger, but not a better or a happier population, I sincerely hope, for the sake of posterity, that they will be content to be stationary, long before necessity compels them to do it.

—John Stuart Mill, Principles of Political Economy

CONTENTS

Acknowledgments   *ix*

1. The Problem   1

2. The Right to a Family   32

3. The Right to Control Your Body   65

4. Sanctions   103

5. The Future   141

6. Unwanted Consequences   177

7. Conclusion: When?   217

Bibliography   233
Index   245

ACKNOWLEDGMENTS

I would like to thank the University of Chicago for allowing me to spend the 2013–2014 year there as a Fellow in Law and Philosophy, which gave me the opportunity to write this book and I also thank Bowdoin College for granting me leave. I am grateful for student and faculty comments at Harvard University, Princeton University, the University of Wyoming, Umeå University, the University of Chicago, Northwestern University, Davidson College, and Lone Star College. I would also like to thank my Bowdoin colleague Jack O'Brien for his great help. Finally, I owe an immeasurable debt to Aidan Penn, who corrected mistakes of every order. Remaining errors and misconceptions are entirely my own.

[1]

THE PROBLEM

The biggest impact a U.S. citizen can have on global environment problems, such as climate change, is having fewer children.

—David Biello, "Human Population Reaches
7 Billion—How Did This Happen, and Can It Go On?"
Scientific American, October 28, 2011

Despite investments in energy efficiency and cleaner energy sources in the United States, in Europe and in developing countries like China, annual emissions of greenhouse gases have risen almost twice as fast in the first decade of this century as they did in the last decades of the 20th century. This places in serious jeopardy the emissions target agreed upon in Rio to limit warming to no more than 2 degrees Celsius (3.6 degrees Fahrenheit) above the preindustrial level. Beyond that increase, the world could face truly alarming consequences. Avoiding that fate will require a reduction of between 40 percent and 70 percent in greenhouse gases by midcentury, which means embarking on a revolution in the way we produce and consume energy.

That's daunting enough, but here's the key finding: The world has only about 15 years left in which to begin to bend the emissions curve downward.

—Editorial Board, *New York Times*, "Running Out of Time,"
April 20, 2014

I'm going to argue here that we don't have a right to more than one biological child. At this point in time, when the world around us is in so much danger from environmental degradation, doing just as our parents did—having as many children as we happen to want—is no longer viable. Given the numbers we have now, it's just not an acceptable option. We are threatened with more population than the planet can bear, and while the future is never certain, the best thing to do when great danger threatens is take steps to avoid it. This is especially true when the danger is something like overpopulation, because that's the kind of danger that isn't certain until it's too late to fix.

What does it mean to say we have no right to have more than one child? The limitation to one child means that two people who procreate should limit themselves to one child between them. This, it is true, is less than replacement value—the population will become smaller and smaller, so naturally this isn't a course we'd want to follow forever. I will argue below, though, that it is the course we need to follow now, and until we have reduced our population to a sustainable number.

To say we don't have a right to do this means a number of things. It recognizes that, as I will argue in Chapter 2, we don't have a fundamental interest in having more than one child. That is, having more than one child isn't something we need to live at least a minimally decent life. It's possible that we don't really need any biological child at all to lead a minimally decent life, but if we do, we certainly don't need more than one. We often say that if someone has a fundamental interest in doing something they have a claim on us to let them do that no matter what the costs, but having lots of children just isn't that kind of thing.

Of course, there are other kinds of rights. Often we say we have a right to choose how to live, even when those individual choices don't reflect our fundamental interests—that's why we can have a right to do things that may be downright bad for us, if that's what is consistent with our own considered choices. This right to choose one's way of living, though, is limited by the harm it does to others. We can certainly exercise rights in ways that are somewhat costly to others, but not to the point where we are doing devastating harm. In Chapter 3, I will argue that in these days, there is a sufficient probability that unlimited procreation will be devastating, and so our right to choose our way of living just doesn't extend to having more than one child.

And, since I support the view that we have no moral right to have more than one child, I will also argue that government legislation to limit how many children we have can be morally permissible. It depends, of course, on exactly what the government does: certain state actions would violate our rights no matter what the reason for them (say, torture for wrongdoing). I will argue, though, that while it would certainly be better if we could reach population goals solely through voluntary actions, there are restrictions that government can appropriately implement if voluntary efforts fall short. There are, of course, other methods that we can promote, and if they work, we need do no more. Economic development generally lowers the fertility rate.[1] Access to contraception generally lowers the fertility rate. If these prove sufficient, so much the better. If they are not enough, though, then it is the role of the state to protect us, both those of us now living and those who will live in the future. This is controversial, but I will argue that it is consistent with what we actually think is just and fair.

There are a number of claims I am not making here. I am not arguing that those in the past or the present who have more than one child are blameworthy. Some of the dangers we face now couldn't have been foreseen by people in the past.[2] And now that it is dangerous, many people don't know this, and many people don't have the means to avoid pregnancy even if they knew it was dangerous. Rather than blaming people, we need to educate people, and where they don't have the means to control procreation, we need to help them so that they have the wherewithal to do that.

Nor am I arguing about what we have a legal right to do. What legal rights we have depends on what the law is, and laws can be changed and frequently are changed. In light of new circumstances, new information, and new moral beliefs we alter our laws to better reflect our needs and our values. And, of course, the laws we already have are subject to interpretation. Others have written on whether American law as it now stands allows limiting procreation, and I won't be discussing that.[3] I will be talking about what the law should be if it is to reflect moral rights, the rights of prospective parents but also those others who are or will be members of society.

Last, I am a philosopher, not a demographer, a statistician, an economist, or an environmental scientist. While I use reliable and up-to-date sources for facts, I don't do my own research in any of these areas. My argument is about what is morally permissible, when and if overpopulation threatens. I do think that it threatens now, but if it does not, and we will only need to worry about this in the future, the question about what rights we do and don't have is still pertinent: this is a book about what morality requires if and when we are threatened with a population that will cause devastating environmental harm. Again, I think we need to worry about this now, but even if this is not true, it is something we need to consider so that in the future we can determine our policies while knowing what our rights and obligations are.

DISCUSSING DIFFICULT QUESTIONS

If we continue to let the population grow in the way that it has, we will leave future humans with lives vastly inferior to our own, if they are able to eke out a living at all.[4] This hasn't gone unnoticed. The number of people we have, combined with our rate of consumption, is already bad—more people at anything like the present rate of consumption will be a disaster. But while many people have offered suggestions as to how to cut back on the consumption of material goods, and how to reduce the amount of greenhouse gases and other pollution that we release into the air, the idea of requiring limits on procreation has not been popular. That government might restrict how many children we have is not generally promoted.

The reasons for this are various. First, it is enormously unpopular with those who rely on public opinion for their support. Politicians don't like to offend voters, on whom they depend. Much as politicians hate to suggest that we might have to cut back on our rate of consumption—much as they have difficulty backing even mild measures, like increasing automobile efficiency—they hate much, much more raising a topic that will be a red flag, population control. Even environmental advocacy groups have avoided discussing it, despite the obvious relevance to environmental protection.[5]

Second, the idea of suggesting that people don't have a right to have just as many children as they want seems deeply contrary to ideals that many cherish. To some, such a suggestion is against basic principles of religion; to some, it cuts against the privacy of the home; to some, it is incompatible with the principles of personal autonomy that justify democracy.

Bill McKibben, in his charming and humane *Maybe One,* argues that while it is best for the environment and for future humans that many of us have no children, or at most one child, government should not get involved.[6] McKibben is optimistic about human nature, and thinks that enough people will be sensitive to the moral arguments against procreation that they will make up for those who have more than one or two children. Even if this turns out to be true, which I, less impressed by the generosity of human nature than McKibben, tend to doubt, I think there is a question of whether it is the most fair way to approach population limits. (See Chapter 2.) For McKibben, as important as it is to limit population growth, government intervention in family size would be "repugnant."[7] In her more recent *Why Have Children?* Christine Overall reaches the same conclusion that McKibben argued for in 1998.[8] She thinks we have a moral responsibility to limit procreation because of the "global dangers" of not doing so, but says, "I am NOT suggesting that this reproductive limit be LEGALLY required or enforceable or that its violation be legally punishable"[9] (emphasis hers), as such restrictions, she later writes, would be "unconscionable."[10] What we should do if people fail to live up to their moral responsibility she does not suggest. Naomi Klein, while excoriating the environmental harm we are doing through current practices of consumption, says population reduction is a "moral dead end."[11]

Of course, we would all agree that if we don't need to force people to limit reproduction, we shouldn't. At the same time, we generally think a global danger merits some sort of enforceable restriction on people, if that is the only way it can be averted. The fact that it is painful, or even repugnant, to think about doesn't actually excuse us from thinking about it, given our options. Instead, we need to think about how to make it as painless, as little repugnant, and as respectful of individuals as possible, if we do have to cross that bridge.

BACKGROUND: POPULATION AND THE ENVIRONMENT

We're familiar with the facts: the word population reached 7 billion in 2011. And we know that this has been an extraordinarily rapid rise: the size of the world population increased during the 19th and 20th centuries from approximately 1 billion in 1825 to 7 billion in 2011. And, the greater the number of people the rapider the increase will be: according to the 2012 "medium" projection of the United Nations, by as soon as 2050 the world will have 9.6 billion people. But that's a relatively optimistic forecast: the same report says that the number could be higher, depending largely on population policies for the next few years—policies it's up to us, as members of society, to determine.[12]

And as we read every day, this high population has resulted in environmental damage: the amount of carbon dioxide in the atmosphere is higher than it has ever been (but not higher than it will be),[13] and the climate is accordingly changing; species are lost at a greater rate than they've ever been; the polar ice cap is melting, and glaciers are melting, the sea level's rising, and, at the same time climate change and local use patterns have produced droughts and water shortages. Meanwhile, even without global warming our numbers create shortages of some basic foods: fishing stocks drop dangerously because of overfishing, and as we use corn to supplement our diminishing supply of fossil fuels, the price of corn for eating goes up. While globally there is plenty of food, under our present pattern of population growth and consumption the need for food can be expected to increase drastically in the future: 40% by 2030, 70% by 2050.[14] Even if we can meet the overall global demand, in individual locations a lack of food (due both to growing population and to climactic change resulting in drought) is expected to produce starvation conditions.[15] (And recently, the United Nations' Intergovernmental Panel on Climate Change has raised doubts about the ability to satisfy global food demand.)[16] The places we live in change, and for the worse; droughts wipe out farmland, topsoil is lost almost at rates 10 to 40 times faster than it is replaced, resulting in a loss of almost 37,000 square miles a year of cropland.[17] (Americans may be pleased to know that their loss is less than that of some places. However, some of the hardest-hit places are those we regard as the heart of the agricultural region, including Iowa.)[18] Meanwhile, megacities grow without the means to make them run efficiently, resulting in huge slum populations living without water or waste disposal (unless we act, "the slum population worldwide is likely to grow annually by 6 million every year . . . to reach a total of 889 million by 2020" (114)).[19] Heat waves increase, and are felt particularly acutely in these growing urban centers.[20] We run short of fossil fuels and of minerals, including the uranium for the nuclear energy that might serve as a substitute for fossil fuels.[21] Shortages, and the prospect of future shortages, result in political unrest, and as we know well, in war. If the population grows enough, these things will only get worse: however careful we may be, we will use up our resources. It's just inevitable.

We know all this—it's in the papers every day. We know that unchecked growth in our numbers will destroy the planet in some sense and will make the lives of future humans, as Thomas Hobbes might have said, poor, nasty, brutish, and very likely short. But they will not be, as Hobbes described life in the uncivilized state of nature, solitary: they will be lives in which we are very, very crowded.[22]

If, on the other hand, we have a sufficiently small population, we can avoid many of these ills. Some resources are sustainable: that is, if we use them at a slow enough rate, we don't need to run out of them, because they can be replenished—water, for example, and topsoil, and fisheries and other foodstuffs. This isn't true of everything, of course: if we continue to use fossil fuels, we will run out of them. They are finite and nonrenewable. However, if we use them at a sufficiently slower rate, we can avoid most of the effects of global warming that arise from their use, which will in turn diminish many of our other losses. There is a certain rate of carbon dioxide emissions that the atmosphere can accommodate, when combined with natural carbon dioxide "sinks" (such as the rain forest).[23] And of course, with fewer people, solar and wind could supply a greater percentage of our energy needs.

Why do some of us doubt the need for fewer people? For one thing, it's just generally difficult for us to face change. It's hard to believe that what we've always done with impunity can in fact be bad for us. We see how difficult it is to modify our diet to include more vegetables and less sugar, or to switch to driving a more fuel-efficient car, and those are things by which we benefit ourselves, and relatively quickly. For thousands of years, growing population seemed to bring benefits—a growing nation was seen as a healthy nation. And individually, the birth of babies has been celebrated as one of the finest moments of our lives, and without any feeling that our personal joy might conflict with the good of others. On the contrary, having a baby has been an intense personal joy that, happily, also helped build a growing, thriving society. Given this, we naturally tend to think that what has been so very good in the past will continue to be good in the future, even when the evidence is against that.

And we've heard at least a few people cry wolf. Thomas Malthus is almost as famous today for being wrong in his predictions about population as for his foresightedness in thinking about it at all. In the 18th century, Malthus wrote his *Essay on the Principle of Population*, which argued that growing population would result in lower wages and higher food prices, until such point that "distress" over lack of food would drive people to refrain from marrying and having children. He was wrong: along with the rising population we have had improvements in agricultural technology, so that many of us have more food than they had in Malthus's day, rather than less. Then, in 1968, Paul Ehrlich similarly predicted a population "bomb" that would result in massive starvation in the 1970s, an alarming forecast that proved to be quite false.[24] On the contrary, in the developed world we are suffering from an obesity epidemic, and while local areas may suffer from a lack of food, this is a problem of uneven distribution, rather than a global lack of food. These failures comfort us. When we know that there have been false predictions in the past, and when a new prediction is one we really don't want to believe, we tend to take refuge in a general skepticism that allows us to avoid thinking about danger—in the same way, perhaps, that some people continue to deny the reality of climate change because it means we need to make "inconvenient" changes to our ways of living.

Third, we have some grounds for optimism when it comes to population. As things are now going, some parts of the globe (especially the United States, western Europe, Japan, and a few other countries) have undergone a decline in birth rate. From 2005 to 2010, 47% of the world population had a total fertility rate of less than 2.1 children per woman.[25] (The fertility rate is the average number of children a woman has over her lifetime.) In the United States, for example, it has dropped pretty much to replacement value: that is, on average, two children per two parents. Many people hope that this trend will spread worldwide, and hope that if it does, environmental catastrophe will be avoided simply by letting people make the personal choices they naturally want to. We don't really need to think about rights and obligations when there's no conflict between what we ought to do and what we want to do.

None of this means we shouldn't be thinking about what might be needed, though. The fact that it's difficult to change our way of thinking is a problem we deal with every day when we get new information, especially when it's information we don't want to accept. Changing takes a lot of education and a lot of determination, but of course it is possible, if we steel ourselves to do it. And, as I will discuss in Chapter 5, it's certainly true that Malthus was wrong, but it's lazy thinking to conclude that if Malthus was wrong in his particular prediction about population size, population size can never be a problem. Avoiding a topic because it's unpleasant, or requires changing our ideas, or because someone once said something false about it isn't something we want to let ourselves do if we want to solve problems.

The fact that the fertility rate has been falling in some places is relevant, though. However, it's also complicated. Even if the birth rate drops, there is something called "demographic momentum" that means the population will continue to rise for a long time. Even though the fertility rate has dropped for 47% of us, and even assuming that it remains at that relatively low rate, the population will continue to grow for another 40 years, as those who are young go on to have their own children.[26] When there is a large number of young people who reproduce their own replacement value, that obviously increases the population for quite a long time—we can't stop growth on a dime, which is why we need to plan ahead.

And although the birth rate has dropped in some parts of the world, in others it has not, and we don't yet know if it will. One-fifth of the world's present population lives in places where the total fertility rate is closer to four children per woman than to two.[27] The United Nations' estimation of future population growth is based on the assumption that the present decline in birth rates seen in some parts of the world will spread to other parts of the world, so that these places will experience a decline in their birth rate, but of course this is as yet uncertain. It will depend, in part, on what we do to support it: there is a huge unmet need for contraception in many parts of the world, and if this need continues to be unmet, we cannot expect the decline in birth rate that we have experienced in the United States and Europe.

This will require a fair amount of change. West Africa, for example, has some of the highest fertility rates, and typically it requires an increase in contraceptive use of 15% to reduce fertility by one birth per woman. If the pace of change in use observed between 1991 and 2004 is maintained, it will take 25 years for fertility in West Africa to a fall from its 2000–2005 level of births from 5.6 to 4.6 births.[28] This will take a certain political will on the part of all concerned, including the will to spend money: there are some 222 million women now who would like to have reliable contraception, but don't.[29] Of course, the longer we delay, the more people there will be who want it, and the more it will cost to meet everyone's needs.

Furthermore, even in those places where the birth rate has dropped, we don't know if that will continue. Birth rates are sensitive to economic pressure: kids cost a lot, and when people are low in funds they tend to have fewer of them. We know that the birth rate dropped during the Great Depression, but not much later we had the baby boom. Both the Pew Research Center and the Max Planck Institute, eminently reputable institutions, have found that the most recent drop in the United States and Europe is a function of the recession, and of unemployment in particular.[30] As the economy improves, we can expect people to have more children. We already see evidence for this: the *New York Times* reports reports:

> The sharp decline in the country's fertility rate during the economic downturn has come to an end, federal data show, as an improving economy encouraged Americans to resume having babies. The number of babies born in the United States in 2012 remained flat, the first time in five years that the number did not significantly decline, according to the National Center for Health Statistics. The leveling off capped a 9% decline in the fertility rate from 2007 to 2011, a drop that demographers say began after the recession took hold and Americans started feeling less secure about their economic circumstances.
>
> The decline "has come pretty close to grinding to a halt," said Carl Haub, a demographer with the Population Reference Bureau, a nonprofit research group.[31]

Last, dropping the birth rate to replacement numbers at this point is probably not enough to save the earth, and the people on it, from environmental degradation. We're doing plenty of harm with the population we have: continuing with this population will, all things being equal, produce at least as much harm as we already have wreaked, and the effects of such harm are cumulative. We need to think how best to encourage fewer than two children per couple—how best to encourage, as long as it is necessary, having just one child.

For this we want to be in a position to address not only the prac-
ticalities but the rights and obligations that are involved. The fact
that we can't be sure exactly what the future holds doesn't lessen
this requirement. One of the biggest moral questions, after all,
is what obligations we have when outcomes are uncertain: what
is our duty when we can't be sure how much we can help? So it is
not time to sit back and relax. Without a discussion of population,
and what people have a right to in terms of procreation, birth rates
may vary according to the vicissitudes of culture or the economy,
rather than with regard to the carrying capacity of the planet. We
need to know what our rights are, and what our obligations are, in
order to make a reasonable decision as to what to do.

CONSUMPTION

There are those who think we don't need to think about population if we focus, instead, on reducing patterns of consumption.
This is reasonable—up to a point. We do need to cut back on consumption of resources. If we didn't consume so much, we wouldn't
use up resources so quickly, and some of our resources could be
used sustainably. And it seems as if this shouldn't be too difficult.
We know that many of us consume way more than we need. Many
in the Western world as well as in some parts of Asia are consuming more per person than has ever happened in the history of the
world, and it is reasonable to believe that such consumption could
be reduced without any great sacrifice. After a certain point, consumption produces diminishing marginal returns: the more you
consume, the less satisfaction you get from each new act of consumption. It's a huge step from having no shelter at all to having a
house, but the step from a very big house to a very, very big house

seems to provide only fleeting satisfaction—which may be why people may feel driven to shore up their fading contentment by buying a very, very, *very* big house. A lot of our accumulation of goods in the Western world is based not so much on material need as on the desire to maintain a certain social status. Status is for most of us an important part of a satisfactory life, but basing status on what things we own involves us in a never-ending possessions race that doesn't yield the lasting self-esteem we want. Without the need to keep up with the Joneses we could relax and do something more fulfilling. And, of course, reducing some sorts of consumption would be good for many of us in other ways, since eating less generally, and less meat in particular, and walking and biking instead of driving, would greatly benefit our health. So at first glance, cutting back on consumption is a win-win proposition.

Unfortunately, while true as far as it goes, this reasoning is incomplete. First, when we speak of excess consumption, we speak only of one part of the world. Elsewhere in the world, 1.3 billion people live in what is termed "absolute poverty": on less than $1.25 a day.[32] This existence on very little money translates into very little food, and very little overall consumption of material goods. This is abject, dehumanizing poverty. Obviously, we cannot expect such people to cut back on their use of resources.[33] On the contrary, we can only hope that they will consume considerably more: we have, if anything, an obligation to help them, not hinder them, in their quest for better material welfare. But of course, as they achieve more acceptable levels of comfort, they use more resources. Charitable institutions often rightly stress that the best response to hunger is not the funds or food we can supply in a crisis, but the development of a healthy local economy that supplies both employment and goods. This is certainly true, but it is also true that this healthy economy will use up many more resources per person. How much more will depend on what level of consumption they reach, but experience indicates that those in developing nations tend to aspire to the unsustainable consumption level exemplified at present by the United States. One cannot blame people for wanting what other people, no more deserving than themselves, have been able to enjoy. While such a desire is not blameworthy, it nonetheless suggests a very dangerous increase in consumption. It is probably literally impossible for the whole world to live at the rate of consumption the richer nations now enjoy, but it's not impossible we might do a huge amount of damage while trying.

And, these poorest countries often have the highest birth rates, so the increased levels of consumption will be spread through a rising population, at least in the short run. (In the long run, development results in lower birth rates.) Again, this is not an argument that the poor should stay poor: such inequality is morally untenable, and in the long run probably practically untenable as well. It's an argument that a significant portion of the globe *should* consume much more than it now does.

This is one reason that cutting back on consumption, as vital as it is for those of us who grossly overconsume, cannot cure all our ills. Second, even if those of us who are the most conspicuous consumers do cut back on our consumption of goods, each child we have is likely to more than outweigh whatever cutbacks we have made. Even if we drive less, and drive hybrid cars, and live in relatively modest houses, introducing another consumer of goods is a net loss to resources.[34] Our children will want their own Priuses and their own (heated!) houses, their own electronics and well-maintained roads and schools, and their children will want their own Priuses and their own houses, and so forth.

Children would be a less of a strain on the environment, of course, if we cut back really radically in the way we live. Perhaps if we had children in a setting in which we had given up fossil fuels altogether, and reduced our furniture, clothes, and food consumption to closer to medieval levels, we would use no more than could be replaced, even if the population continued to increase for a while. No one is going to do that, though. It would introduce an enormous amount of labor that we are very happy to have escaped, and we're not going back if we can help it. We're happy to recycle our lunch bags two or three times, when we actually remember to do that. Change, when that change is easy to do and has no real effect on our comfort, is relatively acceptable. (I say relatively, because the truth is that while they may agree with it in theory, even now most people don't choose the most efficient cars, or the most efficient light bulbs, or make other easy changes.) Giving up on the technologies that actually do make a substantial difference to our general ease just doesn't seem likely.

Experience shows that while we aren't willing to cut back on consumption, we are willing to reduce the number of children we have. We know this, because in places where contraception is culturally acceptable and readily available, the fertility rate has been, as we have seen, dropping. This may be because in households where both parents work, having children seems more and more difficult: working two jobs leaves very little time for childcare. Or, it may be in some cases that, even where time is not so short we don't think it's worth the costs. Some people—maybe a lot of people—would just rather have a more comfortable lifestyle than a larger family. This may strike us as a shocking thought, put so baldly, but certainly we find people arguing that they cannot afford more children when what they mean is that they cannot afford them without some sacrifice to their lifestyle. Or, more generously, it may be that people want to have fewer children in order to give each child they do have more advantages. Whatever the reason, we know that reducing the fertility rate is something we actually are willing to do, since a good number of people have done it voluntarily. It may, then, be a more immediately successful area of focus than large, immediate reductions in consumption, even though reducing fertility sounds much more shocking. At the very least, it's not something that is deeply contrary to present practice.

Given all this, it makes sense that we should think now about whether it can be morally permissible to interfere in human procreation through state regulations as to family size, or whether that impermissibly infringes on human rights. It is certainly to be hoped that the population will become smaller more naturally, and remain at a sustainable level, without anyone feeling that they are being forced to sacrifice what they want for the sake of other people's welfare. But since we can't count on this, we need to consider the arguments for and against an unlimited right to have children. Even if it is consumption and population in combination that pose our present danger, that doesn't mean we're justified in having more children than the system can bear. Contributing either part of the destructive combination is wrong, even if they're only harmful together. A match by itself might not burn down a building—it might take both a match and gasoline. If you know someone is dousing that building in gasoline, though, and you still throw that match on it, you've done wrong.

CHAPTER OUTLINE

Chapters 2 and 3: Rights

It's been widely said, including in the United Nations Declaration of Human Rights, that we have a moral right to procreate, and that this should be reflected in our laws. Perhaps we do. The question, though, is whether a right to procreate gives us a right to procreate just as many times as we might want. One hundred and sixty countries have signed a covenant saying that citizens have a right to food, but this is not taken to be a right to Roman banquets every night—it's a right to be able to access enough food to meet our nutritional needs.[35] The right to work, also enumerated in the Universal Declaration of Human Rights, doesn't mean a right to the best job, or to lots of jobs at once. All these rights have limited scope. Why think our right to procreation should be unlimited?

In Chapters 2 and 3, I will discuss the right to have children, and will argue that even if there is a right to procreate, it is not unlimited. There are bases for legitimate rights claims, and I will argue that when we look at the right to have children, the reasons that underlie that right don't extend to having whatever number of children you may happen to want—don't, indeed, extend to having more than one per person. Having a need for something in order to live a decent life may ground a right, but even if producing a child is essential (for some people) to have a decent life, you don't need multiple children for that. You don't need to have a lot of kids to get the benefits of childbearing—small families aren't inferior to big ones. And, as I will discuss in Chapter 3, while your general right to control your body gives you a right to make a lot of personal choices without intervention, it doesn't give you a right to make choices that inflict serious harms upon others. If we are in a context where unrestricted childbearing is likely to ruin the lives of others, you don't have a right to do that. You don't have a right to act in that way even when you mean no harm by it, even when you are only one of many inflicting the harm, and even when it is a matter of religion.

Chapter 4: Sanctions

In Chapter 4, I will discuss the different strategies we can employ to encourage population limits. We want methods that are effective, that have as few costs as possible (including psychological costs), and that are consistent with other rights held by the individual. While I will argue that government restrictions, complete with (appropriate) sanctions, can be morally acceptable, it would be nicer all around if people voluntarily limited procreation. We need, for one thing, education. In addition, we can make the use of contraception more attractive by making it cheaper and easier to get. We could also provide further incentives such as tax breaks for those who have only one child, or conversely, tax penalties for those who have more. And, if necessary, we can simply make a law requiring that people limit themselves to one child.

This last is, of course, the most controversial. Government interference in how many children we have seems fraught with dangers. For most people, the idea of restrictions on how many children you can have immediately conjures up pictures of China, and the fear of forced sterilizations and forced abortions, and we might well prefer to leave decisions in the hands of (even flawed) individuals rather than to give the state the power to abuse our rights in the pursuit of even a good social goal.

However, state interference doesn't have to mean rights will be abused. The fact that forced abortions and sterilizations are wrong doesn't mean that all state constraints on childbearing are wrong. It means there are ways of regulating childbearing that are immoral. Even if you don't have the right to have as many children as you may want, you have the right to be treated decently. That doesn't mean you can't be sanctioned at all. Sanctions need to discourage dangerous behavior, but without violating the rights of those who have acted wrongly. In this chapter I will discuss ways of discouraging population growth that are effective but at the same time respectful of human rights.

Chapter 5: The Future

However, even if the government can constrain how many children you have without violating rights, there is a question whether it is its business to do that. One thing that is always true is that the future isn't here yet. This raises a number of issues that are relevant when we are deciding what people should be allowed to do. Typically, when we decide whether the government should interfere in someone's actions, we do this by looking at the costs and the benefits to those concerned. You want to have a great party with really loud music, but you have many close neighbors who don't want to be bombarded with Queen. Laws are made that strive to be balanced—you can play music loud enough that it can be heard outside your house, but only up to a certain number of decibels. We give reasonable consideration to the desires of all concerned. But how much do we have to sacrifice for people who aren't actually there? Most of the people who will benefit from our restraining how many children we have don't actually exist yet, and many people question whether we can have an obligation to nonexistent people.

Now, this issue of future people can be exaggerated, because it's clear that environmental degradation is not simply something that is going to happen in the future: it is happening now, and already affects some people in very dire ways. As luck would have it, it so far especially affects people in nonindustrialized nations who have had no part in bringing it about, which in itself should convince us that we already have an obligation to change our ways, regardless of our effect on those in the future. According to a recent report by the World Bank, Bangladesh, which is insignificant on a global scale in the production of greenhouse gases, will be one of the first to be badly hit: it's already experiencing worse flooding than previously, and experts agree that it is threatened by much worse in the way of floods, cyclones, rising sea levels, and very high temperatures.[36] As we know, many of the small island nations are also threatened, also without having done anything close to what Americans and western Europeans have done to cause the harm they will end up suffering. So this is a present harm. And some of the people who aren't yet affected by environmental change are alive now, and will be affected in their lifetime, as drought, heat waves, shortages of fish stocks, growth of slums, and so on, increase, and reduction in the birth rate could help these people avoid suffering that will otherwise occur. So, even without regarding future generations, we would have a case at least for making changes whose effect can be felt in the next 80 years or so.

Still, it must be admitted that some of the most dire effects of population and environmental degradation will be felt in generations as yet unborn, and this raises issues that don't arise when governments engage in more typical trade-offs between individuals. We would be giving something up for people who don't yet exist, who don't yet have rights, and with whom we certainly can't be said to have any reciprocal agreements.

To some, this is straightforward enough: they will say that of course we owe it to future generations to provide them with the basic wherewithal for a good existence: if not the same advantages we ourselves had, at least something close. This is more obviously true if we can do that without great sacrifice. To others, though, the idea that I can now have an obligation to someone who doesn't exist yet seems absurd. In Chapter 5, I will discuss the peculiar moral problems that are attached to acting for the sake of the future. I will argue that it's reasonable to think future people do have a claim on us. In particular, they have a claim on our government, because it is the role of the government to preserve the welfare of the state, and that means it has an obligation to promote the well-being not only of present individuals but those who will come later. "Après nous, le déluge" is not an acceptable philosophy of state action. We don't think the government should be allowed to act in a way that condemns our (even unborn!) grandchildren, and that also holds true for those who come even later.

Chapter 6: Unwanted Consequences

So far, then, in Chapters 1–5, I will have discussed the right to have children (Chs. 2–3), and second, whether state interference in how many children we have can be justified (Chs. 4–5). In Chapter 6, we will look not simply at theory but at practice, and in particular at unwanted consequences that might occur if people took seriously an obligation to have fewer children for the sake of those to come.

The Economy
One dire prediction is that the economy will collapse if we don't have an ever-increasing population: that economic growth is required for a healthy economy, and that a growing population is required for economic growth. Others, though, argue that for a healthy economy to be predicated on constantly increasing population is eventually self-defeating. Running out of resources is itself a pretty dead-certain impediment to economic growth, so we might as well acknowledge that continued population growth isn't something we can rely on forever as the foundation

of a healthy economy. Given this, some thinkers are naturally trying to think of new models. We need to design a steady-state economy—one that is prosperous without growth. We will look at the argument that it is possible, and necessary, to achieve prosperity without an endless increase in the number of consumers. Failing to investigate economic models that don't require this kind of population increase is shortsighted, to put it most charitably, and once again, the time to explore new models for the economy is before the one we are in has fallen under the weight of its own requirements.

Cultural Survival
There has also been pressure for local population growth in places where the fertility rate has dropped radically, on the grounds that the survival of a culture depends on producing more children. Sometimes this is put as a national interest, as in Russia, where Vladimir Putin has put out a plea for Russians to produce more children. The issue more generally, though, is not about the survival of a nation-state as a governmental entity (since national population numbers can often be buoyed by immigration) but about the survival of a particular kind of person, persons who carry forward a cultural project that may be seen as essential to the survival of an ethnic group. I will argue, though, that some cultural change is inevitable and not in itself a bad thing, and that in any case, the survival of a culture does not depend on a particular kind of baby being born in a particular location.

Sex Selection
Many people fear that a reduction in the numbers of children would result in sex selection—fewer baby girls than baby boys through elective embryo implantation, abortions, or even infanticide. The

fear is that if people can only have one child, they will too often choose for that child to be a boy.

This is a complicated issue. It is certainly true that we don't want to promote either sexism or a disproportion in the numbers of women. On the other hand, there is sex selection even in places that don't have a one-child policy. The basic problem is the sexism that creates discrimination against women. As it happens, the status of women generally rises as they have fewer children—they are able to work more hours outside the home, and while there is nothing intrinsically more worthwhile about working outside the home than staying in the home and taking care of children, the truth is it pays better, and better pay results in better social status and greater individual empowerment. When women have a better economic and social status, parents have less incentive to choose to have boys. The effects of having fewer children, then, are mixed. We will see that there are steps we can take to counter prejudice against girls that would work even in a society that does have a one-child policy. And, in the long run, we will see that what we need to do to improve the status of women is to attack the root causes of preference for boys, and if we do address that, the number of children a person has won't dictate any sex preference.

Siblings

Is it bad to be an only child? Do children have a right to siblings? Do we have an obligation to provide a child with siblings he or she can grow up with?

Many people still have the belief that only children are both unfortunate and, very often, morally inferior: lonely, but also selfish and self-centered. Newer research, though, shows that there is nothing inherently unfortunate, much less morally inferior, about being an only child. Not surprisingly, the happiness and the character of only children depend primarily on the way parents interact with them. And, of course, it will make a difference whether a child is an only child in a society that is structured around multichild families, or in one that is designed around one-child families. With a general social change, we can restructure our only kids' social lives to make them maximally rewarding, and without the prospect of the losses that overpopulation would bring.

Chapter 7: When?

Last, we need to think about when we want to implement such changes, and when would be the right time to relax—that is, when we will have reached a sustainable population. This, of course, depends both on our beliefs about facts and about values: will voluntary restraint become widespread? How quickly? Will government interference be necessary? What do we project in terms of depletion of our resources? In terms of climate change? And what is it that we are trying to avoid? A lack of fuel? A lack of food and water? The end of solitude? The end of wilderness? The disappearance of species?

The worst-case scenario is cataclysmic climate change, resulting in death and destruction, and condemning those unfortunate enough to be born after us to lives that will be much worse than our own. This, it seems to me, would clearly be an unacceptable moral imposition on others, and would justify our restraining our own actions. But some will argue (and I would agree with them) that additional values should play a role in our decision-making. Many people think that we should consider, for example, qualities of enjoyment other than the misery that complete ecological collapse would bring about. Even where we have sufficient material well-being to get by, what about the experience of nature, and of wilderness, and of solitude? More speculatively, what about the value of species in their own right, aside from our enjoyment of them—do we have an obligation to preserve them, and to preserve them in their natural habitat, living their natural lives? What we are trying to preserve clearly makes a difference in when and how deeply we need to change our ways. In Chapter 7, I will discuss the different values in question, and the strength of the obligations they place on us.

CONCLUSION

It is time to talk about the right to have children and what that means, so we will be prepared when and if push comes to shove. Obviously, these issues are controversial, and their discussion is painful; to some, it is offensive even to think about population limits, much less to broach actual policy possibilities. Such avoidance, though, is unintelligent. We know that it is inevitable that if the population grows in the way it has so far, we will run out of resources. Technological advances may delay this, but it's hard to see how they can allow us to avoid it entirely. Sure, it is possible that something extraordinary will happen to prevent that: that we will colonize other planets, say, before we have run out of fuel or water. At present, though, there's no other livable planet in sight, so we pretty much need to plan around staying on this one. And on this earth, unlimited population growth would be catastrophic.

Many things make this conversation difficult: the uncertainty of the future, the pain of contemplating intervention in people's family life, and the pain of contemplating what may happen if we don't. But while these things make the conversation difficult, they aren't reasons not to have the conversation. This book is one attempt at such a discussion. The ultimate aim is simply to promote thoughtfulness, and recognition that the number of children one has is no longer simply a private affair. We wish that it were! It was lovely when all we considered was our own ability to raise children well, with no thought to the rest of society. Those days are gone for now, just as those days are gone when we could decide how much fuel to burn, how much fresh water to use up, how many animals we might kill, without any regard for the effect of that on the future.

So we need to discuss these things. The time to decide on morally permissible population policy is before state interference is necessary, and if it is never necessary, so much the better. It is a known truth that you can't teach someone to swim once he is already drowning; you need to teach him in calm water, where help is at hand. If he never needs to use his skill to save himself, the time was still well spent. For us, then, the time to discuss the morality of reproduction is now, before the climate is made unlivable, before ecosystems are destroyed, before wars over resources that are scarce now, like oil, or too likely to be scarce in the future, like fresh water, take away the leisure and the composure we need to craft rational and humane policies. The time to talk is now.

NOTES

1. Amartya Sen, "Fertility and Coercion," *University of Chicago Law Review*, vol. 63, 1996, 1035–1061.
2. I have two children myself. Back in my childbearing years, we thought that replacement value, two children per couple, was environmentally responsible. If everyone had limited themselves to two, maybe it would have been.

3. See Carter J. Dillard, "Rethinking the Procreative Right," *Yale Human Rights and Development Law Journal*, vol. 10, 2007, 1–63; and Luke T. Lee, "Law, Human Rights, and Population Policy," in *Population Policy*, ed. Godfrey Roberts, Praeger (New York) 1990, 1–20.

4. For example, "The Royal Society perceives two critical issues that must be addressed quickly in order to establish a sustainable way of life for all people and avoid undermining the wellbeing of future generations. The first is the continuing expansion of the human population." Royal Society, *People and the Planet*, Royal Society Policy (London),, April 2012, 11. "Longer-term, the stabilisation of the population is essential to avoid further exceeding planetary limits and increasing poverty" (99). Nonetheless, the Royal Society states that such reductions must depend entirely on voluntary efforts: while "[i]n the long term a stabilised population is an essential prerequisite for individuals to flourish . . . this is by no means a coercive prescription" (102).

5. Mireya Navarro, "Breaking a Long Silence on Population Control," *New York Times*, October 31, 2011.

6. Bill McKibben, *Maybe One: A Case for Smaller Families*, Plume (New York) 1998.

7. Ibid., 12.

8. Christine Overall, *Why Have Children?* MIT Press (Cambridge, MA) 2012.

9. Ibid., 184.

10. Ibid., 232.

11. Naomi Klein, *This Changes Everything: Capitalism vs. the Climate*, Simon and Schuster (New York) 2014, 114n.

12. United Nations, Department of Economics and Social Affairs, Population Division, *World Population Prospects: The 2012 Revision, Vol. II, Demographic Profiles*, 2013.

13. Justin Gillis, "Heat-Trapping Gas Passes Milestone, Raising Fears," *New York Times*, May 10, 2013; Ben Tracy, "Carbon Dioxide Levels Highest in Recorded Human History," *CBS News*, May 10, 2013, www.cbs.com/8301-18563_162_57883995/carbon-dioxide-levels-highest-in-recorded-human-history.

14. Food and Agricultural Organization of the United Nations, "Prospects for Food, Nutrition, Agriculture and Major Commodity Groups: World Agriculture Towards 2030/2050," Interim Report, Global Perspectives Studies Unit, Food and Agriculture Organization of the United Nations, Rome, 2006.

15. For example, Niger, where the population may double in the next 20 years (Royal Society: *People and the Planet*, 38).

16. Justin Gilis, "Climate Change Seen Posing Risk to Food Supplies," *New York Times*, November 1, 2013.

17. David Pimental, "Soil Erosion: A Food and Environmental Threat," *Environment, Development and Sustainability*, vol. 8, 2006, 119–137. Pimental estimates that over the last 40 years, 30% of arable land has become unproductive.
18. *New York Times*, "Washing Away the Fields of Iowa," May 4, 2011, Editorial.
19. United Nations, UN-Habitat, *State of the World's Cities 2010–2011—Cities for All: Bridging the Urban Divide*, Earthscan (London) 2011.
20. Brian Stone, *The City and the Coming Climate: Climate Change in the Places We Live*, Cambridge University Press (New York) 2012. Stone notes that 70,000 died in Europe due to the 2003 heat wave, arguably a function of climate change (12). Other experts agree that heat waves pose a greater danger to human life than more dramatic, and more publicized, events like tornadoes, earthquakes, hurricanes, etc.
21. Nafeez Ahmed, "The Coming Nuclear Energy Crunch," *Guardian*, July 2, 2013.
22. See Thomas L. Friedman, *Hot, Flat, and Crowded*, Farrar, Straus and Giroux (New York) 2008.
23. Deborah Zabarenko, "Human Warming Hobbles Ancient Climate Cycle," *Reuters*, April 27, 2008, http://wwww.reuters.com/article/scienceNews/idUSN2541737720080427.
24. Paul Ehrlich, *The Population Bomb*, Sierra Club / Ballantine Books (New York) 1968.
25. United Nations, Department of Economics and Social Affairs, Population Division, *World Population Prospects: The 2010 Revision, Vol. II Demographic Profiles*, 2011, xxi.
26. Royal Society, *People and the Planet*, 11.
27. Ibid., 94.
28. J. G. Cleland, R. P. Ndugwa, and E. M. Zulu, "Family Planning in Sub-Saharan Africa: Progress or Stagnation?" *Bulletin of the World Health Organization*, vol. 89, #2, February 2011, 137–143.
29. Malcolm Potts, Rachel Weinrib, and Martha Campbell, "Why Bold Policies for Family Planning Are Needed Now," *Contraception Journal* (Association of Reproductive Health Professionals), April 2013, http:www.arhp.org/publications-and-resources/contraception-journal/april-2013.
30. Gretchen Livingston and D'Vera Cohn, "U.S. Birth Rate Decline Linked to Recession," April 6, 2010, Pew Research Center, Washington, DC; and "Economic Crisis Lowers Birth Rates," Max Planck Institute, Rostock, July 10, 2013.
31. Sabrina Tavernise, "Fertility Rate Stabilizes as the Economy Grows," *New York Times*, September 6, 2013.
32. World Bank, "World Bank Sees Progress against Extreme Poverty, but Flags Vulnerabilities," Press Release No. 2012/297/DEC, World Bank, Washington, DC, February 29, 2012.

33. "For one billion people who live in extreme poverty, and a further billion who are so poor as to be malnourished, the chief drivers of consumption are the attainment of adequate living standards, including basic commodities and services." Royal Society, *People and the Planet*, 57.

34. Paul A. Murtaugh and Michael G. Shlax, "Reproduction and the Carbon Legacies of Individuals," *Global Environmental Change*, vol. 19, 2009, 14–20; Brian C. O'Neill and Lee Wexler, "The Greenhouse Externality to Childbearing: A Sensitivity Analysis," *Climactic Change*, vol. 47, 2000, 283–324; Charles A.S. Hall et al., "Environmental Consequences of Having a Baby in the United States," *Population and Environment*, vol. 15, #6, 1994, 505–524.

35. The right to food is articulated in the International Covenant on Economic, Social and Cultural Rights, which so far as 160 sovereign signatories.

36. *World Bank, Turn Down the Heat: Climate Extremes, Regional Impacts and the Case for Resilience*, World Bank (Washington, D.C.) 2013, xxii.

[2]

THE RIGHT TO A FAMILY

Blood is thicker than water.
—English proverb

RIGHTS

We talk about rights a lot, and the range of things that get claimed as rights is vast: we debate whether there is a right to die, a right to bear arms, a right to gay marriage, or a right to healthcare; we agree that there is a right to religious freedom, to free speech, and equal treatment, while disagreeing a lot on exactly what these come to in action. Some people claim a right to be forgotten online, and in 2013 US secretary of state John Kerry told a crowd of German students that Americans "have the right to be stupid."[1] We use claims about rights to emphasize the importance of an issue because we agree that rights are important, and that they should be respected. How we know when we have a right remains, however, very hard to articulate, not just because we have poor powers of articulation, but because in a deep sense it's hard to understand when we have a right to something and when we don't. We need at least some idea of what it means to have a right, though, if we are going to figure out whether we have a right to have as many children as we choose.[2]

First, of course, there are two different kinds of rights, legal and moral. Some of the questions just mentioned are debated largely in legal terms: whether, for example, the US Constitution guarantees a legal right to gun ownership. Legal rights can certainly be difficult to understand, but on the whole we do at least have a handle on where they come from. Laws are made by humans, be it a king or a congress of citizens. This means that while there are many debates about the interpretation of a particular statute or ruling, we at least know where to look to get a grasp on what the law entails. In the United States, for example, there is a lot of debate on how the Constitution should be understood, but at least we know that when we try to understand whether there is a right for individuals to own assault weapons, we should look at the Second Amendment.

Moral rights are more difficult. Moral rights are generally understood not to have been created through an act of will, but rather to arise somehow from the moral standing of the entity whose rights are in question. Even those people who think of human rights as "God-given" don't understand God's will to have been arbitrary, but rather based on something about humans that means we should get peculiar consideration. This means that when it comes to discerning moral rights, we don't have any handy authority to which we may turn when we need to know if someone actually has a moral right to something. Instead, we need to think. We need to figure it out ourselves, and this hasn't been easy.

To say we have a right to something is, after all, a very strong statement. Generally, to claim a right is to make a claim on other people, a demand that they must treat you in certain ways. We believe we have a moral obligation to respect rights, and that that obligation is so strong that third parties can intervene and force someone who has failed to respect a right to amend his ways. Not all moral obligations are like this. I really ought to write a thank-you note to the person who gave me a wedding present, but no one thinks it's okay to chain me to a chair to make me do that. Much as my friend deserves to hear from me, I'm not violating a *right* when I don't send her a note, even if I am doing something morally wrong. If, on the other hand, someone has a right, her claim on my action is much stronger: a right provides a "trump," as legal theorist Ronald Dworkin has put it.[3] It outweighs (mere) desires or needs, so that the rights-holder is *entitled* to that to which he has a right, in the way that, say, my friend's reasonable expectation of a thank-you note definitely does not entitle her to have one. As another leading rights theorist has put it, "A right provides the rational basis for a justified demand."[4] It is because this demand is justified that we typically think it's okay, or even required, for third parties to interfere when you fail to respect someone's right—rights are so important that we should, as a group, work for their enforcement.

If people have a right to have more than one child, then the default assumption is that any effort to prevent us from having more than one would be morally wrong, and that anyone who tried to prevent us from having them could justifiably be stopped. Is the right to have children like this?

INTERESTS

To know whether there is a right to procreation, and if so, what exactly it is a right to, we need to know what conditions give you a right to something. Since the introduction of the notion of rights into Western discourse, more theories about their justification have developed than we could possibly review here even if we wanted to, and it would be fruitless to entertain them all.

Fortunately, though, most rights theories have commonalities. Generally, those who study them think rights claims may reasonably be based in either of two kinds of things. Some believe the crucial factor is our status as rational agents. They believe that basic moral rights derive from the particular fact of our being able to reason in particular ways, and from the respect to which that entitles us. This is the consideration that leads us to think we have rights that animals, for example, don't, like the right not to be owned by other people. I will discuss these rights in the next chapter. The other foundation for rights, which I will discuss in this chapter, is perhaps simpler: it is essentially a claim to what we need for basic well-being.[5]

The idea here is that, all things being equal, we have a right to what we need for a decent life. Philosopher Joseph Raz has proposed that " 'x has a right' means that, other things being equal, an aspect of x's well-being (his interest) is a sufficient reason for holding some other person(s) to be under a duty."[6] Well-being is a broad term. It typically includes considerations of happiness (how you feel) and considerations of what is good for you (what makes you better off). Often these are grouped together as constituting your interests. On this view, we can say animals have rights—not the same rights humans have, but still some rights—arising from what they need for basic welfare. This would include a right not to be tortured, certainly, and many would say rights to move around in the way that is natural for them, instead of being forced into tiny pens. Animals don't reason in the way we do, but we know it's against their interests to be treated in certain ways. If the deprivation of something will make our lives miserable, or meaningless, or in any way make it valueless—if it deprives us of our vital interests—we often say that it is something we have a right to.

It's for this reason that some people argue that we have a right to food, since without sufficient food, even if we manage to stay alive, we can't pursue the activities that we generally think make life worth living. Many people argue that there is a right to healthcare, for the same reason—illness may interfere with our being able to do very much at all, so if we are in a situation where other people can provide healthcare, they have an obligation to do that. And in addition to these sorts of rights to things that we need in order to go on and pursue other activities, there are states or activities that are thought to be essential to a good life just in themselves. For example, for most of us, some sort of social interaction is essential to our happiness and to our proper functioning, which is why solitary confinement seems so cruel, even if it is a confinement replete with creature comforts.[7]

Some people have problems with the interest-based theory of rights. They argue that, for one thing, it justifies too many rights claims—since rights claims are so strong, their numbers should be restricted, because otherwise we will be too burdened by people's claims for houses, education, food, jobs, healthcare, clean water, leisure time, transportation, and any number of other things that might be said to be necessary for basic welfare. This is especially true if we think rights based on interest are positive rights—rights that the goods in question should be provided. Whereas negative rights simply call for us not to interfere when someone, for example, goes to vote, positive rights mean we have an obligation to make sure people have what it is they need. We do this sometimes (we do provide K–12 education, free of charge, and think it is our duty to do so), but many people resist the claim that we have to make sure people are provided with *everything* they need for basic welfare. Other people question what it takes for something to be a vital interest—just how important does it have to be? If people have a right to medical care, for example, should that be limited to basic healthcare? Should they get whatever they need to be healthy, even if that is repeated, expensive surgeries? Or what?

These are all reasonable concerns, and the interest-based theory of rights needs to be worked out in much more detail. Still, there is no doubt it has an intuitive appeal: can't we say that a starving child has a greater right to your third blueberry muffin than you do? Don't we often feel that the superrich have no right to their ostentatious indoor tennis courts while some people go homeless? So the idea that there are basic needs that make justified claims on others doesn't seem crazy, even if it is difficult to say what the parameters are on such rights claims.

Are there, then, vital interests involved in childbearing? The right to bear children is obviously somewhat different from the rights to food or the right to healthcare. While it's very hard to imagine someone living a satisfactory life who is very hungry most of the time, or very sick, we all know a number of people who are perfectly happy without children. There's a fair amount of rhetoric around having children that sometimes obscures this. For example, John Robertson has written that

> Procreative liberty should enjoy presumptive primacy when conflicts about its exercise arise because control over whether one reproduces or not is central to personal identity, to dignity, and to the meaning of one's life. For example, deprivation of the ability to avoid reproduction determines one's self-definition in the most basic sense. . . . It also centrally affects one's psychological and social identity and one's social and moral responsibilities.[8]

This, though, while appealing in certain respects, is ambiguous. It is true that I would have been, in some sense, a different person without having had my children, whether I had no children at all or just had different children. I am the person I am because of the relationships I've had, and because of the significant experiences I've had in general, and my relationships with and experiences of my children are among the most profound of these. If they were different, I'd be different. But this doesn't mean that without children I'd have no sense of identity at all, or that my life would be meaningless, as the Robertson quotation might suggest. I'd have a *different* identity, and my life would have a *different* meaning. Most of us in the United States and Europe now have lived within the time of contraception, and thus could, and can, choose how many children to have, but this doesn't mean that those in the course of history who couldn't control their procreation had no identity or had meaningless lives—they just had different lives than they would have had if they had been able to choose how many children to have.

After all, some of the most meaningful lives we know of were lived by childless people—including religious figures, artists, writers, and philosophers. Some of these are people who may have chosen not have children because having them was incompatible with other things they valued—the freedom to do a certain kind of work, for example. Others may simply not have liked children. Still others would have liked to have children if they could, but for one reason or another they couldn't: because of a physical inability, or a partner who was unwilling to have them, or perhaps for lack of any partner. None of this amounts to misery or meaninglessness. Generally, even those who are childless against their will have quite satisfactory lives, notwithstanding lingering regrets over their lack. Having children is not so basic an interest as the interest in sustenance, or health, or social connections.

For this reason, some say we don't really have a right to have any children at all—it's not something we can demand, but a privilege to be cherished. That we don't have rights over other people—including a right to bring them into being—is, to some, persuasive.

Still, it seems to be true that most people want to have children, and that our standard model of a good life typically involves having some children. It may be that this model is based to some extent merely on convention, but that doesn't mean it isn't important to our well-being. Our ability to live up to merely conventional standards often makes a big difference to how we assess our own success or failure in life: what's considered attractive, or a good job, or a valuable talent, often depends on the fashion of a particular period, but they still play a big role in our self-esteem. While it is not perhaps the most basic of interests, for many of us having children is part of our picture of a successful life, so we may concede, at least for purposes of argument, that there is at least a strong interest, if not a vital interest, in having offspring.

But what, specifically, does this interest involve? It seems to me that there are three elements of the right to procreation in which we have an interest: (1) having biological offspring in itself—merely having people out there who bear part of one's individual genetic code; (2) having a family—not so much producing children, but raising them, living with them, having them as fellow travelers through life; and (3) equality—being treated as just as worthy as others to reproduce and have a family. All of these, I will argue below, are important to us, and all are worthy of respect. However, they are all things we can have without having lots of children—merely having one child is enough.

(1) Reproduction

There are those who think that merely producing children isn't that important to us—what we want is to raise them. "We don't seem to have an interest in procreation per se," writes one: "The interest we have is not in procreation itself, namely in merely replicating our genes, but in rearing children who are genetically connected."[9] It's quite possible that the experience of raising our children is our primary goal in having children, at least in the modern world, but our interest in simply reproducing has nonetheless been very strong, and has received strong legal defense. In 1942, the US Supreme Court ruled that Oklahoma's proposed sterilization of chicken thief and armed robber Jack T. Skinner was unconstitutional, Justice Douglas arguing that the law allowing sterilization of those convicted of three or more felonies "deprives certain individuals of a right which is basic to the perpetuation of a race—the right to have offspring."[10]

The simple desire to pass on one's genes, whether or not one rejoices in bringing up the child in question, has been, to say the least, a powerful motivating force through human history. The joys of childrearing and domesticity, while real, haven't historically been a highly touted source of value. Children were not universally seen as adorable, and there was a tendency, for those who could afford to, to have them brought up largely under the auspices of someone else—in someone else's house, or off at school, or up in the nursery with a nanny. For many, the point of having children was not to enjoy their babyhood, toddlerhood, and youth, but simply to carry on the family line. It's not only Henry VIII who worried about leaving enough children to ensure his legacy, even if he was one of the few who could go through six marriages in pursuit of them. We are not immune to the force of evolution, and while most of us are not conscious of generation per se as a motivation to have children, it may nonetheless be one. Whether we want to leave biologically related offspring to secure a dynasty, like Henry Tudor, or simply to feel that something of ourselves remains behind when we are gone, some people do care about biological reproduction in itself, even if we will not spend time with the children we produce.

(2) Family Life

For most of us, though, the primary reason to have children is to partake of family life. We enjoy the company of our children; indeed, for some of us the time we have spent with our children includes by far the most enjoyable moments of our lives. From admiring the perfect little feet of your newborn, through witnessing children's delight when they realize that on Halloween perfect strangers will hand them candy, through watching them master the multiplication table or finally pass the driver's test, sharing someone's childhood is a unique and poignant experience.

This value has been reflected in law. Families are the setting in which we are raised and in which we live our private lives, and laws have been created to protect them from intrusion from those outside, except for the sake of individual family members' welfare. The belief that families are special is reflected in laws of many countries, and the United Nation has claimed this as a moral right for all people: "Men and women of full age, without any limitation due to race, nationality or religion, have the right to marry and to found a family," and "The family is the natural and fundamental group unit of society and is entitled to protection by society and State."[11]

It's true that, as been pointed out, childrearing is far from unending bliss. Some studies present evidence that parents are no happier than nonparents; on the contrary, happiness, as self-reported, actually goes down with having children.[12] It is incontestably true that even when things go beautifully, childrearing is fraught with difficulty. Children take up a lot of time, and they cost a lot of money, and shortages of time and money cause worry, and sometimes a sense of helplessness when we realize that the only way to get the money for college, or even soccer camp, is to work more and thus spend less time with our children. Then too, the company of small children, while extremely rewarding in particular moments, inevitably involves a lot of tedium—all your attention is taken by activities that sometimes just aren't that interesting. And, of course, children tie you down in small and large ways: it's not only hard to pick up and go teach in Europe for a year, it's hard to be spontaneous and head out to the local movie. And there is no stress like the stress of worrying about your children, whose happiness you care more about than you own, but for whom there is so often so little you can do. Even the most relaxed parents worry about whether their children are okay, whether they have enough friends, how they are doing in school, whether they will make the team or whatever ambition it is that they cherish—and of course this doesn't end with childhood. This, as I say, is true even if things go beautifully, and things don't always go beautifully. The agony of those whose children's lives go awry, through illness, misfortune, or bad choices the child itself makes, is unfathomable. Given this, we cannot unequivocally say that having children always makes lives better. Depending on their individual traits and circumstances, some people live as well, or better, without children as they would with children, even if things were to go well with their children. For the unlucky, having children may make their lives much worse.

While this is true, it doesn't necessarily undercut the value of childrearing. To be fulfilling, lives need activities that we find valuable, and for any activity there will be some people for whom it turns out to be a misfortune rather than a benefit. And while it is true that even those who greatly want children may answer psychologists' questionnaires in a way that indicates they are less happy since the birth of their children, this doesn't mean that childrearing has failed to be rewarding. While unusually naive parents may go into childrearing with the idea that it will be a source of constant fun, the fact that it isn't doesn't usually leave us disappointed. The experience is more complex and nuanced than fun. It is, as countless parents have found, enriching, fulfilling, and, with all its failures, satisfying in a way that is more important, for most, than having a lot of great child-free vacations. When we reflect upon it, we may find that many valued activities don't make us occurrently happy, in the sense that we feel that at that moment we are having a good time. When I read about people who climb to the summit of Everest I am struck by how painful each and every footstep seems to be, and yet clearly many of them are getting enough out of this to make it worth the pain, the danger, and the money. (And many choose to return, and more than once.) The satisfaction of an endeavor isn't measured simply by the pleasure of its pursuit.

Last, we should not forget that the time spent raising children until they are 18 or so, while the most commonly emphasized, doesn't provide the only good you get from having children. When one's children have become adults, they provide the more general enjoyment of the society of people you love, and whom you've known and cared for all their lives—an almost unseverable social connection. This is a sense of satisfaction that lasts throughout one's life

So, there are great and unique advantages to the raising of children, and while there are great and unique joys to a number of things, many of which we don't think we have rights to, these joys strike many as more central to our common picture of a fulfilled life. Family is a good endorsed by perhaps all cultures, and toward which we may feel a natural drive.

Of course, childrearing doesn't in itself entail a need for reproduction on the part of the parents: the joys of childrearing, and the joys of continued companionship after childhood, do not necessarily require biological offspring. Adopted children are very obviously loved, and very obviously provide the same full gamut of experiences, and the same opportunity for lifelong relationships. However, for whatever reason, this isn't an attractive option to everyone. Some people may be motivated by the considerations we saw in (1) above, in that they particularly want to share these aspects of the parent-child relationship with their own biological progeny. It may be that some people are so constituted that they wouldn't enjoy adopted children; certainly some people believe that they wouldn't. And, of course, in some places now, local adoption is very difficult: there aren't enough local children who need adoptions, and as mentioned, the adoptive parent needs to meet an articulated set of demands that biological parents don't. Adoptions out of one's own country are an option for some people, but tend to require a lot of money and include a lot of uncertainty as to process and outcome. Whatever the reason, for most people the first choice is to share this experience with those to whom they are biologically related, even if a relationship with an adopted child might in fact yield just as much in rewards.

Given all this, one can make a reasonable case for saying there's a strong interest in reproducing one's genes and for the domestic joys of (biological) family, and that this grounds some sort of right to procreation. I'm not sure this is correct, but it's not unreasonable to believe.

(3) Equality

While the interest in procreation and the interest in having a particular kind of domestic life may not be universal, the interest in equal treatment is. The harms of racism, of sexism, of discrimination against homosexuals, of any discrimination based on irrelevancies of class or status, are obvious. One expression of such discrimination has been the attempt to control or prevent procreation by those in the despised categories. Nazi Germany stands at the forefront of those who have tried to wipe out or diminish certain kinds of people by preventing them from having children, but it is hardly alone. The United States, too, has a history of treating people unequally when it comes to procreation.

The first tool to restrict childbearing was prohibition on the marriage of people whose offspring the majority believed would be undesirable. Laws against interracial marriage began early in the history of the country, and persisted in some places until 1967, when the US Supreme Court struck down Virginia's law against white people from marrying people of other races.[13] Laws specifically against procreation were also fairly common. At the beginning of the 20th century, a wave of interest in eugenics led to popular support for improving the human race (or as many promoters saw it, preventing its degeneration) by keeping supposedly inferior people from having children to whom they would pass on their undesirable traits. First, laws were passed to prevent "unfit" people from marrying,[14] and as time passed, laws grew more aggressive, culminating in a popular movement to sterilize those who, left to their own devices, might recreate others who (it was thought) would be like themselves: epileptics, idiots, drunks, and criminals. By 1935, 28 states (out of the 48 then existing) had passed sterilization laws.[15]

This is a sad history, and it's sadder that the courts initially upheld such laws.

In arguably the greatest mistake of his otherwise distinguished career, Justice Oliver Wendell Holmes affirmed the constitutionality of Virginia's sterilization law, writing in *Buck v. Bell* that sterilization was a sacrifice that citizens could reasonably be expected to make "to prevent our being swamped with incompetence," and that "It is better for all the world, if instead of waiting to execute degenerate offspring for crime, or to let them starve for their imbecility, society can prevent those who are manifestly unfit from continuing their kind."[16]

If restrictions on how many children we have allows unequal treatment in the way that sterilization laws in the past did, we will naturally reject it, because one of the things we most unequivocally have an interest in is equal respect. Neither a strong desire for procreation nor a felt need for family is universal, but a need for equal respect does seem to be so. (Equal treatment may also be entailed by the right to autonomy, which I will discuss in the next chapter, but at present my focus is on our interest in equality, which includes its contribution to our welfare and the fulfillment of our desires.) Even a child, perfectly satisfied with his own portion of cookies, can experience his satisfaction turning to dismay if he sees that another child has more—he doesn't need to read Thomas Paine on the rights of man. Being treated unequally can be a statement about your status and power, and seeing your own status diminished in favor of others' is something that eats away at self-esteem.

This does not require that all people end up with the same goods. When I paddle my kayak by a big house with an unimpeded view of the open sea I often wish I had one like it, but the fact that I don't have one doesn't make me feel diminished as a person (although it would be really great if someone were to give me one). The reasons for this are various. For one thing, while I would greatly enjoy a house on the shore, I'm doing pretty well without one. It wouldn't make a life-changing contribution to my happiness. Then, too, I may believe that those who live in the houses with a great view deserve their nicer settings by having worked much harder than I have. This is quite possible, since I've never worked that hard, and I am quite open to the idea that those who work harder should get better stuff. Of course, at least some of them probably didn't work very hard either—they probably inherited these old, pine-shingled houses from someone who worked hard generations ago. But while that makes their relative advantage somewhat less palatable, it still doesn't arouse resentment, since I, too, have achieved whatever success I've had largely through luck, including the luck of good parents, the luck of intelligence, and so forth. These differences, then, don't bother me, because they are not all that grave in effect and because they don't send any particular message about me.

To be deprived of children when others are not, though, is not the same. The statement made by depriving me of children is of a very different nature: it is a statement about my worth, and about my children's worth, and it is a statement that our worth is very little. It is possible, of course, that people with big houses and lots of money think that those who lack those things are indeed relatively worthless—that no body with less than a million dollars, or five million, or ten million, is worth talking to. Most of us don't think that, though, if only because most of us aren't very rich. We think that the quality of our personhood is not defined monetarily but by our many ineffable traits, so that while money is a boon, it isn't indicative of anything good or bad in what is essential to us. Being denied the possibility of children, precisely because it is thought those children might be like us, is to say that our nonexistence is to be preferred to our existence. It is an insult of perhaps the worst kind. If restrictions on childbearing entailed inequalities in treatment, that would infringe on our interests in an unacceptable way.

This is not to say that no one can be denied the activity of raising a child, if they prove themselves to be unworthy. The most we are given is the chance to raise a child, based on what is assumed to be an ability equal to others'. If we fail in a way that harms the child, the child's right to be taken care of calls for interference. That may well imply that the parent in question is inferior in some respect—either in basic competence or in character—but in this case the differentiation is of a different nature. Removing children from the home after justified findings of neglect or abuse is not a statement that the parent is the sort of person of whom we want no more, so that we want no offspring from them. Rather, we *do* value these parents' children, so much that we want to make sure they have adequate conditions for living. They're as good as anyone else, so they should have as good a chance for a happy childhood as anyone else. It's an affirmation of equal value, rather than a negation. Equal respect is something we are due, and we won't accept policies about procreation that deny this. Even if we accepted the argument that no one has a right even to one child, we'd think if there are going to be children, each of us would have as much of a right to one as anyone else.

ONE CHILD

None of these legitimate interests in reproduction, childrearing, and equal treatment, though, means that we have the right to have just as many children as we want. All of these rights claims can be met by having just one child.

(1) Reproduction

To procreate is to reproduce, passing on one's genes to a new person. Obviously, if you have one child, you have done this. You may see that family resemblance (or not; honestly, one never knows what a child will look like, no matter how many one has); you may tell yourself your own traits have been passed on; you may simply know that you have produced a new person. This doesn't, it is true, guarantee that your genes will be passed on forever—your child may not choose to procreate, and in the worst case, a child might die before the age of procreation (although, in that case, one might, if still able, reproduce again). But for most rights, like the right to pursue happiness, there is no guarantee that your ultimate aims will be met. Your right is the right to act in a way that makes achieving your ultimate aims possible if everything works out well. Thus, you have the right to marry, but you don't have the right to an enduring marriage—you have the right to a chance of one. You hope it turns out well, but if it doesn't, you can't claim your rights were violated, whatever other complaints you may make. Having a right to something doesn't entail the right to multiples of that thing for the sake of insurance. One's rights are not to everything one wants, but to basic goods. The right to food isn't the right to caviar and champagne, the right to education isn't the right to go to the best university but to an adequate education, and any right to pass on one's genes is met by one child.[17]

(2) Family Life

We should acknowledge, first, that when it comes to rearing a child—not just creating one—our rights are not absolute. Would-be adoptive parents have to meet an imposing list of qualifications, and while some of the specifics of the requirements have been controversial (financial requirements, for example, and the preference for two parents rather than one, and parents of different sexes) we don't generally object to the very idea that adoptive parents should have to meet some kind of standard in order to even vie for an adopted child. On the contrary, most people think that it would be irresponsible to let just anyone adopt a child, without any regard for the prospective parent's fitness. And while biological parents are generally given a chance to raise their own children without a prior approval process, their children can be removed from them, sometimes permanently, when their childrearing abilities prove poor enough: abuse or neglect can be enough to justify removing a child from a home. And those who retain the right to rear children don't have the right to rear them just anyway they please—laws require that children have to be educated, for example, in some state-approved manner, and we have such laws because we think this kind of care is morally required. Even if there is a moral right to rear children, it's not unlimited.

Still, those constraints are in place for the sake of the child. Can there be acceptable limits when the parents are capable of raising a child acceptably, given the important role family can play in life?

Yes. After all, the value of family doesn't depend on the number of children in the family. Quality doesn't depend on quantity.

A family of two parents and a child makes it possible for us to do all the things we like to do with children. The joys of intimacy and familiarity, the bonds that develop from long periods of time spent together, a shared history, the sense that there are those you can rely on in any circumstances, are as present here as in a larger family. (Of course, they may equally be absent, whether the family is small or large, if things don't turn out well. Sometimes families don't get along. The right, again, is not a right to the family that fulfills one's dreams, but to a reasonable opportunity for having one.) Quantity of family members does not determine the value of family life: the idea that the bigger the better has been left behind for many things, and surely the same is true of families. Is a family of four kids twice as good as a family with two? A family of eight kids four times as good? No. The point is not to be able to field your own baseball team. While the goods of family are great, and to some people perhaps essential to living the preferred human life, they can be achieved without the participation of lots of children.

It is true, of course, that every child is unique, and thus that each child in a family, no matter how many have preceded him, brings something to the family that makes it different. It is not clear that this gives the parents a right to have just as many children as they may want so as to experience the variety in family that this would engender, though. Reproducing in quantity might give one great joy—the opportunity to know even more people well, to help even more people learn and develop. That is not something you have a right to, though, any more than you have a right to a particularly agreeable child, or one who gets into Harvard or is an Olympic athlete. It's more like my desire to fly to Europe first class, or for a Jaguar XK140, something I'd love to have, but which clearly no one needs to guarantee me. There are any number of experiences that would make my life fulfilled in ways it is not yet fulfilled, but we don't typically feel that I have a right to those. I have a right to certain basic goods, like shelter, but I don't have a right to own houses in a variety of locations, urban and rural, mountain and ocean, even though that would be better than my one small house with a view only of the backyard.

We know, too, that as noted in Chapter 1, many of those who are able to are voluntarily limiting the number of children they have. In many cases, this is due to a shortage of time and money—children cost so much that people choose to have small families in order to support them adequately. In the United States, where college can cost $250,000 or more, that alone induces some people to decide they'll have only one or two children. The fact that a university education costs so much has certainly been a cause for complaint, but hasn't resulted in political protests that the right to have a big family is being violated, because this isn't something we have a right to.

(3) Equality

Violations of the right to equality are egregious, particularly so when the benefit that is distributed unequally is one that people hold dear, and even more so when it is one whose deprivation seems to constitute an insult. However, constraints on the number of children we can have need not offend against the right to equality in any way.

The sterilization laws discussed above were themselves expressions of the belief that different people are more or less valuable, and with that, have different basic rights. When this became most obvious, in the case of *Skinner v. Oklahoma*, mentioned above, the US Supreme Court agreed that such laws were unconstitutional.[18]

While *Skinner* is often cited as a statement about the right to have children, per se, most of the arguments presented actually pertain to the right to equal treatment. The plaintiff, Jack Skinner, had been convicted of three felonies: first, stealing chickens (by "stealth") and then two armed robberies. Oklahoma mandated sterilization for those who had been convicted of two or more felonies involving "moral turpitude," but made explicit exceptions for what we might call white-collar crimes: violations of revenue acts, embezzlement, and political crimes.[19] While a number of objections were made to the law by Skinner's lawyers, the Court said most of them did not need comment: what mattered was that the law treated people unequally, contrary to the equal protection clause of the 14th Amendment. The equal protection clause says that "no state shall deny to any person within its jurisdiction the equal protection of the laws," meaning, in short, that any difference in treatment has to have a rational basis. Oklahoma didn't do this. Justice William O. Douglas compared a chicken thief to an embezzler, and believed that no good reason existed for differentiating the way they were to be punished: the nature of the two crimes was the same, and they should be punished in the same manner. This case was decided in 1942, and the decision (along with the knowledge that eugenics laws were being widely enforced by Hitler's regime) led to the disappearance of eugenics laws in the United States.

This is the way it should be, and there is no need for it to be otherwise. As I say, there are those who believe we don't have a right to even one child, but we do want the human race to continue. (It's true, there are those who argue that this is not, perhaps, a good idea, but it seems to me the rational thing to do is improve individual human lives, and makes our lives less costly to other species, rather than giving up on humans entirely.[20] A world without humans would, it seems obvious to me, be sadly diminished.) Given that we, as a society, want people to have (some) children, even those of us who don't want individually to be parents, there will be children born. The just thing to do is to give everyone an equal chance at having a child.

This may not be obvious. There are those who advocate something rather like the selection of parents portrayed above, only without, they would say, the intrusion of prejudice. Some advocate licenses for childrearing, primarily for the sake of the child, but secondarily because of the costs to society of allowing people who are incapable of raising children properly to have them in the first place.[21] While the intent here is benevolent in ways we can certainly understand, the lesson of *Skinner* is clear: first, that such laws may end up applied according to prejudice, and second, that they simply go too far. Certainly, no one wants an abusive—or for that matter, merely misguided—parent to have the unfettered ability to hurt a child. It is also true that it sometimes takes us far too long to know that a parent is unfit. Still, the idea of preventative restrictions—of simply saying some people can't have a child to begin with—runs counter to our general belief that you shouldn't interfere with people merely on the general belief that they are the kind of person who is likely to do something wrong. For one thing, we cannot be sure who will be an abusive parent. For another, once we begin to choose who may, and who may not, be a parent, before they've had the chance to show us what kind of parent they can be, the potential for unjustified discrimination is all too apparent. We know that in the past single parents have been regarded as inadequate, that gay parents have been seen as inferior, and so forth. Too many ascriptions of incompetence in parenting are simply reflections of our moral beliefs about the parent's way of living, rather than a realistic assessment of the possibility of the child born to such parents having a flourishing life.

While licensing parents makes a differentiation that is too likely to allow prejudice, limiting the number of children all of us has does not. An understanding that, for the sake of people both present and future, each of us should have no more than one child has none of the suggestion of selectivity. It is a rule that would apply to all. We would share the same status, and the opportunity to partake of the same good.

It is true that if this moral rule becomes a government policy, then, like any government policy, it does reflect one kind of inequality: the government has more power than the individual. It is always disturbing, to say the least, when we recognize how great the power of the state is in comparison to the power of any one person. However, we do accept the general necessity for the state to be stronger than the individual. We accept it when we accept the idea of law. We accept it even in things that, arguably, are more important than childbearing. We want these laws to be created within a democracy, where there are some protections for the individual, but we do allow them.

And, if our concern is inequality, we should reflect on the fact that unrestricted procreation is likely to exacerbate inequality in other areas. First, there is the inequality that arises when some people voluntarily restrict their procreation out of a sense of obligation and others don't. As I discussed in Chapter 1, there are a number of writers who suggest that we should voluntarily refrain from having more than one child per couple. A few people have suggested to me that those of us who see the dangers of overpopulation should have no children whatsoever, not because they want the human race to end, but because they know that some people will continue to have a lot of children if left to their own devices, and so believe some of us should have no children to compensate for those who have more than one. There are two problems with these suggestions as to voluntary childlessness. For one thing, it is unlikely that these suggestions would be willingly adopted by enough people to make much of a difference to environmental damage. And, it seems manifestly unfair that some people should do without children in order to make up for what might be regarded as the self-indulgence of others. To allow some to have howsoever many children they may want, while others give up on having children at all to pay for that, is an egregious form of inequality, even if it is a burden that is borne voluntarily. The much more fair way to approach population issues is for everyone equally to be able to have the same number of children, if they so choose: better one per person than more for some, and none for others.

Second, aside from the inequality that arises from burdening the conscientious for the sake of those who are not, the results of overpopulation are, at least so far, experienced unequally in different places. The harms of global warming vary with geographical and economic situation. Climate change will cause some areas to be flooded and yet others to have droughts, while some areas will continue relatively unaffected. Some areas will suffer from wholesale migration to cities that haven't got the infrastructure to cope with the influx, or the means to improve their infrastructure, and others will continue to thrive, at least for a while. It is not surprising that island nations have agitated in particular to prevent the melting of the polar ice caps: they will suffer in ways that other nations won't, even when those unaffected nations have caused the changes that hurt the island nations. Inequality in living standards will be created or, where it already exists, will be exacerbated. Typically, those who are worse off will be worst off, without themselves having caused the harm that is done to them.

Maintaining a right to unlimited childbearing will result in more inequality than restraints on childbearing will itself create. While we may not like the sense of general inequality we experience when we are subject to governmental restraints, people suffer just as much if their inequality results from others simply ignoring their situation when they could in fact respond to their plight.

WHAT IF I DON'T HAVE THE CHILD I WANT?

I have been asked this question frequently in discussions of this topic, and I always suspect that those who ask it have no children. The point being made is that if my interest in having children is to have a certain sort of relationship, or to reproduce certain aspects of myself, I may find that the first child I have fails to do either or both of those things. If we do indeed have a right to these, and the first child doesn't meet my need, the idea is that I should have a right to more satisfactory offspring.

The reason I suspect that those who ask this question don't have children is that anyone who has a child knows that you could have a dozen children without any of them being what you had in mind before you had children. Sports-crazy fathers who dreamed of teaching their child to put a spin on a football may end up with a bookish child who hates to go outside. Scholarly, teetotaling parents may end up with frat brothers whose favorite leisure activity is beer pong. Quiet, retiring yogis end up with children who make the house ring with noise and can't stand to be still. What determines whether a parent has the child he wants is the parent, not the child: the parent simply changes what he wants. We adjust and we love the child we have, rather than hankering after one who would better fit the image we had before we grew to love this one. We get into sports if that is what our child likes; we learn about knights and armor if that's what she is into. The image of the child we planned on before the actual birth completely fades away, and we love the child we have. At least, most of us do, and those who don't—the pushy parent at the soccer game who constantly yells at his son because he's not aggressive enough, or the parent who conveys to his kid that she needs to get into Harvard if she's to get any parental respect—certainly aren't regarded as people who need to have another chance at a child.

Could there be limits to this observation—some children who are so disappointing that they really don't count as meeting a basic interest in parenting? Children where the fault isn't that the parent has some preexisting problem that he hopes to solve through the achievements of his child, but rather where the child is so much a failure on all counts that it hardly counts as having a child? I don't know. Those who've asked me this question have sometimes elaborated and given the example of a child with mental disabilities. In my experience, which I grant is limited to the people I've known with special needs children, such children have been just as loved and just as fulfilling as any child. This is not to say that parents didn't wish their child had had better luck in the lottery of birth, but that they still draw the benefits of having a child. I haven't the experience to say this is always true, though. Perhaps there are children out there who really are so limited in their capabilities that they don't provide what one wants from children, again, not because the parents are neurotic, but because no normal person could find the relationship rewarding. In such cases, I'm not really sure what should happen. If a child dies, it seems to me perfectly reasonable that parents should have another one. If a living child were somehow truly "as good as dead" (as one person put it to me), then perhaps it would be reasonable for those parents to try again. Of course, the right to have a child that is discussed here is not a right that a child should be provided to you, but that you shouldn't be impeded in your attempt to have a child. If, for example, you are infertile, you don't have the right that someone else should give you a child. But perhaps it could be argued that you have the right to have a child who is capable of providing the goods that children provide, and where one cannot do that, you have a right to another try. Presumably such cases would be so few that they wouldn't have much effect on population.

BUT WHAT IF I'M DIFFERENT?

It is true that we are not all the same. Sometimes people object to talk of what sorts of things "people" have a fundamental interest in, because, of course, not all people are the same. What if I feel that whatever other people may be content with, I myself really can't have even a minimally decent life unless I have lots of children?

When it comes to rights theory, individual variation in vital interests doesn't get much attention. A common interest in good health might lead to very different specific claims by different individuals, of course, in that one person might claim a right to multiple surgeries because that's what she needs to live, whereas a luckier person needs only standard vaccinations, but those are both expressions of the same interest in health. Similarly, there might be exceptions to a one-child rule based on such common ends: maybe your child needs a bone marrow match that only a sibling can provide. In that case, both you and your sick child would have needs arising from vital interests (for your child, the interest in life itself, for you the interest in preserving your child's life) that it would only be reasonable to allow for.[22] In these cases, the basic needs are ones we share, even though those needs need to be met in different ways for different people.

We don't hear so much about what should be done if one person needs something very unusual, not as a means to some recognizable end, but as an end in itself: you can't be happy unless you own a Maserati, and so you think one should be delivered tout de suite. It may be that many rights theorists aren't so interested in what you personally happen to want as in what they believe is objectively beneficial. This "objective list" view of what is good for us, of things that are good for us by reason of our shared human nature, is fairly popular.[23] It's the sort of view that holds that even if you really, really just want to lie in bed stoned all day, that isn't good for you because it denies the valuable capacities that make you human. So it may be that we reject idiosyncratic needs because we don't believe their fulfillment really makes you better off.

Or we might accept that what is good for you depends on your desires, but at the same time have trouble believing that people's desires can really be all that different. If you say that you can't be happy, even minimally happy, without something most people do just fine without, our common reaction is to direct to you a therapist, rather than to assume that you are somehow have special requirements for happiness. If I claim, however sincerely, that I can never find any contentment in life if I don't win a Nobel Prize, a therapist would probably try to address the deep-seated insecurities that lead me to pursue status recognition. He'd recognize that the common need for self-esteem has been unmet in my case, and would try to address whatever basic issue has led to self-doubt. He wouldn't recommend that I bribe the Nobel committee, however much he wanted to help me, because he wouldn't believe that the Nobel Prize is really what I need for happiness. He'd think that my real need can be met in different ways. We just aren't that different. Similarly, if someone says he just can't have a satisfactory life without lots of children, I think we would think that something else is going on that needs to be addressed, rather than that he has a unique set of needs. Especially if one child becomes the norm, the psychology that would lead to insistence on more might seem suspect—the need might arise from insecurity or narcissism. (I don't know George Foreman, but five sons named George Foreman, not to mention daughters Freeda George and Georgetta, has always struck me as suggesting a problem.) It might arise in short, not from a vital interest but from a misdirected desire.

Last, in practical terms, there is a limit to how much difference society can accommodate when we are coming up with laws, even where people have truly deep and different needs, talents, and desires. We generally need to make rules for everybody. It's possible that someday technology somehow could allow us to craft laws more narrowly for specific people—letting extra good drivers drive faster than the speed limit, very informed people get medicine without prescriptions, and so forth. In that way, we could, perhaps, ascertain whether there are people for whom having more than one child is truly a vital interest. It seems unlikely, though—that would take a lot of information about a lot of people. So while it's possible, in the meantime we will have to cater to the psychological norm.

CONCLUSION

Some rights, then, may be based on interests, on justified claims to receive, or at least allowed to pursue, what we need to live a decent life. It's reasonable to think that we shouldn't have to give up what we need for a reasonable chance of being happy, of being fulfilled, of having self-esteem and the feeling that we are esteemed by others, at least where that isn't too burdensome on society as a whole. There is no vital or fundamental or basic interest, though, in having lots of children. If there's a vital interest in having children, it can be adequately met by one child. If we discover that we need to limit ourselves to one child for the sake of the common good, no one can claim that this has made it impossible for us to live a good life.

NOTES

1. Eydar Peralta, "John Kerry to German Students: Americans have 'Right to be Stupid,'" *NPR*, February 26, 2013. http://www.npr.org/blogs/thetwo-way/2013/02/26/172980860/john-kerry-to-german-students-americans-have-right-to-be-stupid.
2. Of course, not everyone believes that there are any such things as moral rights. Jeremy Bentham famously called talk of rights "Nonsense upon stilts," in *Rights, Representation, and Reform*, ed. Philip Schofield, Catherine Pease-Watkin, and Cyprian Blamires, Oxford University Press, 2002, 330. My point here is not to defend the claim that there are rights, but to discuss whether, if there are rights as they are normally conceived of, we would have a right to have as many children as we might happen to want.
3. Ronald Dworkin, "Rights as Trumps," in *Theories of Rights*, ed. Jeremy Waldron, Oxford University Press (New York) 1984, 153–167.
4. Henry Shue, *Basic Rights: Subsistence, Affluence, and U.S. Foreign Policy*, Princeton University Press (Princeton, NJ) 1996, 13.
5. As I say, I'm not discussing all theories of rights here. In particular, I'm not discussing John Stuart Mill's utilitarian theory of rights, where rights are a set of rules for behavior we develop because they maximize utility (or happiness). I think that on the utilitarian standard it would be easy to argue that there is no unlimited right to have children.
6. Joseph Raz, "Rights Based Moralities," in *Theories of Rights*, ed. Jeremy Waldron, Oxford University Press (New York) 1984, 183.
7. "Basic rights, then, are everyone's minimum reasonable demands upon the rest of humanity . . . they are the rational basis for justified demands

the denial of which no self-respecting person can reasonably be expected to accept. Why should anything be so important? The reason is that rights are basic in the sense used here only if enjoyment of them is essential to the enjoyment of all other rights." Henry Shue, *Basic Rights*, 19.

8. John Robertson, *Children of Choice*, Princeton University Press (Princeton, NJ) 1996, 24.

9. Daniel Statman, "The Right to Parenthood," *Ethical Perspectives*, 10, 2003, 25.

10. *Skinner v. Oklahoma*, 316 US 535 (1942).

11. United Nations Declaration of Human Rights, Article 16.

12. Nattavudh Powdthavee, "Think Having Children Will Make You Happy?" *Psychologist*, vol. 22, #4, 2009, 308–310; Jennifer Senior, "All Joy and No Fun: Why Parents Hate Parenting," *New York Magazine*, July 4, 2010, http://nymag.com/news/features67024.

13. Chief Justice Earl Warren wrote: "There is patently no legitimate overriding purpose independent of invidious racial discrimination which justifies this classification. The fact that Virginia prohibits only interracial marriages involving white persons demonstrates that the racial classifications must stand on their own justification, as measures designed to maintain White Supremacy." *Loving v. Virginia*, 388 U.S. 1 (1967).

14. Daniel Kevles, *In the Name of Eugenics: Genetics and the Uses of Human Heredity*, Knopf (New York) 1985, 99–100.

15. Ibid., 111–116.

16. *Buck v. Bell*, 274 US 200 at 207, 1927.

17. Again, I am arguing about moral right and moral obligations, but J. Carter Dillard has argued convincingly that to the extent that *Skinner* does establish a right to procreation, it doesn't establish a right to have more than one child, so that contrary to most interpretations, the US Constitution doesn't provide any legal protection for unlimited childbearing. J. Carter Dillard, "Rethinking the Procreative Right," *Yale Human Rights and Development Law Journal*, vol. 10, 2007, 1–63.

18. *Skinner v. Oklahoma*.

19. Ibid., 536.

20. David Benatar, *Better Never to Have Been: The Harm of Coming into Existence*, Oxford University Press (New York) 2006, argues that coming into existence almost inevitably does cause harm, since we all suffer and we have an obligation not to harm. This is certainly an ingenious idea, but in the end the argument fails to convince.

21. Hugh LaFollete, "Licensing Parents," *Philosophy and Public Affairs*, Winter 1980, 182–197, argues that licensing to protect children from abuse or neglect would be warranted. Jack C. Westman has emphasized the more general costs to society of neglected or abused children that he believes licensing

might avoid. See Jack C. Westman, *Licensing Parents: Can We Prevent Child Abuse and Neglect?* Insight Books / Plenum Press (New York) 1994.

22. There are other moral issues connected to having donor children—I don't mean to assume that having a child because another child needs something from it is unproblematic in itself, just that this is the kind of case where the need for more than one child might be genuine.

23. For example, Richard Kraut, *What Is Good and Why: The Ethics of Well-Being,* Harvard University Press (Cambridge, MA) 2007.

[3]

THE RIGHT TO CONTROL
YOUR BODY

*Biologists guess that the result of a rapid warming will be the greatest
wave of extinction since the last asteroid crashed into the earth. Now
we are the asteroid.*

—Bill McKibben, "Worried? Us?" *Granta*, Fall 2003

I've argued that we don't have a fundamental interest in having
more than one child. We can live an extremely good life—happy,
successful, fulfilled—with just one. (And most people can probably live a perfectly good life with none.) This may not settle the
question of whether we have a right to have as many children as we
want, though. Many people who speak about rights will say that
interests are not the only source of rights. It is commonly claimed,
after all, that we have a right to do things that are actually against
our interest, things that harm us in significant ways. These rights
aren't rights simply to get what makes us better off, but rights to
a certain sort of control over the way we live, in large ways and
small.[1] Controlling our actions won't necessarily make us better
off (we might choose to do something quite self-destructive), but
it still allows us to shape our lives in the way we want, however
peculiar that may be.

One of the claims we meet frequently is that we have just such a right to control our own bodies: control over my own body is so basic, so important, that it means other people have an obligation to leave my body alone, even when I use it to do things that hurt me. This is why, it is argued, we don't make people give blood against their will, even when there is a real need for blood and potential donors would not be harmed by giving it. I don't have to give up my right to bodily control for your sake. Most people believe I can't be (justifiedly) made to give up bodily control even if that might make me better off—say, when you force me to live off fruit, vegetables, and tofu for a month. That's why many people believe I can choose to smoke, even when that will obviously do me harm. Given this emphasis on bodily control, proponents of complete freedom in procreation may argue that control over reproduction is wrong because reproduction is something that involves the use of our bodies, and the right to control our own bodies is basic and inviolable.

Even if we stipulate that a right to control the body exists, though, the question is what exactly that includes. This is something that has not been discussed as much as we might think, given how frequently the right to bodily control is referred to. What I will do here is argue that the most plausible grounds of the right to complete control of the body are three: first, that, as John Locke famously said, it is our property; second, that control over the body is essential to autonomy, to our being able to function as persons who can live according to our own decisions and own values; and third, that the denial of bodily autonomy results in an unjust denial of equality. While all of these are reasonable grounds for rights, however, it will turn out that none of them entails a right to have more than one child.

PROPERTY

For me, to think of the body as property is peculiar: I think of my body as something I am, rather than something I own. I agree with J. E. Penner, who argues that for something to be conceived of as property it has to be separable from me, something I can give up, transfer, and so forth.[2] While it's true that parts of my body are separable from myself, my body as a whole is not. I also think of property as being subject to social conventions that dictate what sorts of things can be owned, how they can be transferred, and so on, and that this is *my* body seems to be true regardless of conventions.

However, not everyone shares this intuition. John Locke said in the *Second Treatise* that even in the state of nature, before the development of laws and conventions, "every man has a property in his own person; this nobody has any right to but himself." This makes the acquisition of other sorts of property possible: we mix our body's labor with something, and when we do that, that thing becomes ours.[3] For Locke, the fact that we "own" our bodies before the establishment of any sort of government emphasizes that this relationship is basic and unvarying: I might or might not own my particular Prius at different times of my life, but my body is always my own, which means the possibility of acquiring (other) property is also basic. What exactly this ownership gives me, though, is not immediately clear. Does my ownership of my body mean I can do whatever I want with it? Does it mean I can use it in a way that harms others?

One of the most well-known contemporary illustrations of the claim that the body is property is found in Judith Jarvis Thomson's "Defense of Abortion."[4] Thomson defends the right to abortion with a series of analogies, many of which weigh property rights against the right to life, and which are used to show that the right to property at least sometimes has greater weight than the right to life. Even if we agree that the fetus is a person, she argues, and that persons have a right to life, it doesn't follow from this that the fetus has a right to use *your* body, even when it needs your body in order to live.[5] If a famous violinist desperately needs to use your kidneys in order to live, he has no right to them, and if his supporters kidnap you and hook him up to your body, you can justly unhook yourself and leave him to die. It is not merely that we have the right to defend ourselves in any way we can against an incursion: Thomson denies that.[6] Rather, as she explains, your right to unhook yourself rests on the fact that the violinist is using *your* body in order to live, and because it's yours, he has no right to use it without your permission. Thomson says the same thing is true of a house that you own. If a woman is trapped in her house with a rapidly growing child, a child growing so big so rapidly that if it continues to do that it will crush the woman to death, the woman doesn't have to let it do that.

> [W]hat we have to keep in mind is that the mother and the unborn child are not like two tenants in a small house which has, by an unfortunate mistake, been rented to both: the mother *owns* the house. . . . If Jones has found and fastened on a certain coat, which he needs to keep him from freezing, but which Smith also needs to keep him from freezing, then it is not impartiality that says "I cannot choose between you" when Smith owns the coat. Women have said again and again "This body is *my* body!" and they have reason to feel angry, reason to feel that it has been like shouting into the wind.[7]

Given this, Thomson can go on to argue that the right to life means no more than the right not to be killed unjustly, and it is not unjust to deny someone who has no other claim than need the use of your body or your house, or, for that matter, your coat.[8]

It's a clear and consistent exposition. However, it doesn't succeed in showing that we have an unequivocal right to control our property. If our claims to control something are in all other regards equal, then the fact that I already own that thing does tip the balance in my favor. But if our need is sufficiently unequal, the case is altered. I do believe in the rule of law, and don't think I should be kidnapped for the use of a violinist no matter how needy and no matter how talented. And in the end I agree with Thomson's conclusion that we have the right to abortion. I think it is obvious that fetuses are not persons and don't have a right to life. Despite these points of agreement, I don't think Thomson's argument works in the way that she wants it to.

I am sympathetic to the critic who asked about our duties to a toddler who appears on the doorstep during a terrible blizzard. He argues that even though it is our house, we have a moral obligation to take the toddler in, and I think most people would agree to this. A toddler can be a pain to have around, and who knows how long you'll have to take care of him? Still, to keep him out in the snow because you have a right to enjoy your own property as you choose just seems wrong. Some might say this just shows that rights don't constitute the only source of obligation. They might say that while you have the *right* to refuse the toddler access to your house, of course, you morally *ought* to help the toddler. For most people, though, this would suggest that while we can blame you for not helping the toddler, we can't justifiedly *make* you help the toddler, since that would violate your right to property. I think this is wrong: if we have to stage a toddler home invasion to get the little guy out of the cold and into your house, that seems completely fair. In the same way, we are justified when we grab your water bottle and use it to extinguish a nascent forest fire, despite your complaint that it's your water and you don't care if the forest burns down, or when we take your new Mont Blanc to do an emergency tracheotomy, even when you argue that it's an expensive pen and you'll never want to use it again after it's pierced someone's throat. Your right to your property is a right to control it in some circumstances, but not all circumstances. As I say, I don't think that is relevant to abortion, but it is relevant to the right to the body when that is construed as property. That is, the right to control is limited, and one thing that limits it can be others' extreme need.

It is true that, at present, most people recognize very little obligation to use their property to aid others. While they may agree that this is the sort of thing a really good person would do, many seem to feel it's not such a stringent obligation that they should feel guilty if they fail to help others with donations of food, clothes, or money. They certainly don't think they can justly be forced to help people in need. But although people often fail to act positively to *help* other people, they do recognize a much stronger obligation not to *hurt* other people. They accept that the right to property isn't a right to use it to harm those around you. (Logically, of course, the distinction between harming and not helping can quickly become muddled, and the argument that we should avoid harm to others might entail a duty to aid in at least some cases, but for present purposes we don't need to enter into that discussion.) Even if I don't think I have an obligation to let strangers use my house when they are in need, I do recognize that others can rightfully stop me from using my house as a toxic waste dump that will cause cancer in everyone in the neighborhood. I don't have a right to do that, because that use of my property is too dangerous to others. I don't even have a right to play extremely loud heavy metal music on my very own speakers placed carefully facing out of my very own windows, even though it won't cause the neighbors physical damage. The fact that it will drive them crazy is enough to justify stopping me.

Similarly for my use of my body. It's true, of course, that insofar as the body is property, it isn't just any old piece of property—it's my natural and inalienable property, and thus very different from my house or my speakers. To say that a right of ownership is inalienable isn't to say it is unlimited, though. There are ways in which other people aren't allowed to interfere in my use of my property and other ways in which they are. If unlimited reproduction is indeed very harmful, the fact that controlling it curtails the use of property I own is not, in itself, sufficient to show I have a right to do it anyway.

AUTONOMY

So the argument that we have a right to completely control our body because it is our property doesn't work. However, while that is a weak argument, the claim that there is a right to control one's own body doesn't depend on it. There are aspects of the body that distinguish it from mere property (and it's possible that Thomson herself, despite her use of property analogies, may have had these other aspects of the body in view). A more important issue than ownership is the question of autonomy—generally, our capacity for a certain kind of self-government. Here, it may be argued that the body is peculiarly tied to aspects of autonomy that relate to identity and integrity, and that this means any incursion into control over the body constitutes an attack on the person in the most fundamental sense.

Autonomous Decision-Making

How does this work? The term "autonomy" generally denotes a kind of self-government, but when people speak of our autonomy they may refer to more than one thing. First and foremost, they may refer to the ability to reflect and evaluate—the very abilities, many people think, that make humans special in a way that other animals are not. Dogs may well think, in the sense of figuring out how to get out of the yard, but humans have the capacity to form values, and to choose goals in accordance with values. To many people, it is this ability to think about what is good and what is bad, what is right and what is wrong, and generally to decide what we think is the best life to live that makes us valuable ourselves, and that makes us distinctively persons.

For some, being autonomous in this internal sense requires a kind of independence from influence when we reach our own decisions. For Immanuel Kant, and those who follow him, this is the only ground upon which respect for humanity is properly based. It differentiates us from animals, who aren't responsible for their actions; it makes us susceptible to praise and blame; it is what gives us unconditional value. And since we respect your ability to make your own decisions, we refrain from interfering in the operations of the mind through, say, brainwashing. As a much more contemporary thinker describes it,

> Human rights can then be seen as protections of our human standing, or, as I shall put it, our personhood. And one can break down the notion of personhood into clearer components

by breaking down the notion of agency. To be an agent, in the fullest sense of which we are capable, one must (first) choose one's own path through life—that is, not be dominated or controlled by someone or something else (call it 'autonomy').[9]

Some contemporary proponents of autonomy no longer stress the Kantian idea of the complete independence of thought. Psychology tells us that we are influenced in many ways we can't control, and the idea that our values should be absolutely unaffected by outside influence has largely been rejected. Humans are, after all, a supremely social species. We still can value autonomy in the sense of critical reflection, though.[10] We can't help but be influenced to some degree by the values we are taught, but we also have the capacity—unless, perhaps, it is stunted by a rigidly totalitarian education—to think about those values, to reflect on whether they are correct or incorrect, and decide which of them we actually want to endorse. It is in this way that we find ourselves changing our political or religious affiliation, revising our opinions about what actions our society ought to permit and what it ought not, and amending our own life goals in light of experience and thought. Our very belief in democracy—a system in which we respect people's ability to decide for themselves what should be done—reflects the extent to which we respect these rational and moral qualities. Because of its fundamental importance, then, we say we have rights to protect our capacity for autonomous reflection.

But does this exercise of judgment have anything to do with control of the body? Well, yes: the body plays a crucial role in all this. First of all, the body we have, and the way that it works, fundamentally affects our sense of identity. It shapes the way we see ourselves and it shapes the way others see us, which in turn further affects the way we see ourselves. And the limits of the body determine the way we experience the outside world, which, of course, affects what sorts of information we can take in. If we had very different bodies, or bodies with very different capacities, we would arguably be very different people with very different kinds of thoughts. It's true that in popular movies we sometimes see plot lines that revolve around characters who have switched bodies but retained their original psychology, but these are fictions—it's not at all clear that I would stay the same if I were to inhabit, for a prolonged period, the body of an ant. There is a recognizable sense in which I *am* my body.

So, my body, with its peculiar modes of perception, shapes my experience, and its physical capabilities shape my activities, and both of these shape my sense of myself. Does this give us rights as to how our bodies may be treated? Certainly. One may reasonably argue that it forbids others (and possibly ourselves) from doing things to our body that directly interfere with our ability to reason.[11] Great physical suffering or the effects of extreme poverty might literally keep us from being able to think: those who wish to control the minds of subjugated peoples may force them to labor to the point of exhaustion and keep them badly nourished, precisely to keep them from having the time and energy to reflect. Furthermore, physical control over people that prevents them from accessing the skills or knowledge they need for informed decision-making would also be a form of bodily control that undercuts the possibility of autonomous thought.[12] It's not that we need complete control over our bodies: people who are physically handicapped often can't control their bodies in the ways normal-bodied people can, and yet they are fully agents. Rather, we need *some* basic goods of the body to allow proper mental functioning.

While this shows that certain conditions are necessary for us to fulfill our potential as reflective persons, it doesn't show anything about the right to reproduce. Having children isn't essential to the rational agency that makes us persons. With children or without children, we are able to think in the way that makes us persons: to reflect, to assess values, to consider what we want to be and how we want to get there.

There is no reason, then, to think that we have a specific right to control reproduction in order to protect our standing as valuable autonomous agents, worthy of respect. If we end up in a situation where governments actually have to push us when it comes to reproduction, we will still be people who reflect and evaluate.

Autonomous Action

However, there are other sorts of rights we associate with autonomy. These aren't rights essential for *being* autonomous, in this internal sense, but instead are rights that protect our ability to *express* autonomy. These are rights to act in the way that we've decided we want to act. For many, the value of autonomy does not depend solely on its role as an internal operation constitutive of moral agency—the real point of autonomous reflection is that you can then *do* what you decide is right. This means it's not enough to let people *think* properly—we need to show respect for them by letting them *act* in accordance with their decisions. We can't develop as complete persons or live satisfactory lives without some sense that we can act in light of our considered choices. James Griffin says of our autonomous decisions that we must let these decisions be expressed in action:

> And none of this is any good if someone then blocks one; so . . . others must also not forcibly stop one from pursuing what one sees as a worthwhile life (call this 'liberty'). Because we

attach such high value to our individual personhood, we see its domain of exercise as privileged and protected.[13]

As Gerald Dworkin says of autonomy, "By exercising such a capacity, persons define their nature, give meaning and coherence to their lives, and take responsibility for the kind of person they are."[14] Being able to reflect and evaluate doesn't have much meaning if we can't act on the decisions we reach.

Indeed, on many accounts, we should respect people by allowing them to act not only on their rational decisions, but on their irrational ones as well. If you make a bad choice, I may try to talk you out of it, but most people think I'm not allowed to interfere just because you are mistaken: I can be totally right that it's not a good idea for you to quit work and drive to Alaska to meet the fabulous person you've been chatting with online, but I'm not allowed to lock you in the basement until you get over it. Assuming you are a competent adult, I can to try to persuade you, but, in the end, I've got to let you go. We respect people's right to live according to the decisions they make, to choose what to do and then do it. The ability to create our own lives by making our own decisions gives us a certain value and constrains other people in the way they can treat us. Autonomous action—the freedom to do what we want to do, to live the way we want to live—is, for many people, really more important than the mental process we use to decide what it is we want to do.[15]

We can see, then, why control of the body is especially connected to our autonomy. We exist as persons with bodies, and it is through our bodies that we live—that we speak, that we write, that we vote, that we express love. It's our most elementary vehicle of action, and being cut off from it cuts us off from basic aspects of self-expression. Indeed, insofar as I identify with my body, control of it by someone else seems to constitute control of me. Crimes against the body—whether it is enslaving someone, or rape, or assault—are seen as much worse than crimes of property like theft or embezzlement, even if those attacks on the body leave our rational capacity entirely intact. If you invade my body physically, you seem to have attacked my agency. Violating my physical integrity diminishes my overall sense of psychological integrity, the sense that I am someone in charge of my own life, and so that violation can be uniquely destructive.

For this reason, the body gets special protection. Autonomy in this sense has been described largely in physical terms, as being about "what to put into my body, what contacts with my body to permit, where and how to move my body through the public space," and for good reason.[16] If we are going to allow people to act on the decisions they've made about their lives, they can't be chained up, or locked away in towers like Rapunzel. And just as proper nutrition and healthcare are probably necessary for internal agency, as discussed above, so are they also necessary for putting one's decisions into action—if you are too weak, sick, or exhausted to move, it's impossible to act in order to achieve your life plans. This is one major reason many people argue that there is a positive right to healthcare, and food, and basic shelter, all things that are required for the body to be able to function. The body is, in this sense, basic to action, unless we are angels or ghosts, so without control over it, our decisions remain unacted upon.[17]

What does this mean for the right to reproduction, though? Does the right to control our bodies in some ways give us the right to control it in all ways? Does it entail that we have a right to have more than one child?

As important as autonomy is, and as important as the body is for the expression of that autonomy, we know there are limits. We all recognize that my right to swing my fist ends where the other man's nose begins, and we recognize that it's furthermore fair to interfere proactively with my fist-swinging when we see that its hitting someone's nose is on the near horizon. We know that as vital as free speech is to both individual autonomy and a functioning democracy, I'm still not allowed to yell "Fire!" in a crowded theater. The importance of sex and reproduction is much greater than being able to punch someone in the nose, of course. However, even here, in these intimate uses of the body, there are limits to what we can do. I'm not allowed to steal sperm from the sperm bank to make myself pregnant, even though these actions wouldn't directly involve an invasion of others' bodies, and the donor may have been indifferent to the ultimate recipient of the sperm he sold. I can't use extortion to force a doctor to give me fertility treatments, even if I really need these. I'm not allowed even to steal the drugs I might need to help me have my own child. And I think most people would think I don't have a right to have a child if we foresaw that my child would somehow cause a contagion that would kill millions.[18] My right to do what I need to to support my reproductive activity is not unlimited. Reproduction may express my deepest desires, but that doesn't mean I can do whatever I want to achieve it. The right to autonomy is important, of course, and so is the right to reproductive autonomy. But all these rights are limited, and they are limited by a consideration of other people. If what we want to do is going to cause serious and unjustified harm, it's beyond the permissible claim to express our desires through action.

What about Religious Belief?

However, it is true that constraining reproduction may involve interference in more than physical processes. For many people, religious beliefs merit special consideration. Expressions of conscience occupy a primary position in the beliefs we center our lives on, and religious beliefs are generally accorded a high priority within beliefs of conscience. They tend to be deeply tied to our identity, and we try to respect them: prisoners, for example, who have been deprived of many of their rights to liberty, are widely thought to have a moral right to have their religious preferences respected, and for that reason to be given food according to their religious dictates. (In the United States, both the 11th and 5th Circuit Court of Appeals have confirmed prisoners' rights to kosher food, apparently accepting the argument offered by one plaintiff's lawyer that "prisoners surrender many of their physical rights at the jailhouse door, but they do not surrender the fundamental right of conscience.")[19] A prisoner who just would really, really enjoy a Chicago-style hot dog, on the other hand, has no right to demand one, because mere desire, unrelated to conscience, doesn't have the same weight—it's not thought to be so important an element of the self. Even if we don't have a right to have children per se, it might be that stopping us from having children prevents some of us from exercising the right to freedom of religion, if our religion requires that we don't constrain childbearing. The right to procreate might be something some of us have, as it were, indirectly: a given religion might or might not have a policy on childbearing, but if it does, and if we have a right to do whatever our religious beliefs dictate, some of us would have a right to whatever childbearing practice our religion commands.

This obviously isn't just a hypothetical. After all, the only realistic way of limiting births is through the use of contraception, in particular what some refer to as "artificial" contraception—condoms, birth control pills, and so forth. Some religious bodies, most notably the Catholic Church, condemn the use of artificial contraception. Some even believe it is wrong to use even "natural" contraception—abstinence—insofar as that is used specifically to avoid procreation. (This includes the "Quiverfull" movement among certain evangelical Christians.) A one-child policy would almost inevitably make it impossible to live according to these standards. While in theory those who allow natural contraception—such as the rhythm method—for avoiding pregnancy do make it morally permissible to avoid conception, we know that this too often doesn't work. Realistically, it is very difficult for people to practice periodic abstinence effectively enough to be sure they will avoid pregnancy. Even those who can show tremendous self-control can have great difficulty in using the rhythm method, just because it can be hard to predict the precise timing involved. And, as we know from experience, not many people even have that much self-control. If they do conceive after failing to use contraception, resorting to abortion to avoid having a child is once again contrary to the same religious precepts. For those who disapprove even of the rhythm method, the only recourse seems to be the avoidance of romantic liaisons altogether, which again isn't likely to happen in significant numbers. People want to have sex, and with sex comes children, unless people use contraception.

Given this, it is naturally argued that a one-child policy would violate people's right to the free exercise of religion, and that, no matter how positive the goals, we can't violate religious rights to achieve them. The question, though, is exactly what the right to the free exercise of religion entails.

John Locke, sometimes referred to as the "father of liberalism," remains influential in our understanding of political rights. Locke is famous for the position on property discussed above, but his influence extends to very different topics. His *Letter Concerning Toleration* was published in 1689 and addresses the specific issue of religious freedom. It's an outstanding humanist document.

Contrary to the practice of his time, contrary to the prevailing belief that religious uniformity was essential to civil stability, Locke advocated toleration for religious difference. He argued for what we have come to regard as the separation of church and state for reasons of principle and of practicality. It was not, he said, the job of the government to determine what religions individual citizens might follow: "[T]he care of souls is not committed to the civil magistrate."[20] Nor, he said, was religious interference even practical—laws against any given practice would not change people's convictions, and religion is a function of inner conviction. He cast doubt, too, on the motives of those who engage in religious persecution: demands that others conform to their own practice "are much rather marks of men striving for power and empire over one another, than of the church of Christ."[21] The document is a sensitive, persuasive, and penetrating argument for acceptance of variations in both religious belief and religious practice.

However, while Locke argues strongly for toleration, he does not believe that laws need to make exceptions for people whose religious beliefs run contrary to what the law demands of everyone. Locke's position is that while you should not make a law in order to get someone to change his religious practice, if you make a law for a good civic reason, and it merely happens to run contrary to religious belief, that is fair enough. The religious person needs to obey the law. The example Locke uses is of child sacrifice—if a sect were to practice child sacrifice for quite sincere religious reasons, of course the magistrate (the representative of state power) can stop them, because child murder is generally not allowed, and since it is generally not allowed, there is no reason to allow it as part of a religious practice. If a practice is generally allowed—such as killing a calf—then we cannot outlaw it just when it's part of a religious ceremony that we happen not to approve of. But just as we should leave its religious use aside when we assess the acceptability of calf-killing, we should leave its religious use aside when we assess the acceptability of child sacrifice. We generally assess it to be wrong, so we may also outlaw it as part of a religious practice: "These things are not lawful in the ordinary course of life, nor in any private house; and therefore neither are they so in the worship of God, or in any religious meeting."[22]

This is one approach to religious freedom, and I think it is the best one, but it is not the only one. Some people believe that in fact we should allow exceptions to laws for reasons of religious belief—that we should "accommodate" religious beliefs, so that the religious are exempt from duties of obedience that fall on others. This accommodation view says we need to weigh the interests of the state in getting obedience to the law, and if the state doesn't have a compelling interest in requiring obedience, an exception to the law should be made to allow for religious practice. There are obvious limits to the latitude given to religious practice—no human sacrifice is going to be allowed—but where precisely those limits should be is a matter of some debate. The general position of those who favor exceptions to the law for religious groups, though, is that religious practice is special and we should give it special consideration when it comes to the general requirement that we need to obey laws. And it is this that Locke thought was wrong: for him, the essence of the separation of church and state is not favoritism toward religious practice, but neutrality.

Modern lawmakers have taken both approaches, at times. The US Supreme Court held to the Lockean doctrine in *Employment Division v. Smith* (1990) when it argued that the state could justly withhold unemployment benefits from persons who had been fired for violating the state law against peyote use. The two men in question had been using peyote as part of a religious ceremony in

the Native American Church. Both worked in a drug rehab clinic
with a policy of no drug use for employees, and when their peyote
use was discovered they were fired. They then filed for unemployment benefits from the state of Oregon but were denied. In its decision upholding Oregon's denial of benefits, the US Supreme Court
argued that while usually unemployment benefits do extend to
someone who is fired because of behavior that is for them a religious duty, this isn't true when the activity in question is illegal
Peyote wasn't made illegal just in order to deprive a religious sect
of its use, and the rule against hiring drug users in a rehabilitation
facility was presumably for the sake of more successful rehabilitation, and certainly not to interfere in religious ceremonies. A religious exception to the law would allow some people to do what
is illegal for others, and undercut the rule of law. Given this, the
Court said:

> To make an individual's obligation to obey such a law con-
> tingent upon the law's coincidence with his religious beliefs,
> except where the State's interest is "compelling"—permitting
> him, by virtue of his beliefs, "to become a law unto himself" . . .
> contradicts both constitutional tradition and common sense.[23]

This, clearly, is Locke's idea: if a law is passed that isn't aimed at
religious practice in particular, it doesn't constitute religious discrimination. In terms of the Freedom of Religion clause of the
First Amendment to the US Constitution:

> Although a State would be "prohibiting the free exercise of
> [religion]" in violation of the Clause if it sought to ban the
> performance (or abstention from) physical acts solely because
> of their religious motivation, the Clause does not relieve an

individual of the obligation to comply with a law that incidentally forbids (or requires) the performance of an act his religious belief requires (or forbids) if the law is not specifically directed to religious practice and is otherwise constitutional as applied to those who engage in the specified acts for nonreligious reasons.[24]

We shouldn't set out to discriminate against a religious practice, but we shouldn't let the religious person be a "law unto himself," either. On this interpretation of the right to religious freedom, then, it wouldn't be an infringement of religious freedom to tell people they can have only one child, even when we foresee that, practically speaking, this would be a goal they could achieve only by the use of contraception. The law would not be created in order to discriminate against any religious group, and if it happened to do so, this would still be an acceptable use of the state's power.

However, this Lockean view has not been the unique or even the prevailing view. In 1993, after, and in part in reaction to the *Smith* case cited above, the United States passed the Religious Freedom Restoration Act This says, among other things, that the *Smith* decision had gone too far in eliminating the requirement that the government justify burdens placed on religious exercise. RFRA, as it is called, says that governments should not substantially burden religious exercise without compelling justification, and that the compelling interest test that was set forth in Federal Court rulings prior to the *Smith* decision is a "workable test for striking sensible balances between religious liberty and competing prior governmental interests."[25]

This legislation has since been restricted to federal laws, but there it has caused exceptions to general, neutral laws in a way that Lockean doctrine would not have allowed. Most recently, in what is called the Hobby Lobby decision, the United States Supreme Court affirmed the right of some corporations to exceptions from neutral law on the grounds of corporations' "religious beliefs," in particular relieving Hobby Lobby and other qualifying corporations from the obligation to participate in the provision of contraceptive health care as (otherwise) required by the Affordable Care Act.

While the extension of religious rights to corporations is certainly novel, the Court has at other times used the accommodation approach to conflicts between law and religious practice. For example, when Amish parents protested that their religious freedom was violated by a Wisconsin law requiring all children to attend public school past the eighth grade, the Court agreed with them.[26] The Amish had argued that exposure to high school would undercut their children's religious affiliation by exposing them to contrary values, and the Court's decision was that parents should not in fact be compelled to send their children to high school, although other parents would need to adhere to the law. The law in question was certainly not enacted with the discriminatory aim of discomfiting the Amish. Instead, it reflected the religiously neutral intent of advancing education, but the Amish were nonetheless allowed an exemption.

Even in this case, though, the argument was not that religious beliefs should triumph over the interests of others. The Amish relied largely on farming skills for their sustenance, and there was evidence that they had successfully maintained themselves in this way without schooling beyond the eighth grade. Thus, the judges concluded, the lack of greater education did not make it likely that the Amish would be a burden to the state. Generally, the issue in accommodation has been taken to be whether (*a*) the law would impose a substantial burden on an individual's religious practice, and, if it does, (*b*) whether the state has a compelling interest in requiring obedience to the law. Since the state had no compelling interest in forcing education on the Amish, and since the Amish claimed that further education would prove a substantial burden, the decision was made to favor the Amish.

I myself think that the Lockean doctrine of neutrality is more fair and ultimately more workable than the accommodationist view. However, even if we agree with the general principle that there can be good reasons to make accommodations even to neutral laws, that doesn't mean that people have the right to have as many children as they want. The test is whether the state has a compelling interest in requiring a certain kind of behavior. We know the costs of overpopulation would be extreme, and that the only way to avoid this is to limit children. If we do find ourselves in a situation where voluntary efforts are insufficient and we need state regulation of family size, the need will be dire. The state has a compelling interest in protecting present and future citizens from environmental disaster, and if we are in a situation where population growth will bring that about, we can't let individual religious belief about the unacceptability of contraception interfere.

Furthermore, there is no evidence that the use of contraception really undermines the foundations of established churches. Many Roman Catholics use birth control as it is, while still considering themselves Catholics.[27] It is often the case with modern technologies that it takes a while for established institutions to figure out how to deal with them, to determine what doctrinal response is consistent with their overall mores. Often the first response is to oppose use of the new thing, only to accept it as familiarity grows. While attempts at contraception have certainly been around for a long time, the advent of the birth control pill made it easy and effective to use, and that and the growing equality of women have caused a re-evaluation of contraception on the part of many religious institutions. Many churches have changed their stance on the use of contraception, without any seeing any collapse of their organizations.[28] The reinterpretation of doctrine in light of new information and new understanding is only rational; if a church is generally robust, a change in some of the less central of its teachings shouldn't lead to general doctrinal anarchy. On the contrary, interpreting teachings in light of greater understanding of morality should only enhance the church's prestige.

The Limits of Autonomous Expression

When it comes to expressing autonomy, there is a huge constraint, and that constraint is the amount of harm it does to other people. It's not simply a cost-benefit calculation: it's part of the idea of having a right that we do allow people to act in ways that result in more harm to others than benefit to themselves, precisely because we want to respect personal choices as to how to live. But there is a limit to how *much* priority personal choice receives.

First, most of us agree that my liberty extends only so far as is compatible with the liberty of others. It's for that reason we believe my liberty to pursue my religion doesn't give me the right to interfere with your practice of your religion, even if my religion says that your religion shouldn't be allowed. Second, even though it is implied in the notion of rights that we can do things that don't contribute maximally to social benefit, we don't have the right to do really *great* harm. Even the most stalwart defenders of rights have conceded that where my action causes sufficient harm, it goes beyond something I have a right to. Rights are implicitly contextual. We say we have a right to free speech, but, at the same time, we agree that we don't have the right to yell "Fire!" in a crowded theater. What we mean is that freedom of speech in a social and political context, where that is part of fruitful public discourse on policy, is generally of paramount importance, whereas yelling "Fire!" in a crowded theater does a huge amount of harm with no benefit (or maybe the benefit of you being able to express your hostile emotions, but that just isn't enough). Even political speech can be constrained in various ways: most people agree with John Stuart Mill that while it's fair enough to write a newspaper editorial claiming that corn dealers starve the poor, it's a very different thing to say that same thing to an angry mob gathered in front of the corn dealer's house.[29] The second one is simply too harmful. All rights are bounded by some consideration of harm to others, and we know and accept this.

How much damage we allow before saying you've exceeded what you have a right to varies with the importance of the action we're thinking of interfering with, and calculating this is where things get difficult. Typically, we appear to think that my right to use my body can be quite severely circumscribed—conscription may force me to risk my body in the line of fire, laws against trespassing keep me from going lots of places, and generally the use of my body to frighten, irritate, offend, or annoy others in public spaces isn't permitted. No one thinks that this somehow infringes illegitimately upon my agency. And, of course, I can be physically imprisoned for years, or even life, if I behave badly enough. We are used to the fact that we live in a society of people whose interests are just as strong as our own, and that even our desire to go naked, urinate in public, have sex on the quad—really relatively innocuous uses of the body—must yield to the interests of others who don't want to see it. There is a much stronger justification for circumscribing the uses of the body that can lead to severe and irreparable harm to others.

It is new, of course, to think of reproduction as being harmful to third parties, and that's part of why the idea seems bizarre to those whose outlook is more determined by past tradition than by looking forward to future effects. In the past it wasn't harmful to society; on the contrary, it was generally beneficial. It was reasonable, then, to conclude that the decision whether, when, and how often to reproduce was a private one that should be left to the parents. If, though, reproduction does become dangerous, the right to reproduction changes. For example, while arguing for strong reproductive rights, and opposing governmental interference in reproduction, Amartya Sen concedes that "despite the importance of reproductive rights, if their exercise were to generate disasters such as massive misery and hunger, then we would have to question whether they deserve full protection."[30] The European Convention on Human Rights provides a right to respect for one's "private and family life," but then goes on to say, "There shall be no interference by a public authority with the exercise of this right except . . . in the interests of national security, public safety or the economic well-being of the country, for the prevention of disorder or crime, for the protection of health or morals, or for the protection of the rights and freedoms of others."[31]

This book is written as a hypothetical—whether or not we face overpopulation that warrants state regulation in reproduction will depend on a lot of things, including how much we consume, and whether voluntary actions decrease the rate of growth enough. That the situation is dangerous is not hypothetical. We know that our patterns of consumption are destructive, and we show no signs of stopping them. In combination with too many children, they will be absolutely destructive. They will be destructive in some ways very soon, and in other ways later, but the outcome would undoubtedly qualify as a catastrophe. We don't have a right to wreak this much havoc.

EQUALITY

It may be that the most salient issue when it comes to bodily control is our standing in society. What's important isn't just whether we can do what we want with our body, but what it means if someone else is preventing us from doing what we want. When someone else prevents us from doing what we would otherwise choose to do, that in itself seems to be a sign of unequal standing: it's a conflict of wills, where they get what they want, and we don't. This is why it seems so different if an accident of nature prevents me from having children, rather than a man-made regulation. We don't think of accidents of nature as showing disrespect, because nature isn't the kind of thing that has different attitudes toward different people. If it just so happens we aren't physically able to have children, we may be sad, but we aren't indignant. When other people prevent us from doing something, though, it often seems like an insult. It depends: if the effect isn't intentional, we may forgive it. The idea that a governmental law might threaten to fine us $50,000 for having an extra child provokes outrage, but apparently we don't resent it anything like as much if we have fewer children because four years of college can cost more than $50,000 a year. The effect is the same, and the cause lies in decisions that others have made, but as long as those decisions were not made with the specific intent of depriving us of the ability to do something we don't see it as an attack on our autonomy or our dignity.

It's a question of equality. As we saw in Chapter 2, we have an interest in equality because the sense that we are equal to others, and that others recognize that, is essential to our well-being. When it comes to rights based on autonomy, equality is just as important. Our right to express our autonomy is as strong as the right of any other autonomous agent. We all have a right to equal respect: equal respect for our ability to make decisions and respect for our right to act on our decisions. When someone else interferes with my choices, it may be seen as a suggestion that the person is superior to me, and I bitterly resent such a suggestion. It categorizes us as two kinds of people, the type with the right to express decisions through action, and the other without that right, and this isn't a division of humanity that we accept. This seems to be true even if the action we're prevented from performing is quite trivial. Witness, for example, the almost comic uproar over New York City mayor Bloomberg's innocuous plan to fight obesity by eliminating large sodas.[32] People could still buy just as much total soda, only in smaller portions, but it struck a nerve in many New Yorkers who already saw the mayor as inclined to be high-handed. The idea that other people have better ideas than we do about what we should drink, and that those other people have the power to enforce their ideas where we don't, seemed to drive people crazy.

Equal standing, then, is extremely important to us. Still, this doesn't mean we oppose any law that interferes in bodily action. As has been mentioned, we accept many laws that regulate where we can place our body, what we can place in our body, and generally that make physical demands on us. What seems to make the difference in whether we accept bodily restrictions is (1) whether the benefits of interference appear to be sufficiently great in relation to the costs (thus, we may accept conscription in World War II but not for Vietnam); (2) whether the burden is equitably shared (if we think drugs are [de facto] outlawed only for minorities, we do feel resentment, because then the law is no longer a statement about drugs but instead is a statement about a particular kind of people); (3) whether we participate in the allocation of power (no one wants to be in someone else's control without having had any say in the matter). If the surgeon anesthetizes me before operating, I've lost control, but through my own choice. It's very different from being chloroformed by a stranger. Even if I don't approve of a policy, if I had at least a vote in the matter, I am more willing to consider that it is not unequal treatment. In that case it's the voice of the majority, and I am in the minority, but at least my vote counted as much as anyone else's.

This means that constraints on procreation have to be done right. It means there must be a good reason for such constraints, one where benefits greatly outweigh burdens. It means that constraints must apply equally to everyone—not more children for some and fewer for others. And it means that such a decision should be made through the normally accepted practices of a democracy, not by the fiat of a ruling class. All these conditions can be met. While people should typically be able to control their bodies, going where they want and doing what they want, we recognize that they can't always do that, and that it is sometimes the job of the government to stop them. In some contexts, reproduction may do no harm at all to others, and in some it may impose only a moderate burden on others. In both of these, we may well say that reproduction is within one's rights. When, however, we are in a context where unlimited reproduction poses a severe burden on others, constraining it is justified—because when procreation will, as Daniel Callahan has described it, "exhaust non-renewable resources, irrevocably pollute the environment," or create "an unmanageably large number of people,"[33] we go beyond what we have a right to do, even if our own conception of the good includes numerous children.

COMPLICATIONS

Of course, harmful reproduction is complicated in ways that Holmes's example of punching someone in the nose is not. When it comes to having children, the harm we do to others is indirect, whereas the harm we do to the person we punch is quite direct: we do it on purpose, we do it all by ourselves, and the effect is almost certain. Harming people by having too many children is none of these, and sometimes that makes a difference in whether I'm doing something I don't have a right to do.

Negligence and Mistakes

The first of these is the easiest to address. Whereas the person who goes to punch you in the nose intends to cause you pain, people who harm through procreation don't intend it. Some people become pregnant unintentionally—it's unplanned. Others intend to get pregnant, but their motivation is simply to live a good life, complete with the social rewards of having children. Insofar as there are specific intentions toward others at all, these are benevolent: potential parents intend to provide good lives to the children they have. They may, too, intend to provide themselves with lifelong relationships, to express love toward their partner, or to please the parents who are eager for grandchildren. Obviously, there is nothing bad in any of this.

Can you blame someone for an action if the act is motivated by benevolence and reasonable self-interest? It depends. Someone who has a perfectly nice motive, considered in isolation, can nonetheless be found blameworthy if there were other things that should have been motivating him that weren't. Take the notorious (real) case of the mother of an aspiring 13-year-old cheerleader, who took out a contract for the murder of the mother of her daughter's rival (hoping this would dispirit the other girl so much she would drop out and make room for the would-be murderer's daughter on the cheerleading squad).[34] Obviously, her benevolent motivation to help her daughter make the cheerleading squad is not enough to show she's not blameworthy, because she should have been motivated more by general considerations of justice. This, to be sure, is an extreme case. More typically, we find people who have benevolent motivations but who just haven't thought about the more negative effects their actions will have. This is often referred to as negligence. If a parent feeds her child exclusively on candy because she enjoys the happiness the child feels at every meal of M&Ms and Mars Bars, we blame her, because we think she is negligent: she should have thought more about the child's health. Perhaps more commonly, people will behave in a way that has a positive effect on themselves, but without thinking of the effect it will have on third parties. So, it's not unreasonable in itself to buy myself something nice when I see it is offered at a cheap price, but it is not a good purchase if there's pretty clear evidence that the item is stolen. I should pay more attention; I should not let the advantage to myself blind me to the fact that this really can't be a bicycle that was acquired legitimately if it's a $2,000 bike offered up for $100. I have an obligation to think about it and not to encourage bike thieves by looking only at what is good for me.

So yes, we can blame people who are motivated by the sorts of desires we generally regard as positive, if they lack other motivations such as enough concern for others to make them think about the effects of their action on those others. And, perhaps more importantly, we can also say an action is wrong even if it is not blameworthy. This is important, because part of the reason we don't want to say having more than one child is wrong is that it seems to suggest that nice people are really blameworthy. Thus, we are apt to conclude, having more than one child can't really be wrong.

This doesn't follow, though. Good people can do wrong things because they are mistaken, or ignorant through no fault of their own. It's only recently that the population has risen so astronomically, and it is something many people aren't aware of, or aren't aware of very vividly. It takes a while for people to understand that they need to change their ways, even when it comes to something they care about a lot, like their own health—how many people continue to do things they know are bad for them, eating bad food, failing to exercise, and even smoking? For many people, if a behavior has been acceptable for most of their lives, or if they've believed it was acceptable, it's hard to reconceptualize it, even when there is overwhelming empirical evidence. And of course, there are lots of people who aren't even aware of the basic facts.

This doesn't mean they aren't doing something wrong, though, if they have more than one child in a situation in which overpopulation is a real threat. It's wrong in that it's a voluntary action that brings about a really bad effect. For example, I can say I did the wrong thing when I give the diabetic person a sugary treat, not knowing he's diabetic—it's not blameworthy, but if I had it to do over again, it's not what I would do. It was a mistake. Good people can do the wrong thing because being good doesn't make you omniscient. What we need to do is educate people, so that they do know when there is an issue with overpopulation, and of course law—when we teach the rationale for it, and with the publicity that normally attends it—is a good way to do that.

Incremental Harm

When it comes to overpopulation, it's a joint enterprise. No one set of parents is wrecking the environment all by themselves, even if it's the Duggars with their 20 kids. Obviously, we can hold people responsible for a harm even when each person contributes only a little to creating it. If I and my nine cousins all plot to poison Grandma, we can't avoid responsibility by each giving her only 1/10th of a lethal dose. Even though each of us can truly say that his dose alone wouldn't have killed her, we are responsible for her death, and no one would dispute this. Responsibility for the environment can break down a little differently, though—while we are jointly responsible for creating such harm, we may feel that there is, at the same time, no good reason to avoid harmful acts because our abstinence alone won't make any difference. In the case of poisoning Grandma, we can imagine that all 10 of us have to participate for the harm to be done, so that if anyone of us bows out, she will be saved. In the case of environmental degradation, however, my action alone won't change the result. If my action by itself won't change the outcome, who cares what I do? I don't have to worry about it.

This issue comes up all the time when individuals make decisions concerning pollution: if I walk to work today, rather than drive, does that really make any difference to global warming? No. It may be a nice statement of principle, but if it doesn't actually do any good, and it's cold out, and I feel like driving to work, is there really any reason not to do that? Similarly for having children: it's true that what I do won't determine whether there is harmful overpopulation. This isn't to say it has no effect whatsoever; each and every person born consumes an enormous amount of goods, especially in the US, and so I do have an effect. Furthermore, there are situations where what I personally do may be the single act that tips the balance from acceptable effects to unacceptable effects: I can be the one who drives and makes the difference that crosses the threshold from harmless to harmful.[35] That said, there is a sense in which what I individually do isn't going to save the world. So why should I deprive myself of something good when it may have no perceptible effect?

It's a good question. It's a question that comes up all the time, too: so many of the things we think that we ought not to do are only harmful if a lot of us do them, and so many of the good effects we'd like to achieve can only be achieved if most of us act together. The question here is often how to make such group cooperation a reality, so that individual efforts aren't wasted.

Here is where law is useful. Consider Grandma again. Say that we each give her 1/10th of a dose, but we know that, as a matter of fact, her weak heart means she only needs 9/10 to keel over and die. If each of us defends himself by saying that the reason we gave her the poison is that we knew the other nine were going to give her theirs and thus that our individual 1/10th would make no difference, the law still isn't going to let us off. (Why would we each give the poison, in that case? Let's say it's because the deal we've made is that anyone who doesn't administer the poison doesn't get a share of Grandma's estate. There is a self-interested benefit to acting, and no harm to not acting.) The law will say we all committed murder, even though my personal contribution really didn't make any difference.

In the case of overpopulation, the harm isn't intentional, but the causal responsibility—or lack of it—is the same, and that is why the law needs to step in. Laws can be ugly, and it would be great if we didn't need them. In an ideal world, when a problem called for collective action, we would come up with a plan of action, deciding what we, as a group, need to do, and we would each voluntarily do our part. Problem solved! However, as we know, this tends not to happen. Maybe it's because we have trouble focusing on incremental harms. Maybe it's inertia. Maybe it's because we doubt that other people will do their share. (See Chapter 5.) In any case, we know that collective action in the absence of law has proven difficult, especially when we are trying to bring about a change of behavior. Joel Feinberg has argued that one reason to pass laws against environmental damage is that they make the wrongfulness of incremental harms easily identifiable—you are breaking a law when that law itself was put in place for the general good. You don't have to calculate the complexity of collective incremental damage, but can just rest on the awareness that what you are doing is a violation of a just law.[36] This in itself gives weight to the claim that it is morally wrong, in a way that we can recognize.

In sum, you don't mean any harm, and you are not uniquely responsible for the harm that is done. The harm is nonetheless something you have no right to inflict.

CONCLUSION

It has been said, correctly, that

> a distinctive feature of rights claims generally, and of a moral right to reproductive freedom in particular, is that the rights' possessor is morally entitled to make her own reproductive choices even when those choices may not produce the most good for all affected, or will not best promote her own good when others are not significantly affected.[37]

Liberty is a good thing, and we should have as much of it as is consistent with living in a society of many billions of other people, all of whom have interests equal to our own, will allow. But that does not entail the right to use our bodies in ways that will have *disastrous* consequences to the lives, liberties, and happiness of others. When we reflect, we recognize this.

In the long run, much of our desire to be left to make our own decisions is probably based on emotion more than on an estimate of the moral justifications involved. We just don't like being bossed around. How much we dislike that, and whether our dislike of having regulations that boss us around is greater than the dislike people feel who suffer the results of our actions, varies. Here, once again, interests enter in. While we don't like being told what to do, we may dislike that most when what we're told to do seems contrary to our interests. And of course, we resent it if a regulation interferes with a right, even if it's not a right we had an interest in exercising. Third, it bothers us if the proposed intervention seems to serve no useful purpose. Last, if the sanctions for the proposed intervention are excessive—more than seem warranted by the harm of the practice the regulation is meant to prevent—that also arouses opposition. And, of course, it's much, much worse if the sanctions proposed seem downright inhumane.

As we've seen, though, regulating the number of children people have need not offend in any of these ways. Our strongest interest in having children can be met by a small number of children—bigger isn't better when it comes to families. While we have a right to control our body in most ways, we don't have a right to use it in just any way we see fit, especially not one that can drastically reduce the happiness of future people. The purpose of such legislation would be avoidance of great harm to others, and education can let us see that. Last, the sanctions attached to such legislation need not be extreme, as we will see in Chapter 4.

If there is a high probability that our actions will cause great sufferings to others and deprive them of the liberties we ourselves cherish, we are doing something we don't have a right to do.

NOTES

1. There is a difference at the foundational level in these two theories about the origin of rights, and some people who believe in autonomy rights don't believe rights can be based on interests, and vice versa. They can merge to an extent in practice, however, since one might hold an interest theory of rights that claims that one of one's interests is in autonomous action.
2. J. E. Penner, *The Idea of Property in Law*, Clarendon Press (Oxford) 1997, Chapter 5.
3. John Locke, *The Second Treatise of Civil Government and A Letter Concerning Toleration*, Basil Blackwell (Oxford) 1948, 15. Of course, we know that Locke says this right to property was limited by there being as much and as good left for others, which might be relevant to using up the goods future people will need: "Nor was this appropriation of any parcel of land by improving it any prejudice to any other man, since there was still enough and as good left, and more than the yet unprovided could use. So that, in effect, there was never the less left for others because of his enclosure for himself; for he that leaves as much as another can make use of does as good as take nothing at all" (17–18).
4. Judith Jarvis Thomson, "A Defense of Abortion," *Philosophy & Public Affairs*, vol. 1, #1, Autumn 1971, 47–66.
5. Thomson effectively undermines the argument that the fetus is a person in the article, but is primarily focused on showing that even if the fetus is a person, the pregnant woman has the right to abortion.
6. Ibid., 53.
7. Ibid., 53.
8. Against the argument that the pregnant woman is responsible for the fetus's need for her body, and therefore owes the use of her body to the fetus, Thomson uses another property analogy: if you have your house fitted with special screens to keep out "people seeds," who, if they get inside, will attach themselves to the furniture and eventually become babies, you don't owe the use of your house to a people seed if it happens to get in, despite your precautions (58–59).

9. James Griffin, *On Human Rights*, Oxford University Press (New York) 2008, 33. I do not mean to imply that Griffin accepts the entire Kantian picture of autonomy.

10. See, for example, Gerald Dworkin, a champion of autonomy who nonetheless says, "Our dispositions, attitudes, values, wants are affected by the economic institutions, by the mass media, by the force of public opinion, by social class, and so forth. To a large extent these institutions are not chosen by us; we simply find ourselves faced with them. . . . It is very unlikely that the development of such dispositions is something over which individuals have much control or choice." *The Theory and Practice of Autonomy*, Cambridge University Press (Cambridge) 1988, 11.

11. Whether we have rights to do things to ourselves that undercut our ability to make decisions is controversial. One argument is that we don't, and that this is a reason we shouldn't be allowed to do things like drugs—it interferes with reflection. Others argue that the second aspect of autonomy, freedom of action (discussed later), means that we should be able to choose what to do to ourselves, even if it is destructive of valued mental capacities.

12. James Griffin, in *On Human Rights*, argues that respect for autonomy requires the provision of education and some minimum level of goods. (See 33ff.)

13. Ibid., 33.

14. Dworkin, *Theory and Practice*, 20.

15. There are, of course, those who think autonomous action is overrated: see Sarah Conly, *Against Autonomy: Justifying Coercive Paternalism*, Cambridge University Press (New York) 2013. In the discussion here I merely reflect, for purposes of argument, the value that most people attribute to personal liberty when it comes to actions.

16. Joel Feinberg, *Harm to Self*, Oxford University Press (New York) 1986, 54.

17. We don't want to overstate the necessity of complete bodily control for agency, though. For one thing, bodies are inherently limited. As mentioned above, handicapped people who have lost some of their control over their body—the ability to talk or to walk—can clearly still be fully functioning agents. Their lives may be harder, in part because of social circumstances, and in part because it is intrinsically more difficult to get where they want to go and to express what they want to express, but they are still full-fledged people, pursuing their own goals. Indeed, we are all circumscribed by circumstance to some extent, in that we can't fly or run a two-minute mile. So we should not overstate the degree to which bodily control is necessary for agency. No one can do just whatever she might want to do with her body.

18. Example courtesy of Kristi Olson.

19. Luke Goodrich, deputy general counsel at the Beckett Fund for Religious Liberty, quoted by Emily Hardman in the Beckett Fund's press release, May 14, 2013.

20. John Locke, *Letter Concerning Toleration*, 127.
21. Ibid., 123.
22. Ibid., 145.
23. *Employment Division, Department of Employment Services v. Smith*, 494 US 872 at 885 (1990).
24. Ibid., 872.
25. Religious Freedom Restoration Act 42 US Code §2000bb.
26. *Wisconsin v. Yoder*, 406 U.S. 205 (1972).
27. According to a Gallup Poll in 2012, 82% of those who identify as Catholic believe that the use of birth control is morally permissible. Frank Newport, "Americans, Including Catholics, Say Birth Control is Morally OK," Gallup, May 22, 2012, http://www.gallup.com/poll/154799/americans-including-catholics-say-birth-control-morally-aspx.
28. Flann Campbell, "Birth Control and the Christian Churches," *Population Studies* (Population Investigation Committee) vol. 14, #2, November 1960, 131–147.
29. John Stuart Mill, *On Liberty*, Chapter 3, in *Utilitarianism and On Liberty*, ed. Mary Warnock, Blackwell (Oxford) 2003, 131.
30. Amartya Sen, "Fertility and Coercion," *University of Chicago Law Review*, vol. 63, #3, Summer 1996, 1039.
31. European Convention on Human Rights, Article 8.
32. *CBS News*, "Heated debate over NYC Big Sugary Drinks Ban Plan," July 25, 2012, http://www.cbsnews.com/heated-debate-over-nyc-sugary-drinks-ban-plan/;CNN, "Controversy Fizzing over Bloomberg's Soda Ban," June 4, 2012, http://news.blogs/cn.com/2012/06/04/controversy-fizzing-over-bloombergs-soda-ban/.
33. Daniel Callahan, "Ethics and Population Limitation: What Ethical Norms Should Be Brought to Bear in Controlling Population Growth," *Science*, vol. 175, #4021, 1972, 492.
34. Anne McDonald Maier, *Mother Love, Deadly Love*, St. Martin's True Crime (New York) 1994.
35. See Shelly Kagan, "Do I Make a Difference?" *Philosophy and Public Affairs*, vol. 39, #2, 2011, 105–141.
36. Joel Feinberg, *Harm to Others*, Oxford University Press (New York) 1984, 227–228.
37. Dan Brock, "The Moral Bases of a Right to Reproductive Freedom," in *Should Parents be Licensed?* ed. Peg Tittle, Prometheus Books (Amherst, NY) 2004, 228. Reprinted from "Funding New Reproductive Technologies," by Dan W. Brock, in *New Ways of Making Babies: The Case of Egg Donation*, ed. Cynthia Cohen, Indiana University Press (Bloomington) 1996, 213–230.

[4]

SANCTIONS

We don't have a right to have more than one child. It doesn't follow from that, though, that the government has the right to stop us. What it is morally justifiable for the government to do to stop me from doing wrong depends on a lot of things. I don't have the right to read my son's diary, but if the government prevented me from doing that by installing 24-hour surveillance cameras in every room of my house and posting the images in the village square, I'd think they were doing the wrong thing. It would work, but it wouldn't be acceptable. In this chapter I will argue that in this case, government sanctions—punishments—can be morally justified, if they are done right, and I will argue that they can be done right.

However, when it comes to stopping an undesirable behavior, punishment shouldn't be the first thing we think of. There are other steps we can take that would be preferable to all involved, so we should start by looking at those. After all, if we can effectively fight population growth without the use of coercion, that would be better for everyone. Sanctions, no matter how justified, always come with costs. There is the literal cost of enforcement—finding out those who have broken the regulation, and then subjecting them to legal proceedings. There are, perhaps more significantly, palpable psychological costs. For one thing, there is general resentment when we are told we can't do something. Even reasonable things like speed limits can get us angry when we actually get a ticket. We may admit that speed limits are on the whole a good thing, since we know letting people drive just as fast as they themselves think is safe will too often be dangerous for other people on the road, but actually being stopped by a policeman, made to show our license or to use a breathalyzer, and worse, having to pay a fine, is still irritating: we think other people shouldn't speed, but we tend to think that we what we, personally, were doing wasn't really dangerous and that the police must surely have better things to do.

Then, while all interference is irritating, interference that costs us our privacy tends to be felt as much more painful than other sorts of restrictions. We at least acknowledge that the government has a legitimate role in policing the highways, but when it is seen as intruding into our home, our sense of invasion is, naturally, much greater. It is true that there is a sense in which having a child is never a private act, since by its nature it involves another person, the child. And it fails to be private in its greater effects—the reason to impose such a law is that the cost of having too many children is too great on society. If childbearing had no such public effects, there would be no reason to interfere. Still, there is another sense of "private" in which we do think of childbearing as private. The reason we (almost all of us) choose to have children is so that we may live with them. Through having them we are crafting the sort of personal life we care about. As we saw in Chapter 2, many of us have children so that we have someone to love, someone who will (ideally) love us, someone with whom we will live in intimacy for years. We typically react with resentment, frustration, and even anger at the idea that someone outside the family—someone we don't even know—could interfere in the way our family is run, including especially who the members of that family will be. Even when outside pressures do affect how many children we have—when, as mentioned, we refrain from having another child simply because it costs too much, from day care right through college—we don't react with the same resentment as we do at the idea that someone will *intentionally* keep us from having children.

This resistance to government interference in the domestic sphere can be exaggerated, to be sure. There are many intrusive regulations we now accept as not only permissible but absolutely obligatory: regulations against domestic violence, for example, which obviously do intrude into the realm of the family, but which we now all applaud. Government regulations as to child welfare in general—requirements that children be educated, and maintained with some specified level of shelter, nutrition, and healthcare—are now seen as necessary in a decent society, and our indignation is only aroused when, through a lack of resources or bureaucratic oversight, these regulations aren't actually enforced and a child is neglected or abused. Some regulations, such as laws against spousal abuse, aroused some opposition when they were first enforced, opposition by people who made these same arguments against public interference in the private realm. We've adjusted, though, because we know they provide a benefit that out-weighs any associated harm.

That said, there are still psychological costs to legal interference with our actions in general, and especially great costs to interfer-ence in the domestic realm. Some of these costs may be transient, and diminish as we adjust our expectations, and some may not. If it is possible to avoid these, and still achieve what we need to, of course, we should do that. We want to rely on sanctions as little as possible when we are trying to get people to behave properly: voluntary compliance is more effective and less costly all around.

EDUCATION

Most of us refrain from stealing because we think we shouldn't steal. It's not that we're afraid of getting caught as much as that we just think it's wrong. If people were only kept from stealing by the fear of getting caught, we'd need way more policemen, and maybe way worse punishments, than those we now have. Instead, we have a shared ethic based on certain beliefs: that stealing hurts people, that I don't have a right to other people's stuff, that a world in which theft was rampant would be really unpleasant in a lot of ways. In the best world, we would share an ethic that we have no right to unlimited children in the same way. It would be ideal to have information that is convincing, and thus to change the public perception, rather than to rely on coercive measures. First and foremost (and this will still be true even if we do put a law in place), we need to understand the costs of rising population. This is something very few people seem to grasp. When, in 2011, the population reached 7 billion, that did get some attention in the newspapers. However, while particular aspects of environmental degradation (especially climate change) do attract our attention, there has not been as much public education as there might be, either as to the extent of such damage or how that might be prevented. If we read respectable newspapers or listen to public radio (and of course, a lot of people don't), we hear particular discrete facts: that there is a fishing moratorium on much of Georges Bank because there aren't enough fish left, that Mt. Kilimanjaro is losing its snow,[1] that we've just had the hottest summer/coldest winter on record, that people in Bangladesh are losing the land they live on because of rising oceans. But we don't get a bigger picture of human use and environmental change. It's not that no one has written about this—there are lots of good books out there. It's not much fun to read about destruction, though, when it is real, and a lot of these books aren't easy to read, precisely because they are trying to be informative: they're often long and have charts and graphs that most of us don't enjoy. Of course, that's no argument against reading a book! But it means that if we want to learn, we need to make an effort—it doesn't come as easily as looking at a headline or watching a commercial.

Part of this lack of coverage is perhaps because the phenomenon of rising population and its general effect on the environment is not really news: instead, we focus on each particular new effect. Another reason may be that mechanisms of fighting climate change, and other effects of rising population, are not profitable. Hotels may tout their "green" policy of not changing your towels every day, restaurants may advertise that they serve only sustainable fish, but usually only insofar as they think these changes will increase their net revenue, in decreased costs or increased sales.[2] For the most part individual industries have little to gain from promoting the preservation of the environment in general, and have even less to gain from promoting smaller families. So, while we are the passive recipients of all sorts of messages if, say, we just watch TV or trawl the Internet, we aren't being taught even the basics of Environment 101.

What we need, then, is public education—education from nonprofit organizations, to be sure, but also from the state. Outside of schools, we don't usually see state education of this sort in the United States, either because we think it's dangerous in a democracy for the state, with all its power, to be affecting our views on policy, or because vested interests don't want the state to send particular messages they see as running counter to their own advantage. School education is a good option, though: education about climate change is becoming widespread, and education about the effects of population could easily be included. How dangerous population growth will be is uncertain, of course, since we don't know whether people will continue to reproduce at the rates they have, but that, too, can be a fruitful area for discussion: one thing teachers (and others) deplore in young people is their view that when it comes to climate change, it's all over, nothing can be done. Teaching them that in fact much of the fate of the world is in their own hands can only be a good thing. So the more education in schools the better, on not only the problems but possible solutions.

Education of adults has been more problematic. Occasionally we do see public service announcements in the service of indisputable goods. There are ads that tell us, in vivid ways, that we shouldn't smoke, that we shouldn't text and drive, that we shouldn't drink and drive, that we shouldn't do drugs. These aren't messages that are particularly factual in their presentation—they tend to rely on graphic testimony (a particular person who's been crippled following an accident caused by texting) or vivid images (the egg frying in the pain as the narrator says, "This is your brain on drugs"). If they work, though, that is only to the good. Of course, it's hard to tell how well they do work—people are certainly still driving drunk, and drugged, and while exchanging texts and drunk driving and drug use (and in some places, texting while driving) are also sanctioned through laws that punish you if they catch you doing it, so what education by itself would achieve isn't known.

It's probable that how well education works depends in part on how much we want to engage in the activity it tells us to avoid—while we are ready to believe that asbestos is dangerous because we didn't have a deep desire to use asbestos anyway, we often resist learning things that would mean we'd have to change. Whether it's global warming or the caloric content of junk food, we're good at denying unwelcome facts. However, we do have evidence from other places that positive campaigns to promote fewer children might be successful. We know that Singapore in the 1970s embarked on a widespread popular campaign to get people to have no more than two children, and that campaign was completely successful.[3] This was not merely an educational campaign, but one that also included incentives (see below), and it was problematic in a lot of ways that mean it's not a program we want to imitate (again, discussed below). Still, education probably played a role in its having an effect.

We know, too, that in sub-Saharan Africa, the region with some of the highest fertility rates in the world, public information about contraception and explicit family planning messages spread through mass media (mainly radio) has made a difference: exposure to it "is directly related to greater knowledge and use of contraception, intention to use contraception in the future, preferences for fewer children, and intention to stop childbearing."[4] And in the last analysis, education on these issues couldn't hurt: the more we know about population, about resource scarcity, about climate change, the better. The more we know about contraception, so that we may control the effects of sex, the better. (There are those who oppose teaching about sex and contraception on the grounds that it encourages young people to have sex, but the majority view is that we don't need education to encourage us to have sex; we've got that down just fine without education playing any role at all. We need education to help us choose when and how to have sex.) Education is a good thing in general, and education about policies of general interest, a good thing in particular.

Of course, some of the things I'm counting as education might strike some people as being more like propaganda than education. Posters saying "Stop at Two" and showing (just) two cute children sharing an umbrella, such as those that Singapore used, aren't relaying actual facts about the disadvantages of overpopulation. Like advertising, they rely more on images than facts and more on appeals to emotion than to reason. They aren't presenting lies, either, but they aren't appealing to us to use our rational capacities to decide what it's right to do.

This is true. If an emotional appeal does manage to convey a fact, though, however it does it, that in itself is educative. As it happens, we know that often this is the best way to get information across—to be quick and vivid. A sign that says "Don't Drink and Drive" doesn't present us with a lot of statistics on the correlation between blood alcohol levels, coordination, judgment, and traffic fatalities. It just tells us what to do. Nonetheless, if it encourages people to think correctly that drinking and driving is dangerous, it has educated them. If a lengthy presentation on the chemistry of intoxication in the human body is something no one would actually stop and read, then that fails to educate. Whereas advertising typically doesn't convey facts at all, or suggests actual falsities (that if you buy this car, most of your time in your car will be spent on a scenic road at sunset with a laughing, model-attractive person at your side, rather than backed up at a red light behind a long line of other cars worried about how late you are), public service announcements can get us to accept truths.

Incentives

Sometimes, though, education isn't enough. We know that it is hard to get people to modify their behavior even when that is obviously in their own interests—to change what they eat, for example, so they can lose weight and generally be more healthy. Even when we've been properly educated as to the facts, we can have difficulty understanding in a way vivid enough to motivate us.

Knowledge and motivation seem to reside in two different parts of the brain. This is even more so if the harm in question is happening to someone else far away—so that if we ourselves are not suffering from a lack of fresh water, or living space, or arable land, or fish to catch, if we don't see clouds of air pollution over our own heads, it's hard for us to take this in in a way that prompts action.

Not surprisingly, then, many campaigns to change our behaviors call for more than education—they call for rewards and burdens we can feel immediately, so that the right behavior really attracts us. The population reduction program in Singapore, mentioned above, was effective, and it used not only education but incentives and disincentives. However, it's not a program we want to emulate. Many of the incentives and disincentives put in place by the government of Singapore hurt poor people much more than others, so that the poor were especially discouraged from having more than two kids. It was harder to get public housing for large families, and maternity hospitals charged progressively more for each additional birth after two, something obviously harder to deal with for those less well off. Voluntary sterilization was rewarded by priority in the allocation of public goods like housing and education, and for a brief period, a cash reward of 10,000 Singaporean dollars was given exclusively to less educated women who volunteered for sterilization after their second child. Sometimes the fact that a policy has a disproportionate effect on the poor is an accident—planners hadn't thought through the effects enough to see that this is what would happen. That's not what happened in Singapore. The government actually wanted more educated, more affluent women to have more children, and wanted less educated women to have fewer.[5] This is not the model we want to follow: we're all in this together. We have an equal responsibility, no matter what our class, our education, or our status. This isn't to say that it's wrong to provide incentives and disincentives in regard to population growth, though; rather, it means that we have to be careful how we do that.

So we want a system of incentives and disincentives that would, insofar as possible, be experienced in the same way by different people. It may be that none will be experienced in literally the same way—rich people have advantages in life from having money, and it is possible this will inevitably affect how they experience all rewards and losses. From a position of comfort, even very attractive incentives won't have the same motivating power, and you are cushioned against at least those losses that are short of disastrous. This, though, is a problem with any social system that allows great economic inequality, and not specific to any particular policy. But while we may not be able to entirely avoid differential impacts, we can craft a system that is as equal as possible in its effects.

Making Contraception Easy

A second area where a growth reduction plan was effective was Indonesia. Facing the prospect of a very large population in a pretty tightly confined space, Indonesia embarked on a massive campaign to get people to have fewer children, and it worked. A fertility of rate of 6 in 1970 was reduced to one of 2.59 by 1999, and while it is always difficult to disentangle causes, most think this was at least largely a result of the concerted effort made by the Indonesian government. The hallmark of this program was free, easily available contraception. The program established more than 2,200 clinics from 1969 to 1973, but more significantly engaged in positive outreach efforts, eventually setting up local village family planning groups. These very local groups were supposed to, among other things, motivate others to use contraception, and to provide contraception and advice on how contraception should be used.[6] The fact that the contraception was free and very easy to get, requiring no travel at all, clearly made its use more attractive. Rates of contraception use increased from 10% of the population to 49% in 20 years.[7] While contraception was not the only factor involved (the education of women also helped), the easy availability of contraception is thought to have played a huge role.[8]

This is the sort of thing that developed countries could easily do. The ease of access, in particular, makes a difference, and perhaps especially to young people. While in these countries condoms are generally easy to get, and cheap, many contraceptives to be used by women are often obtainable only after a visit to a doctor, which in many cases will require more money than many can afford, as well as time and travel. Even if it's just getting on the bus and going downtown, travel can put people off. It's not, of course, that people think, "I'd rather have an unwanted pregnancy than take a tedious bus trip," but rather that people plan to go, but just not today—and put it off indefinitely when each day they feel that today, like yesterday, they just don't have time. And, of course, they don't plan to get pregnant in the meantime—but things happen that are unplanned. There continue to be those, of course, who oppose gynecological services in high school health clinics on the grounds that available contraception will encourage young people to have sex, but again, the evidence of history is that people don't really need encouragement to have sex. They need encouragement to use the contraceptives that will prevent some of sex's unwanted consequences.

The relatively recent decision making the day-after pill available without a prescription is a step in the right direction, since at least it eliminates the time and money required for seeing a doctor, but free would be better than cheap, and, for that matter, picking it up anonymously would be better than having to face the pharmacist.

(This may not seem like a big deal, but to a 14-year-old girl, it often is.) These and other forms of birth control could be made much more accessible than they now are. In the United States, the recent Affordable Care Act attempts to make birth control free for those who buy the policy, and this will make a big difference, but you do have to buy the policy (not something open to teenagers), and most of the surest forms of birth control require a doctor's prescription, and sadly, doctors are not found in every neighborhood. Difficulty of access can be a significant disincentive—the more local the provider, the better.

We need to fund family planning and fund it in an effective way. We need contraception to be easy to get—not after a ride across town to a strange place, but at the local school. Since teenagers are notoriously poor planners, some call for the much wider use of so-called LARCs, long-acting reversible contraception—contraceptive patches or IUDs (intrauterine devices).[9] With a LARC, instead of taking a time out from sexual activity for the male to put on a condom or for the girl to insert a diaphragm, for example, the girl is using birth control as the default option. When the time comes and she actually wants to get pregnant, the method is removed. This way, teens who often don't plan to have sex and therefore haven't taken appropriate precautions are ready in advance if the situation develops.

And, of course, while teenagers are probably the group most in need of help in obtaining reliable, easy-to-use contraception so as to avoid pregnancy, these same things can happen to anyone—a failure to foresee where an evening will lead, or a difficulty in getting to the primary care physician or contraceptive clinic, can lead older people, too, to experience unwanted pregnancies. Some argue that the contraceptive pill is safe enough that it should be available over the counter, and given the risks involved in pregnancy, perhaps we should give this serious study.[10] Over-the-counter availability of birth control pills has been endorsed, after all, by the American College of Obstetricians and Gynecologists (in 2012).[11] Just as we allow the "Plan B" emergency after-intercourse contraceptive to be sold without prescription, it is plausible that the advantages of easy access outweigh disadvantages in the case of preventive contraceptive pills, too.[12]

When it comes to reducing the fertility rate, the developed world, especially the United States, is of prime importance because we are the worst of the consumers—using more energy and producing more carbon emissions than anyone else, and for the sake of things we don't need. Expanding the availability of contraception would also make a significant difference in fertility rates around the world, though. It is estimated that 215 to 220 million women globally have an unmet need for contraception—that is, there are that many women who would like to plan their pregnancies and have smaller families, but who can't because they have no access to contraception.[13] The barriers in these cases are various: sometimes contraception is too expensive, sometimes it is too hard to get, or sometimes misinformation leads people to think contraception is too dangerous to health. The number of contraceptive methods available also makes a difference—as there are more options, there appears to be more use.[14] Other times the medical profession itself creates barriers, requiring unnecessary tests, follow-up visits, or other procedures that are costly and time-consuming.[15] Local clinics that can educate women (and their male partners) about the use of contraception, and about the safety of contraception, and that can provide free contraception should make a huge difference.[16] Some of these women who lack access to contraception live in the countries that at present have the highest fertility rates: Uganda, for example, has a reported unmet need in 38% of its women, and a fertility rate of 6.7 children per woman.[17]

So the availability of contraception and reliable information about contraception would be a huge help here. Regardless of our worries about population, it seems the humane thing to do: if millions of women need help to do what is safer and healthier for them and their families, and we can provide that help without much cost to ourselves, helping should strike us as a duty. For those who are unmoved by the plight of individual women, the prospect of global overpopulation should add sufficient urgency. There are, it is true, other reasons people don't use contraception. In some areas cultural traditions lead people to prefer big families, sometimes with an ideal of as many as seven children, as in Niger, apparently.[18] Here, too, though, education can make a difference, not just about the use of contraception but about the dangers of overpopulation both globally and locally—including in the family, where families with fewer children might plausibly be able to provide better health and better education to those children they have.

We might also consider other options: in Indonesia, two methods were not stressed, for fear of giving religious offense in a country where the support of Muslim clerics was vital to success—abortion and sterilization. While abortion remains a politically fraught issue in some Western countries, notably the United States, and is in any case never what one would want to promote as the preferred manner of birth control, sterilization is for some people a good choice. Sterilizations could be free. Indeed, some have suggested a cash stimulus for sterilizations. David Benatar suggests we do this only after the person has had the desired number of children (in his case, two) so that the poor are not unduly pressured into being denied the parental experience by the need for the cash reward, and this seems wise.[19] Still, if offered to those who truly want it, it is effective and can be (especially for men) a relatively simple solution.

These steps are not without costs, but not costs as great as later dealing with the poverty and disruption that will arise if we face extreme overpopulation. It has been estimated that eliminating unwanted pregnancies through contraception would give us a population by 2100 that is three billion fewer than if we don't eliminate unwanted pregnancies and continue our present practices as usual.[20] We in the developed world can encourage local changes and make them affordable. It would help too, of course, if religious opposition to contraception and abortion stopped, and religious leaders focused instead on preservation of the earth they believe God created. As Bill McKibben has pointed out, we've already done a good job at being fruitful and multiplying—"We can check this commandment off the list."[21] Of course, many religious followers already ignore injunctions against contraception, but for some they make the use of artificial birth control truly problematic. Emphasis on abstinence as a means of avoiding pregnancy is largely pointless, in practical terms: in many parts of the world women have no say in whether or not they will have intercourse, and men too often do not worry about the consequences. And even where women and men have better options and realistic understanding of the outcomes, we are, as we know, all too human—shortsighted planners and optimists and sometimes simply weak of will.

It's true that we don't really like to help other people much, and this is especially true when the need seems indirect. However much we may claim to respect choice, we don't typically feel compelled to make it easier for people to choose, so helping people choose how many children to have may feel like an unnecessary burden. While we may admit we should help people who are starving, we don't always do that, and having more children than you might have liked doesn't strike a lot of people as so bad that we need to intervene (and we can see that indeed, we haven't). The argument for helping others to have fewer children so they can in turn keep from burdening yet others with the consequences of overpopulation may seem even less compelling. Helping so that some people may fail to hurt other people often seems just too removed.

This conception of action, though, is peculiar. Imagine that there is a fire, and we can put it out only with the use of water from your hose. Imagine, though, that the hose is not long enough to reach the endangered building. Would you deny water to those who want to form a bucket brigade, on the grounds that there are too many intervening steps between your resource and those who are trapped in the burning building? No. When we each play a crucial role, we are each responsible, even when the eventual effect is out of our own hands.

Those who stress the importance of voluntary action are inconsistent, after all, if they make voluntary action impossible by denying people the means to do what they would choose on reflection. Those who stress the importance of individual decision-making when it comes to family are inconsistent if they don't move to make it possible for others to make family planning decisions. We need, then, to make this possible.

Financial Rewards

Leaving the specifics of contraception aside, there are other ways to incentivize having fewer children. We could create tax breaks for those who have only one child. At present in the United States we have just the opposite—automatic deductions for every child you have. Population issues aside, a number of people have argued that this isn't fair. The childless already subsidize those who have children, through shared costs for schools and public services in general. It seems reasonable that rather than childless people having an extra tax burden relative to others, they should have less of a burden. And in addition to simple fairness, the tax break (for the childless, or for those who have only one child) could encourage people to have fewer children.

We know, after all, that financial pressure makes a difference to how many children we have. As noted in Chapter 1, recent declines in the birthrate have been attributed to the recent recession. More generally, we are familiar with engagement in personal financial planning when it comes to how many children we can afford. It's something we are used to dealing with, and furthermore used to dealing with without finding it a morally unacceptable intrusion. Financial rewards for fewer children might make a difference, and if so, would do that without arousing resentment.

We can make it easier to have fewer children. And we can change the cultural appreciation of small families. Changing culture seems like a massive undertaking, until we realize that our culture is always changing, and that in many cases we try to control that change, and in many cases we have controlled that change. We have tried to change from a culture that believes that some races are naturally inferior to others to one that thinks that is nonsense. We've worked on changing from a culture where women were regarded as incapable of doing traditionally male activities with any degree of success. As I write, there is a big public relations campaign underway on television to end domestic violence. In none of these cases have we concluded that culture can't be changed. We know that some people change more easily, and some less easily. Some may well not change at all. But we don't give up on change when that is called for morally. We persuade, and we encourage, and we help.

Disincentives

Those are all things that make having fewer children easier, rather than things that make having more children harder than it would otherwise be. While incentives are naturally more attractive, and don't seem as oppressive, it can also be justifiable to offer disincentives, burdens that a person has to bear if he does have more than the desired number. Traditionally, offering incentives has been seen as much less intrusive than offering disincentives, and therefore as easier to justify:

> Attempting to influence a person's decision by providing an incentive to choose one alternative rather than another does not limit a person's liberty to decide, or at least does not do so in a way which is per se morally objectionable. Instead, it increases a person's liberty or freedom to choose a certain alternative by eliminating or compensating for a feature which might restrain him from choosing it.[22]

Sometimes the difference between an incentive and a disincentive feels pretty clear to us, and sometimes it is hard to see that there is a difference at all. It depends, in part, on where we start from: If the baseline is no cookie, but one cookie if I eat my vegetables, that could be seen as an incentive—I'll be better off with the cookie than I otherwise would have been. If the baseline is one cookie, and you threaten to take it away if I don't eat my vegetables, that's considered a disincentive. Even if no cookie is considered the baseline, if the prospect of no cookie is bad enough, it may feel like being threatened with a burden when you are told that is the way it will stay if you don't eat your vegetables—just as if you were saying, "I'll take away your cookie if you don't eat your vegetables," which is normally viewed as a disincentive. The difference isn't always clear in practice. That said, at least in theory we can distinguish when we are being encouraged to do something by having that made more attractive to us, and when we are being discouraged from doing the alternative by having that made less attractive to us.

Consider, again, taxes. As said above, we could offer a tax break to those who don't have more children. Or, we could disincentivize having more children by charging more taxes to those who do—the opposite of our present system. As discussed above, when private individuals have children, that is a public burden. Even aside from the future environmental effect, children are (through no wrongdoing of their own!) a burden on public resources—not, in normal circumstances, an unwelcome burden, but nevertheless a burden in the sense that they have costs for those who themselves don't benefit from their presence. Water, sewers, roads, fire departments, law enforcement, and public education—all of these are paid for in part by someone other than the parents, and it is the contribution of these others that makes having children as cheap as it is—cheap, that is, relative to what it would be if the costs weren't shared.[23] It is not unreasonable to think that those who choose to use more public resources should pay more. It's true that those who use more water from a town system (rather than a well), for example, do pay more to the local municipality, but they aren't (typically) paying their full costs. In a system of fair taxes, those who use more would pay more. To make such a system equitable, rather than a lump sum (such as is now given as a tax deduction to those who have children), we would arrange the tax liability according to the income of the individual, a sliding scale so that all are equally disincentivized despite the different amounts they must pay. This is similar to the way we now calculate taxes, and a method we generally accept (but without the loopholes that allow for unfairness).

As I've said, it's hard to imagine any policy that really affects rich and poor in just the same way when the disparity between the two is very great. This policy could at least do relatively well in that respect, though, and compares favorably to some other suggestions. Cutting welfare benefits to those who have more than a certain number of children, for example, is clearly inequitable, since only the poor will feel it. The argument for this kind of inequitable arrangement is apparently that those who receive welfare benefits are already parasites on society, and thus can justly have their income differentially restricted. Even if this were true (and I don't think it is), it ignores the fact that when it comes to the environment, we are all parasites—and those who consume more than their share are the most parasitical of the lot. What we need are disincentives that are fair and effective, and that don't pick out one class or population as somehow blameworthy. We need policies that discourage all of us from having more children than we can all—now and in the future—live with.

Coercion

It's the idea of coercion—of actual laws against having more than one child—that really bothers people. Bill McKibben argues that we should have no more than one child, but that government intervention would be "repugnant" and unnecessary. He's not opposed to encouraging people to have fewer children through governmental action, apparently, since he is in favor of the federal government providing more funding for contraception, but he is against laws that would require action that isn't entirely voluntary.[24] Christine Overall similarly suggests we should limit how many children we have, but says again that this should be voluntary: "If two people agree to reproduce together using their own gametes, they are entitled not to be interfered with or prevented by third parties."[25]

I've already argued, though, that we don't have a right to have more than one child. Those who want to argue that it would still be unacceptable to punish people for doing that need to make either of two claims. They could argue that sanctions are unnecessary, because we can achieve a reduction in population without them, and punishing people where there is no need is inhumane. Or they could argue that even if the threat of sanctions is the only way to get people to do what we want, the only sanctions that would be effective when it comes to restricting how many children we have are sanctions that aren't morally permissible. They may argue that certain types of punishment are unacceptable, no matter what they accomplish, and so we shouldn't use them or even threaten to use them. A regulation against having more than one child would just be unenforceable. If we accept either of these arguments, the fact that we don't have a right to more than one child doesn't mean the state can forcefully stop people from having them. Given this, both of these arguments deserve discussion.

Are Coercive Laws Necessary?

First: can we achieve voluntary restraints on how many children we have through the more palatable means we've just outlined: education, incentives, and disincentives? If so, it is true that adding threats and punishments into the mix just seems both mean and stupid: why get someone to do something by threatening to hurt her when there are much less painful methods available?

What if, though, education just doesn't motivate us? What if an appropriate system of incentives and disincentives doesn't get us to change our ways? If they are enough, that is great. However, they might not be. For one thing, not everyone will be convinced by education. No matter how obvious a truth, there will be some who deny it. And while peer pressure has a strong effect—we are more likely to believe something simply because we know that other people believe it—this isn't always enough.[26] Peer belief pushes us one way, but we also feel a disinclination to believe something if we see that believing it would cut against our own interests—if we see it would make us unhappy, or require us to do actions we don't want to do. We'd rather retain the false, comfortable belief. We know this as wishful thinking—a tendency to believe that things are the way we want them to be. Wishful thinking has long been recognized: John Stuart Mill wrote in 1843 that when a person has a "violent inclination" to think something is true,

> It makes him shrink from the irksome labor of rigorous induction, when he has a misgiving that its result may be disagreeable . . . It operates, too, by making it look out eagerly for reasons, or apparent reasons, to support opinions which are conformable, or resist those which are repugnant, to his interests or feelings; and when the interests or feelings are common to great numbers of persons, reasons are accepted and pass current, which would not for a moment be listened to in that character if the conclusion had nothing more powerful than its reasons to speak in its behalf.[27]

In contemporary times, social scientists have verified our tendency to believe what we want to believe. This can encourage us to doubt truths, even facts that are strongly publicized and backed with what ought to be convincing evidence. We tell ourselves we are being independent when we resist a widely accepted truth but in fact we may simply be running away from what Al Gore called inconvenient truths rather than really using our own judgment.

Perhaps equally common is simple selfishness. Even when we think that what we are doing is harmful to others, we sometimes do it anyway. It is perhaps more common for selfishness to lead us to deny that when we favor ourselves we're hurting someone else, but there are times when that just doesn't work, and we act selfishly all the same. This isn't just true of what we might normally think of as self-centered or egotistical people—it's a common and understandable human tendency, one we work to overcome, but sometimes not successfully. We tell ourselves that our own circumstances are distinctive, or that we are especially deserving, or that in some way our interests should get special consideration. The lure of selfish rationalization is difficult to resist and we succumb.

Last, even when people are relatively unselfish, in some circumstances it's quite rational to believe that it doesn't make sense for us to make a sacrifice. We're giving up something when we don't have a child we'd otherwise like to have. If we don't think other people will make that same sacrifice, there seems to be much less reason to make the sacrifice ourselves. For one thing, being one of the few to give something up may make us feel like chumps, as if we've been taken advantage of. It's not fair for us to suffer more than others.

This in itself, while it reduces our motivation to do the right thing, doesn't necessarily mean we shouldn't. Sometimes some of us do have to bear the greater burden if a goal is going to be accomplished. If the goal isn't going to be accomplished, though, then our sacrifice is truly in vain.

If we believe that not enough people are going to give up having a second child to make our own choice effective, it is actually reasonable to say, "Why should I give up doing what I want to do when it won't even do any good?" We need a big enough number of people to limit how many children they have for that to really make a difference: if I don't think enough are going to do it, what is the point? Some might say that other people's failure in this regard merely strengthens our own duty: if there are people who aren't going to cut back on the number of children they produce, that only means that the rest of us must cut back even more, and have no children at all. That way we can make up for those people who continue to have too many.

It is problematic, though, to plan a policy that requires unequal sacrifice. For one thing, it doesn't seem fair to those who do bear the burden—they give up the one child they want and have a right to just because someone else is going to have more than their share. And, in part because it is unfair, the motivation to act this way is not a motivation that is likely to be widely shared—when we perceive that other people aren't doing their share, we generally don't do our share, rather than doing more:

> People may not want to implement their considered judgments, or to be altruistic, unless there is assurance that others will be bound to do so as well. More simply, people may prefer not to contribute to a collective benefit if donations are made individually, with no guarantee that others will participate; but their most favored system, obtainable only or best through democratic forms, might be one in which they contribute if (but only if) there is assurance that others will do so as well.[28]

I want to feel that my sacrifice is making the world a better place. If no one else is going to do the right thing—or if not enough other people are going to do the right thing—then I can lose my motivation to do it myself.[29]

Laws that involve sanctions can change this. Knowing there is a law in place raises our expectations of cooperation from other people. If we expect them to cooperate, we are ourselves naturally more willing to cooperate. For one thing, it relieves any feeling that I'm being unfairly put upon, bearing the burden for others who don't do their share. More importantly, law shows me that my sacrifice will actually be effective, because I'm part of a group that I can expect to act as I do.[30] In cases like this, where the problem arises from the activities of a group, it takes collective action for the problem to be solved, and what law does is make collective action much, much easier than it would otherwise be. The law coordinates, and the law organizes, and the law provides an incentive for right action.

And does law accomplish its goal solely by punishing people? Do we all obey the rules only because we're in fear of being harmed if we don't obey? No—it's more complicated than that. Avoiding punishment isn't, for most of us, the only reason, or even the main reason, we obey the law, and this is a good thing. If I think my neighbor will obey the law if and only if he calculates the probability and costs of getting caught and decides lawbreaking isn't worth it, I should feel nervous. Whenever I'll be away for a week he'll be pretty sure he can steal my bike and sell it before I'm back, and if the fear of actually suffering the sanctions is the only thing stopping him from stealing, he'll go for it. If, on the other hand, he has internalized the belief that the action in question is very wrong in itself, and if he believes that it furthermore is an act that his society believes is very wrong, and if he thinks his action will violate a cooperative schema that he and his neighbors have entered into voluntarily and for their mutual good, then he's more likely to act in accordance with the law than if he's just afraid of getting caught.

Law can have this effect, without the need for a policeman in every home: it can change our opinions about what it is morally permissible to do. As was said above, what we really want in order to change behavior is a change of moral values, a change of social mores, and having a law in place often has the effect of convincing individual citizens that this is a norm they really need to adopt themselves. Law is in itself a form of persuasion. When society passes a law and says that conformity to this law is so important that it will spend time and money to enforce it, that sends a powerful message about what society believes. As legal theorist Richard McAdams explains it, we tend to want to do what other people will approve of. We generally believe that laws, at least in a democracy, express the attitudes that other people hold toward an activity. If a law is passed making something illegal, then we think that most people disapprove of it, and we will often change our behavior so that we don't do what others disapprove of.[31] So, law changes our preferences as to action. This is more than a temporary change of behavior just to keep from getting in trouble with other people—it is an internal change of mind that can persist.[32] Of course, people do disobey laws, but generally the mere fact that something is a law provides a strong motivation to act in accordance with its dictates.

It is true that this expressive power doesn't arise with every law. People have to believe in the general legitimacy and benevolence of the government. And even within a legitimate government, if people are quite convinced that a law is not expressive of majority attitudes, it won't have this effect. In the United States, the use of marijuana has been a violation of law, and, depending on the particular place and time, often one accompanied by quite severe punishments. At the same time, while there are any number of people who have not smoked marijuana, I expect we'd be hard put to find a single American high school where it isn't available. (It's hard to know this, but I know that every year I ask my students to raise a hand if they went to a high school where marijuana wasn't available, and I've never had a single hand raised.) While there are certainly lots of individuals who don't smoke marijuana, and there are some individuals who disapprove of it, it's probably hard to find any individual who believes that it is generally disapproved by others. (Because marijuana use in itself is so widely accepted, those who want to justify laws against it have tried to make popular the claim that it is a gateway drug, that however benign in itself, it leads to the use of drugs that are harmful. Apparently this argument has not gained widespread adherence.) It's presumably because we think most people are okay with the use of marijuana that we have finally made a number of changes in the law, as more municipalities and states make the possession of marijuana legal. Again a law only changes attitudes if we believe it actually expresses the will of the society we're in.

And even where we don't think a law expresses majority approval, we may find that law motivates us to obey, again without reference to sanctions we'd suffer if we broke the law. Many people believe that there is an obligation to obey the law just because it is the law. We might think we have an obligation to obey laws because of the security laws bring us—we don't want to promote a general breakdown of law and order. Or we might think that lawbreaking is wrong in itself, all things being equal—we might think that respect for democratic government requires respect for democratic laws, even if those laws are misguided (unless perhaps the laws themselves are undemocratic). Whatever the reason, most people seem to feel that there is some claim to obedience in the simple fact that something is the law.

This, then, is one difference between a disincentive, such as an extra tax, and a coercive law, a law that has sanctions attached.

A disincentive, since it is a burden attached to an activity, might do the exact same amount of harm to the individual as the sanction attached to breaking a law. The message that the two send is different, however. In the first case you believe you are not being punished—you're just being discouraged from a particular course of action, but the decision is still a personal one. No one thinks it would be wrong of you to do the thing that's disincentivized—it might be imprudent, but you aren't violating any rules. In the second case, society is announcing that you are doing something wrong, something that the collectivity deems to be unacceptable, so unacceptable that they've made a law against it. The material effect is the same, but the message is very different. In some cases, then, law can do what no combination of education, incentives, and disincentives can accomplish.

Sanctions

Given all this, do we actually have to punish people for having more than one child?

Well, I've argued that laws send a message, and that we are sensitive to that. Having a sanction attached is part of the very message the law sends. It says breaking this rule is so bad that getting compliance is worth the costs (to you, and to society) of punishing you. It says, further, that breaking this rule is so bad you *deserve* a punishment. And part of the moral weight of the law is expressed by the particular sanction we attach. While I'm not a fan of the death penalty, I certainly believe that severe penalties for murder do send the right message—that murder is as bad as it gets. Sanctions for having more than one child will convey a message about how serious this issue is.

And even though I've argued that most of us obey the law because it's the right thing to do, rather than from a fear of getting caught, we know that isn't true of everyone. Some people won't care about the law, either because they continue to disagree with it, despite its expressive function, or because they just want to make an exception for themselves. For some people, the policeman on the corner *is* the only reason they don't steal. So, for these reasons, I think we do need sanctions when it comes to regulations about how many children we may have.

But what kind of sanctions? When it comes to one-child policies, people have imagined horrific things: when an "illegal" child is born, it has to live a closeted existence to escape detection—if detected, it will be killed or imprisoned. (This is the story in *The Shadow Children* series by Margaret Peterson Haddix.) Or when detected, it will be stolen away by the army and the family punished. (The *Terra Nova* television series was about a family that went back in time 85 million years in order to retain their illegal third child. Perhaps strangely, the modern world from which they escape is depicted as horribly overcrowded, which might be thought to make the two-child policy not unreasonable.) Or all children must face trials that ensure that a certain number of them will die. (In Alexei Panshin's *Rite of Passage* about life on a huge space ship, "free-birthing" is regarded as despicable, and a population increase is prevented by dropping all 14-year-olds on alien planets to survive by themselves for a month, with only a limited number getting through the month without getting killed.) And so forth. We seem to think that anyone who wants to limit population will by that very token be ruthless. (In the science fiction world, overpopulation itself is often depicted negatively, so there is no consensus as to recommendations for what we should actually do.)

Basically, we imagine a world dictatorship, indifferent to human life, but (somehow) worried about the suffering that will arise from overpopulation, and ruthless in its quest to prevent that. And we don't like world dictatorships that are indifferent to human life and ruthless in their quests, whatever that quest is for.

In the present world, government restriction on reproduction is associated with the People's Republic of China, and the reputation it enjoys is not good. While in China the enforcement of the one-child policy has usually been through fines, violators of the policy have sometimes been faced with forced abortions and sterilizations. Naturally we find these repugnant. China is not a democracy, and its governmental actions are not transparent, and our dismay at the government's use of power over the individual is increased by this. Even in a democracy, though, bodily invasion of this sort would be felt as horrific. Bodily invasion is a personal assault, and when it comes from the government it seems all the more an injustice. This is one of the reasons we disapprove of torture as a punishment, even for the most heinous crimes. The body seems so vulnerable, so personal, so human, and the bureaucracy that invades it so powerful and so cold and impenetrable.

We shouldn't do these things. We don't accept the invasion of the body in these deep, significant, frightening ways. And some people will then conclude that if we find these sanctions unacceptable, then *no* sanctions are acceptable. If we find these actions unacceptable, that may seem to suggest that even if we accepted that, in theory, governments have the right to restrict how many children someone has, there might be no morally acceptable way to actually do that. The only way to literally prevent people from having children does appear to be to sterilize them, or to force abortions on those who are pregnant, and so, we conclude, prevention is unacceptable. The theoretical discussion as to whether there is a right to have however many children one wants may appear to have no practical import if we can't act on that knowledge without acting immorally. Showing that there is no right to a certain action without suggesting any acceptable way of preventing such an action may seem pointless.

Second, and more importantly, if the only way of enforcing a policy violates rights, that may suggest that the actions that policy is intended to prevent are ones we have a right to: preventing your action violates a right just because what you are doing is something you have a right to do. If I violate your right in preventing you from voting, that's because you have a right to vote. If I violate your right in stealing your property, that's because you have a right to keep your property. If I violate your right in forcibly preventing you from having more than a certain number of children, that may seem to be because you have a right to have as many children as you want.

However, in this last case, such a conclusion would not follow. First, even if the only ways to stop people from having an excessive number of children were ones we rightly condemn (and I'll argue there are others), it wouldn't actually follow from that that you have a right to have as many children as you want. The mere fact that I cannot, practically speaking, find a way to stop you from doing something without violating one of your rights doesn't mean that what you are doing is actually morally acceptable. Consider this example: say that I have correctly posted my legally and morally acquired land with "No trespassing" signs. Let us say that you see the signs but nonetheless decide to cross my property: not because you are fleeing a raging bull and jumping the fence onto my land is the only protection, not because you are starving and your only means of sustenance is my tomato patch, not because you are a victim of a long line of oppressive capitalistic dealings that have unjustly deprived you of property and allowed me to amass it. No, you are a propertied, secure, well-fed individual, who just prefers walking through my yard to going the long way round to your destination. I think we would agree that you have no moral right to walk through my property. Let us say, too, that the only way I can stop you is to shoot you. It so happens that I can't call the police because my phone is down, through no fault of my own, and anyway, the police are so far away that by the time they got here you would be long gone, and given your complete lack of criminal history, there would be no way to identify you through DNA, fingerprints, or a lineup, and thus extract from you any recompense for what you have taken by your wrongdoing. I have already tried to stop you by verbal excoriation, and it hasn't worked. There are no neighbors who can help me. Being slight of build and untrained in the martial arts, the only physical means of stopping you that I have is the gun I keep for self-protection. Unfortunately, my only gun is a .357 Magnum, whose force is such that when shot, you will die. Would it be morally acceptable to kill you, given that you are violating my property right? I think we would say no. You aren't presenting any threat to me; you're just trespassing. Even though you are doing something you have no right to do, I have no right to kill you to prevent you from doing it. Does the fact that I can't, morally, stop you mean that you have the right to walk across my property? I think we would again say no: in this case, you are doing what you have no right to do, but there is no morally acceptable act I can take to prevent you.

This, to the extent it goes, offers some defense against the argument that (a) accepting that we don't have an unlimited right to have children entails that we must countenance forced abortions and sterilizations; and that (*b*) since we can't countenance those, you must have a right to have as many children as you want. We can say that those practices are unacceptable, but there is a no correlative right to do what they prevent. They are practices that are almost unimaginably physically invasive and emotionally traumatic, and to subject someone to such treatment, even for a legitimate social goal, seems too much: like using torture on murderers to deter potential murderers. Even if he's guilty, even if he's dangerous, many would say he has a right not to be tortured. It's just not an acceptable way to treat people; or, as it might be put, it violates fundamental rights. Sometimes, practically speaking, the means of prevention can be too harmful to be justified, even where there is a real infraction.

So, even if there were no permissible way to stop you, it wouldn't mean you had a right to do what you intended.

This wouldn't be very helpful as a practical point, however, if we had no suggestions as to what sanctions on excessive reproduction could be acceptable. There would be no way to enforce the law. However, in the case of reproduction, there are morally acceptable ways to stop you from having more children than are compatible with the health of the planet.

Punishments do not have to be physical to be effective. Fines can be effective in stopping undesirable actions. So can losing privileges, such as taking someone's driver's license for violating the law, but fines in themselves might be enough. People think of abortion and sterilization because they are the only way to literally prevent a pregnancy, but when we pass laws, we don't generally try to literally prevent anyone from breaking the law. We don't actually expect complete compliance. We would like it, no doubt, but we know we won't get it, either because of moral limitations or because of the practical costs of prevention. We have typically been willing to accept that less-than-maximally effective sanctions are acceptable as ways of discouraging people from doing what they have no right to do, even when what they are doing is really dangerous. For example, we don't don't do all do all we might do to prevent murder, even though murder is unambiguously bad. Detecting all possible murders would take too much in the way of surveillance, and far too many policemen, and would leave far too few resources left over for other useful pursuits. We don't even adopt punishments that might have the greatest deterrent effect because we think those are just too inhumane. We're not supporting the right to murder when we refrain from drawing and quartering murderers, even if that would scare more people away from murder. We reach what is really a compromise, doing what seems an acceptable amount to reduce the number of murders, knowing that they won't be entirely prevented.

Can we expect a system of fines to get sufficient compliance? It seems likely, if the fines are heavy enough. For one thing, we already know that decisions as to childbearing are extremely sensitive to costs. As said in Chapter 1, the fertility rate has dropped in western Europe, the United States, and some parts of Asia, and this seems to reflect the costs and time involved in childrearing—not only the actual outlay in child expenses but the costs in earning power that are lost when parents spend more time with children and less at work. This has changed the pattern of childbearing for many people. As it is, of course, financial costs for day care or lost earning power affect people differentially according to income, so that richer people can afford more children than can those who are less well off. One advantage of a fine system is that it can be made equitable. To bring it about that fines would have an equal impact on people of different incomes, we can use a sliding scale in assessing amounts, with much greater fines for people with much greater incomes. Again, this would work in some ways like a tax system, except that it could be made more equitable than the tax system is. And, importantly, the message sent by a fine is qualitatively different from the message expressed by a tax, because a fine conveys the message that what you have done is unacceptable to those around you.

And, of course, these practical inhibitions would be combined with education as to why the policy needs to be adopted, as discussed above, as well as positive incentives (like free and convenient contraception) to make conforming to the law easy. We would see a general change in the cultural meaning of having larger families as smaller families become the norm and are seen to be socially preferable. Ultimately, as with all regulations, the most efficient way to make it effective is something we may have to discover after we've tried it a while, when we see what it takes for the law to be effective. We don't want to apply sanctions that don't yield the desired change in behavior, and we don't want to apply sanctions that are heavier than required for common compliance. We can discover the best approach once we stop refusing to look at the issue and give it our full attention. For now, the main point that needs to be made is that there is nothing about a one-child policy that entails unacceptable sanctions, and there is no evidence that acceptable sanctions would be ineffective. This is something that could be done in a respectful, effective way.

Again, we naturally hope that sanctions never prove necessary. With education, with a system of appropriate incentives and disincentives, with enough people of good will, it is possible that we can show the self-discipline to do what is required, and bring ourselves and our descendants to a better future.

NOTES

1. There is some dispute as to whether this is due to global warming or to deforestation, but both of these are affected by population pressure.
2. This is a generalization. I am sure there are individual businesses who engage in environmentally good practices even where that diminishes their overall profit, and who try to educate people as to why that is important. When I look at larger businesses, though—those that advertise on television, for example—I don't see much of that.
3. Federal Research Division, *Singapore: A Country Study*, Library of Congress (Washington, DC) 1991, 73–75: "In a manner familiar to demographers, Singapore's demographic transition to low levels of population growth accompanied increases in income, education, women's participation in paid employment, and control of infectious diseases" (74).
4. Charles F. Westoff and Akinrinola Bankole, "Mass Media and Reproductive Behavior in Africa," Demographic and Health Surveys: Analytic Reports No. 2, Macro International, Calverton, MD, 1997, ix.
5. Federal Research Division, *Singapore: A Country Study*, Library of Congress (Washington, DC) 1991, 73–75.
6. Ashok Barnwal, "Success of the Indonesian Population Program: Lessons for India," *Journal of Development and Social Transformation*, vol. 1, 2004, 43–50.
7. Charles P. Wallace, "Column One: Popular Population Control: Indonesia's Family Planning Program Has Become a Model for the World. A Mix of Moderation, Madison Avenue and Islamic Teachings Has Overcome Staggering Odds," *Los Angeles Times*, September 27, 1993, quoting Kenneth R. Farr of the US Agency for International Development.
8. Federal Research Division, *Indonesia: A Country Study*, Library of Congress (Washington, DC) 1993, 109.
9. See Nicholas Kristof, "Politicians, Teens, and Birth Control," *New York Times*, November 12, 2014.
10. James Trussell, Felicia Stewart, Malcolm Potts, Felicia Guest, and Charlotte Ellertson, "Should Oral Contraceptives Be Available without Prescription?" *American Journal of Public Health*, vol. 83, #8, 1993, 1094–1099.
11. Committee on Gynecologic Practice, "Over-the-Counter Access to Oral Contraceptives," Committee Opinion, The American College of Obstetricians and Gynecologists, No. 544, December 2012.
12. Elizabeth Nolan Brown, "Over the Counter Birth Control Pills? Not in America," March 26, 2014, http://reason.com/archives/2014/03/26/over-the-counter-birth-control-pills-us.
13. Robert Engleman, "Trusting Women to End Population Growth," in *Life on the Brink*, ed. Philip Cafaro and Eileen Crist, University of Georgia Press (Athens, GA) 2012, 223–239.

14. Martha Campbell, Nuriye Nalan Sahin-Hodoglugil, and Malcolm Potts, "Barriers to Fertility Regulation: A Review of the Literature," *Studies in Family Planning*, vol. 37, #2, 2006, 87–98.

15. Ibid.

16. James N. Gribble, "Fact Sheet: Unmet Need for Family Planning," in *Population Reference Bureau: World Population Data Sheet 2012*, Population Reference Bureau, Washington, DC, July 2012, www.prb.org/Publications/Datasheets/2012/world-population-data-sheet/fact-sheet/unmet-need.aspx.

17. Ibid.

18. Ibid.

19. David Benatar, "The Limits of Reproductive Freedom," in *Procreation and Parenthood*, ed. David Archard and David Benatar, Oxford University Press (New York) 2010, 101.

20. Corey J. A. Bradshaw and Barry W. Brook, "Human Population Reduction Is Not a Quick Fix for Environmental Problems," *Proceedings of the National Academy of Science*, vol. 111, #46, November 18, 2014, 16610–16615.

21. Bill McKibben, *Maybe One: A Case for Smaller Families*, Plume (New York) 1998, 198.

22. Michael D. Bayles, "Limits to a Right to Procreate," in *Ethics and Population*, ed. Michael Bayle, Schenkman (Cambridge, MA) 1976, 42.

23. Ibid., 47–48.

24. McKibben, *Maybe One*, 12.

25. Christine Overall, *Why Have Children*, MIT Press (Cambridge, MA) 2012, 29.

26. See the pioneering work of Muzafer Sherif, *The Psychology of Social Norms*, Harper and Brothers (New York) 1936.

27. John Stuart Mill, *A System of Logic*, Harper and Brothers (New York) 1891, Book V, Chapter 1, 514.

28. Cass Sunstein, "Preferences and Politics," *Philosophy and Public Affairs*, vol. 20, #1, Winter 1991, 3–34.

29. Indeed, a cynic might argue that under a voluntary system, even if others do cut back on the number of children they have, someone might rationally take advantage of this to have more himself, since their sacrifice has already addressed the problem: Michael Bayles writes, "[I]f most people voluntarily limit the size of their families, then it will be in the interest of a particular couple to have more than the set number of children. For they will reap the benefits of an extra child and not significantly lose any of the benefits from a limited population. On the other hand, if others do not limit the size of their families, then it is still in the interest of a couple to have more than the set number of children. For if they did limit the size of their family, they would suffer all the disadvantages of an unlimited population and sacrifice the benefits of additional children" ("Limits to a Right," 48–49).

30. Richard McAdams "Focal Point Theory of Expressive Law," *Virginia Law Review*, vol. 86, November 2000, 1649–1729.
31. Richard McAdams, "An Attitudinal Theory of Expressive Law," *Oregon Law Review*, vol. 79, Summer 2000, 339–390. See also Robert Cooter, "Expressive Law and Economics," *Journal of Legal Studies*, vol. 27, June 1998, 585–607.
32. As shown in the work of Muzafer Sherif, *Psychology of Social Norms*.

[5]

THE FUTURE

From a moral point of view, the problem is not whether we can peer into the future and determine what future human beings will need and desire. It is possible to conceive—as distinguished from imagine—that future generations will be so different that our social ideal will no longer pertain. . . . I am only asserting that since we cannot know what their social ideal will be, we should act on the assumption that it will not be all that dissimilar from our own; we have no special reason to think otherwise. Hence, the course of responsible behavior in this generation would be to take what we do know, and can reasonably project, and act accordingly.

—Daniel Callahan, "What Obligations Do We Have to
Future Generations"

I have argued in Chapters 2 and 3 that we have no right to have more than one child in any situation where that threatens great harm to others. In doing that, I used various comparisons: that we don't have a right to yell "Fire" in a crowded theater, that my freedom to swing my fist ends at the other person's nose, and so on. Many people will argue, however, that there is a big difference between my intent to punch someone in the nose and having more than one child. The objection is that the harm we do through over-population is a future harm, enough in the future that the people we are protecting aren't even born yet. This, they say, changes the moral stakes. For one thing, the more distant in the future an act is, the more difficult it is to predict it—we can't even predict next week's weather very well, they can reasonably say, so how can we worry about how our actions will affect people 20, 40, or especially hundreds of years from now? There is no need to beat yourself up, much less make actual sacrifices, to avoid dangers that might not come to pass anyway.

Second, even if we could accurately predict the future, some will argue that the fate of future people has no moral importance for us. Future people will have rights when they eventually come into being, but they don't have rights yet. So we don't have any obligations to respect their rights. Those of us who are now existing, though, do have rights, and even where our rights aren't in question, the importance of our welfare places others under an obligation. Making us give up something we want (more children) for the sake of others who don't exist is wrongheaded—it's like saying my child can deprive me of my property now, merely because my will says he will inherit it when I die. The fact that he *will* have a right to the old clock doesn't mean he has a right to it *now*, and if I decide I want to sell everything in the house, clock included, to buy myself a Caribbean cruise, I haven't violated his rights of ownership.

Further, some people endorse a more complicated argument as to why we don't need to cut back on the children we have for the sake of future generations. They argue that we can't really wrong future people even if we allow overpopulation to make their lives really, really bad. The argument is that if it weren't for overpopulation, those people wouldn't be there at all, so they can't complain about the very poor conditions they are born into. Better options just weren't available for them. Unless their life is truly so bad that they'd be better off dead, or unborn, we haven't harmed them by bringing them into existence, even if we bring them into existence in a depleted, denuded world. On this scenario (known in philosophical circles as 'the nonidentity problem') that they are alive at all trumps all the disadvantages attached to their lives.[1]

These arguments are significant. I have argued that our right to control central aspects of our own lives, including the use of our bodies, is limited by the harm we may be doing to others. What might otherwise be an acceptable act becomes unacceptable if it results in serious disruption to others' lives. However that argument only works if we make the assumption that the harm to others that is in question really counts when we are weighing the costs and benefits of our action. The injury they will suffer has to be the sort of injury to which we should give serious moral consideration. If harm to people who don't yet exist has no weight when we are making our decisions as to what to do, we are likely to reach a very different conclusion when it comes to the permissibility of restricting reproduction.

Again, when we seek to justify government interference, we look for some harm that the interference prevents or some benefit that it conveys. Costs need to be sufficiently outweighed by benefits for a law to be worthwhile. It may irritate me to have to wait at crosswalks while dawdling pedestrians amble by, but the interruption to my progress can be outweighed by the harm that would foreseeably occur to pedestrians if they had to dash wildly across the street, dodging oncoming vehicles. The law giving pedestrians priority at certain places is justified.

Granted, sometimes we do enforce laws against theft even when the person who's been stolen from isn't harmed by it (you take the rich guy's sculpture from the least favorite of his many summer homes, and he doesn't notice), but at least we think the harm is one from which he could suffer: the loss of a sculpture is the kind of thing that usually does constitute a substantial harm, even though this happens to be a case where it doesn't. But when it comes to actions that do no harm, or almost no harm—the theft of a daisy, or paper clip, or putting the tip of your toe onto my private lawn—we don't think interference, much less punishment, is justified.

We need to justify intervening in your life, and in order to do that we generally need to show that this is the kind of thing that does significant harm. Can we do that when it comes to overpopulation? Yes. I will argue that when it comes to the likelihood of environmental degradation arising from increased population, the harm *is* certain, so that questions about unpredictability do not, on the whole, come into play. As to the second question, whether we, who now exist, can owe anything to those who don't yet exist, I will argue that one primary role of the state is to look after the interests of those who will come as well as of those who are now citizens. Last, the question isn't whether those who come later have grounds for complaining about the conditions of their existence, but whether we could have created a better world with happier people if we had limited population growth.

PROBABILITY VERSUS CERTAINTY

When I go to punch someone in the nose it is virtually certain that I will do him some harm, even if that is only some passing pain. It's always possible that I won't—perhaps a sudden microburst will suddenly push us out of range of each other. Perhaps the punch lands and requires medical treatment, and in the course of the treatment a dangerous tumor is discovered and my punch ends up saving the victim's life. This is pretty unlikely, though, so when I start in to hit him I am very likely to do him some harm, and more harm than good. In the case of overpopulation, though, many people argue that we are talking about a much more distant future, and that that significantly changes the moral status of the action. The more distant the event, the less sure we can be that it will actually come about: the more time, the more variables (typically) and with that we have that much less predictability, less certainty.

Some people who say we shouldn't worry about climate change in particular, and overpopulation in general, argue just this way: when it comes to averting dangers in the future, we are off the hook. We don't know with absolute certainty, they will say, that the climate will continue to change in the way experts predict, since we've never been in just this situation before. Indeed, we've been surprised already by unpredicted changes. Granted, the surprises have all been bad ones—the temperature is rising faster than we thought, not more slowly—but skeptics can say that just goes to show we are dealing with a new area of experience and shouldn't trust our own dire judgments. Even if severe climate change does occur, the more speculative will argue, there may be ways to avoid its effects, and the effects of overpopulation more generally. Desalination may provide plenty of fresh water for drinking, farming, and industry; new agricultural methods are developed every day and may provide plenty of food. The disappearance of rare metals may be compensated for by new technologies. Or perhaps future people will have very different psychologies and enjoy just the things that we hate: shortages, crowding, landscapes without any vestige of nature—maybe fighting for resources will even come to seem an amusing pastime. Or we may colonize new planets, where the population that exceeds the earth's resources may live happily. So, they will say, no need to give up a sure good thing (the children we want now) when that may be unnecessary.

This just won't work, though. First, we know that we are suffering from climate change now. The changes we have produced are already being felt all over the world. Those who worry about merely a future of environmental degradation are really the optimists. We see this in the *New York Times*:

> The effects of human-induced climate change are being felt in every corner of the United States, scientists reported Tuesday, with water growing scarcer in dry regions, torrential rains increasing in wet regions, heat waves becoming more common and more severe, wildfires growing worse, and forests dying under assault from heat-loving insects.[2]

And, of course, similarly across the globe, as reported by the Intergovernmental Panel on Climate Change.

> The I.P.C.C., composed of thousands of the world's leading climate scientists, has issued three reports in the last seven months, each the product of up to six years of research. The first simply confirmed what has been known since Rio: global warming is caused largely by the burning of fossil fuels by humans and, to a lesser extent, by deforestation. The second, released in Japan three weeks ago, said that profound effects were already being felt around the world, including mounting damage to coral reefs, shrinking glaciers and more persistent droughts, and warned of worse to come—rising seas, species loss and dwindling agricultural yields.[3]

Environmental degradation is not a merely future issue. It is happening now, and people are being harmed by it. It is happening, in fact, more rapidly than we had expected, so as concerns certainty versus uncertainty, all the news is bad. And many of the greater harms that will occur in the future will occur in the near future, soon enough that we know that science fiction possibilities for salvation won't have materialized: "The world has only about 15 years left in which to begin to bend the emissions curve downward. Otherwise, the costs of last-minute fixes will be overwhelming."[4]

It is true, as was discussed in Chapter 1, that it is not population alone that brings us to this pass. The way some of us live, the amazing amounts of resources we use, and our ever-increasing CO_2 output, has accelerated climate changes. Asked to cut back, we have instead increased our production of greenhouse gases. I certainly agree with those who say that the industrialized world doesn't have the right to consume at a rate that wreaks havoc on the economies and the lifestyles of others. We don't have the right to indulge ourselves in ways that destroy the lives of others. Practically, though, we are, as I've argued, more likely to be willing to cut back on how many children we have than on our patterns of consumption. If we can reasonably foresee that we will not cut back in any significant way in consumption, proceeding as if we *are* going to cut back at some very near date is unreasonable. Doing what you want on the grounds that some other person or persons could possibly act in a way that would offset the harm of your act is selfish, especially when you know that, as a matter of fact, they aren't likely to do what would be needed. If I am driving down the street drunk, it's always possible that everyone in the crowd in front of me will perform fabulous backflips to get out of the way, but I can pretty much bet that they won't. Excusing myself by saying they could have avoided the harm I sent their way doesn't work. We can't expect future people to be able to reduce consumption when we haven't so far been able to do that ourselves. And, in the long run, unimpeded growth would eventually have the same effects, even if we cut back considerably on our rates of consumption and pollution. There is just a limit to how many of us the planet can support, even if we were to cut back—as the evidence suggests we won't.

So we don't have to think about the future if we are estimating whether population could have an effect on us—it is having an effect already. In terms of probability, the probability of harm is 100%. It is true, though, that the case for limiting population is stronger if we consider not only the interests of those now living but also those who will live, because considering harm to the future means we are considering the interests of a much greater number of people. Generally, we consider harms more significant the more people they affect—while all avoidable deaths are regretted, plane crashes with 350 victims upset us more than plane crashes with 3, just as acts of mass terrorism make us more upset than does a single murder, even though the perpetrators of both may be equally contemptible. And, we naturally take greater pains to avoid these larger harms. Given this, the suffering of those who are yet to be born is relevant to the argument presented here, since it increases the numbers of those we will harm. The first question, then, is whether harm to future generations, as well as the present harm we already know about, is likely. And, of course, the answer is yes.

There may have been some confusion here. Whether or not population will continue to grow at a dangerous rate of increase for the foreseeable future *is* uncertain. The effects that will be felt if it does continue to grow are *not* uncertain: they will be devastating. As to the rate of population growth, it is true, we don't know if the population will grow at the rate it has in the past: as has been discussed, while the population over the last 100 years has grown at an unprecedented speed, the fertility rate over much of the world has recently been dropping. While in China that has been a result of government interference, in the United States, western Europe,

and parts of Asia, it has been merely a function of parental preference and the availability of contraception. If this decrease in fertility holds where it has so far occurred, and if it spreads to other
parts of the globe, the population will continue to grow for some
time, as we saw in Chapter 1: the UN predictions about population
assume that the drop in fertility rate will hold and indeed spread,
but the population will continue to grow because of demographic
momentum. If the fertility rates drops to the replacement rate
of 2.1 everywhere, eventually growth will end, but probably not
before we have reached an unsustainable number. This uncertainty
about whether the population will grow in more dangerous ways
shouldn't be confused with uncertainty about the effects of population growth if it does continue to grow, and of course whether it
continues to grow is up to us, and whether, as recommended here,
we have significantly fewer children than we have been having.

Those who argue that the effects may not be great tend to
rely on a bad argument. First, they say, correctly, that past predictions about disastrous effects of overpopulation have proven
false. Second, they conclude that since past predictions of disaster
proven false, present predictions will prove false as well. This is a
conclusion based on wishful thinking rather than reason.

It is true, as was briefly discussed in Chapter 1, that we've
gone through a couple of population scares (not that everyone
was scared, but the question at least made some informed people
nervous) and that those frightening predictions proved incorrect.
Thomas Malthus, writing between 1798 and 1826, argued that a
growing population would outstrip food supply, with catastrophic
starvation becoming inevitable.[5] That didn't happen. Again, in
1968 Paul Ehrlich argued in his popular neo-Malthusian book,
The Population Bomb, that starvation would be widespread in the
1970s and 1980s.[6] That didn't happen, either. While there have

been and continue to be food shortages in many places, the cause is not an absolute lack of food but political systems that are unstable and/or allow vastly unequal distribution of goods. On the whole, we consume more calories than we did in the past, and of course many populations are more threatened by obesity than by starvation. Malthus did not foresee the great strides we would make in agriculture, including the fruitful use of land that in Malthus's time wouldn't have been regarded as arable, and many critics regard Ehrlich's book as sensationalist, making predictions that were attention-getting but unreasonable even given the limited information available at the time. And so when some people look at the danger of general environmental degradation and argue that the best way to combat it is to limit human population, other people resort to the fact that Malthus was wrong, and that Ehrlich was wrong, and conclude that since they were wrong . . . what exactly?

When we talk about environmental degradation now, we're not talking about food supply. (It's true that food supply comes up—some predict that global warming will reduce American production in the Midwest by 40%—but that is not the exclusive or even primary focus.)[7] And it's not 1798, when the first copy of Malthus's *Essay on the Principle of Population* was published, and it's not 1968, when Ehrlich published his book—we know more and have better science. Nor are current predictions of environmental destruction made on the basis of the theories of 1 or 2 or even 10 or 20 people—it's being studied all over the world, through the combined efforts of experts in many fields, and they agree.

When we aren't engaging in wishful thinking, we realize that the fact that several theories concern more or less the same topic does not make them the very same theory. Believing that if Malthus and Ehrlich were wrong, any other prediction of overpopulation must be wrong is like saying that if one attempt at a flying machine failed, they all must fail, and the Wright brothers should stick to bicycles. And for that matter, Malthus's basic principle, that the increase of the population is necessarily limited by the means of subsistence, is clearly correct. He was just wrong in his estimate of how much food land could produce. Skeptics may say it's arrogant to believe that we know more now than Malthus did, but honestly, how often do we deny that we know more about science than they did in 1798, or even 1968? It's only when we don't want to believe the results of our science that we become so modest in our estimates of its truth.

So we cannot go from the fact that Malthus (and his 20th-century followers) did not correctly predict improvements in agricultural production to an assumption that the quite different problems we face now—most notably, global warming, but many others, as discussed in Chapter 1—can somehow be compensated for or fixed by improved technology. We don't see any way of doing that.

In the end, though, whether the harm is certain to occur may not be the morally pressing question. If a harm is probable enough, it behooves us to take steps to prevent it. And when this is a harm to other people, which we could prevent without the violation of basic rights or the production of too much harm to ourselves, it becomes a moral duty that we should prevent it. We sometimes allow people to gamble with their own futures, but to gamble with someone else's is quite a different matter.

Consider leaving a loaded gun on a school playground. It isn't certain it will hurt anyone. Maybe no one will find it. Maybe a custodian will find it and put it away safely. Maybe a cautious and authority-loving child will find it and turn it over immediately to a teacher. Many of these are more likely than the discovery of technological fixes that will allow unlimited population growth, but no one would let me off the hook for leaving the gun there. The flimsy excuse that it *might* not cause any harm would cut no ice with anyone. If a child finds and shoots someone with the gun, my saying correctly that it could possibly have turned out okay won't convince anyone that I should be excused.

Someone might reasonably object that leaving a gun on the playground is very different from having children. When we consider how we should behave in terms of probable harms, we need to consider not only the harm our act may do in the future, but the benefit that comes to us from the same act. This is a question we confront all the time. It is more probable that we will kill an innocent person when we drive than when we walk. Yet we drive and are not blamed for thereby endangering others. At this point in time, in most societies, it's very hard to live without driving—we wouldn't be able to work, or get groceries, or take our children to the doctor without hopping in the car, even though that's inherently risky. So we do accept dangerous practices when they are beneficial enough that the advantages outweigh the disadvantages.

On the other hand, we all agree that drunk driving is extremely blameworthy, even though most people who drive drunk don't end up killing anybody at all, and those who drive drunk and get home safely get some benefit out of it—they are home, where they wanted to be. Drunk drivers are self-indulgent: they don't need to be drunk in the first place, and being drunk, they don't really need to drive. We condemn them because they are doing something potentially dangerous that they don't need to do, and trusting to luck that it will turn out. It is, really, a balance: how much harm will the act do if it does end up harming someone? How likely is that harm to occur? How much do we gain from doing the action in question? What options do we have for achieving the same, or similar, benefit without engaging in the dangerous practice? In the case of having more than one child, where you can avoid that, and where the evidence is out there as to what continuous population growth will likely do, I would argue that you are too much like the drunk driver for moral comfort.

FUTURE PEOPLE DON'T HAVE PRESENT RIGHTS

Another argument against our obligation to refrain from having unsustainable numbers of children is that insofar as we refrain for the sake of future people, we are mistaken, because future people don't have rights. As said, many future environmental harms will happen to presently existing people, just later in their lives, but some of the worst ones are predicted to occur to people who aren't yet born, so this question is significant. The argument is that while future people will have rights once they are born, they don't have rights now. As in the example above, someone's future right to property doesn't give him control of that property at the present moment. The future right to vote doesn't mean we can't interfere with you casting a vote when you are still underage. In the case of people who aren't yet born, they are, obviously, not in a position to bear any rights whatsoever. So whatever harm we may do them can't be a violation of their rights.

This is a common argument. I think, though, that it is misconceived, and in at least three ways. First, not all our obligations involve rights. We can have duties to help people whether or not their rights are in question. Second, even though future people don't yet possess rights, a good case can be made that we have an obligation not to preemptively make it impossible for them to exercise basic human rights once they are born. Last, even if we didn't, as individuals, have obligations to respect the rights of future persons, there is good reason to think that the government does have an obligation to look after the rights of those who will come, and to act now as is necessary to protect them.

As to the first, I think we all agree that how we should treat other people isn't just a function of who has what rights. An ideal of moral duty that limits our duties to respecting rights is sadly arid. It is only a minimal criterion for right action, and one that could be embraced by people we would generally think of as morally contemptible: selfish, misanthropic, even downright nasty. Imagine a parent who conceives of his child's birthday celebration as requiring no more than what the child has a right to—which might after all be nothing, since a right to cake and presents isn't one we generally recognize. Why volunteer to help in the schools, since they don't have a right to my time? Why send food to earthquake victims, since by rights it's my food, and not theirs? Why treat others pleasantly when no one has a right to more than that you not attack them? Usually, we think we should benefit people whether or not their rights are at stake, especially if the alternative is that they exist in great need. Typically, we think even more strongly that we shouldn't hurt other people, even when it's within our rights to do so. As we generally consider rights, it's within our rights to be as mean as possible to everyone we know as long as we don't actually harm them physically: we can say, "You're stupid and ugly!" when they greet us, tell them their new grandchild looks like a newt, insult their past performance in anything from cooking Christmas dinner to landing a job, and deprecate the possibility of future improvement, but does anyone think that someone who lives this way has treated people they way he ought to? Again, how much we normally think we ought to do to help others may be limited by how much helping would hurt us, but as I have argued in Chapter 2, limiting ourselves to one child won't hurt us much.

Rights, then, are not the only thing we need to pay attention to. However, it is true that rights are generally believed to make especially strong claims on us. While we think we should help people in need even when their rights are not at stake, we tend to think that if their rights are at stake, we can do more: we can force people to respect rights. If you tell me I'm ugly and stupid, other people may chastise you, but typically they don't think they can forcibly prevent you from saying that. If, on the other hand, you fail to respect my right to bodily integrity (you try to hit me), it is okay for someone else to step in and keep you from throwing that punch; indeed, we think it's obligatory to do something, even if it's just calling the police. Sometimes we've allocated authority to some recognized body to do this (like law enforcement), and sometimes it's okay for private individuals to step in, but everyone agrees that when my right is violated, forcible intervention is justified. If you find out that your neighbor is keeping someone as a slave, you have a very strong duty to step up and make sure that stops.

Given this, it is fair to say that the question of rights is important, even though it doesn't exhaust all of morality. And some people will argue that future people don't have present rights. Since they don't have rights, we can't be forced to do anything to help them, or even to refrain from harming them. Maybe we aren't very nice people if we do nothing to make their lives better, but being a selfish, misanthropic, and downright nasty person is our privilege. If we choose to have fewer children so that those who come will have decent lives, that is nice of us, but no one can make us refrain from an action for the sake of people whose rights aren't being violated.

I think part of this argument is correct. In some cases, certainly, the possession of a future right places no one under a present obligation in regards to that right. I think that's true of inheritance, as mentioned above. My son's right to inherit means nothing until I'm actually dead. In other cases, though, it's not so clear. When it comes to the exercise of rights to basic interests, I can see a case being made that future people will have a basic right to certain living conditions. Those potential rights do place us under a present obligation to provide a decent chance of living, if a person is going to be born at all. Similarly, if we think of rights in terms of autonomy, I can see the argument that if we know a person is going to be born, we now violate his rights if we do something likely to deprive him of the ability to make choices in how to live.

It's true I can go ahead and sell the clock my son hopes to inherit. But what if I am planning to become pregnant next month, and now set about doing drugs whose residual effect will cause my future child severe brain damage? When I do this, I deprive that child of the ability to learn, think, and be self-sufficient. On any view of rights, he may be said to have a right to do those things: he has a basic interest in doing these things, as described in Chapter 2, and it is typically believed that these are the conditions required to exercise autonomy, as described in Chapter 3. If we know people will come into being and we preemptively deprive them of the conditions they need to exercise their fundamental rights, it does seem we have violated an obligation to them that these basic rights be respected. We normally think that children who are born with fetal alcohol syndrome, for example, have been wronged by their mothers, even though they weren't persons at the time the harm was initiated. Such a mother has so distorted the conditions of her child's existence that it will not be able to thrive, and to that extent has violated a right to a fair chance at life. It is true that mothers have special obligations to their children that the rest of us don't share, but when it comes to depriving people of the conditions they need for exercising their rights, the obligation is general.

Consider the Racist Superscientist: he hates an entire race of people (by which we can understand a group of people with some shared biological trait that gives them an appearance we associate with race). He considers the possibility of (somehow) feeding all of the existing population a drug that would cause severe brain damage and reduce their intelligence so much that they will no longer be able to function as reflective, active members of society. Then he considers that, unfortunately, since these people currently exist, they have rights, and he would be violating their rights. Despite his hatred, he is a respecter of rights, so he refrains. Instead, he develops a kind of gene intervention that will cause the genes to mutate in a way that only affects their offspring. This way, he causes their descendants to be born with the handicaps he wished for their parents/ancestors. Surely we would think he is violating the rights of those who will be born disabled through his efforts, even though the action he takes precedes their actual existence. It's as if he had set a bomb that would go off in the future—the only people who will die are people who haven't yet been born, but surely we could say their right to life was violated, even if the bomber is dead by the time the harm occurs.

In a similar context, Joel Feinberg refers to "anticipatory rights." When we speak of a child who can't yet walk, we don't yet say it has the right to walk freely down the sidewalk, since it can't. However, we anticipate that it will eventually (assuming it survives) have a right to walk freely down the sidewalk. Cutting off its legs on the grounds that it doesn't yet have this right would clearly be wrong.[8] The exercise of almost any right requires certain material conditions. I can't exercise my right to vote, for example, if there is nothing like a polling place where I can cast one, and no way to count the votes. Many people believe we have a right to education, which is why the state provides it for free, but no one can exercise this right unless there are schools and an educational system in place. In many cases, these requisites for the exercise of a right need preparation long before the right itself is to be exercised, and in some cases, before the person who will exercise it has even come into being. You can't, after all, instantly produce an education system at the moment the child is capable of receiving education. These material conditions can only be met if steps are taken before the birth of the person who will exercise the rights.

In the same way, creating a generally bad environment will deprive future generations of the conditions needed to thrive. In both these cases, it seems plausible to say that rights have indeed been violated, even though the action that violates them was started before the entity who holds the right was born. My child's right to inherit the family clock is always provisional—his future right depends entirely on my conveying ownership to him, which I am morally free to do or not. As long as I own the clock, I have the right either to convey it to him or to choose not to. Some rights are conditional in this sense, dependent on whether another person bestows them or not, whereas others are unconditional, or, as we sometimes put it, inalienable. When it comes to these, where the person has a claim that doesn't depend on the will of another person, we need to make sure we are not (now) undercutting the (future) exercise of the right. This may not be a definitive argument, but I think it is one with at least intuitive plausibility.

Last, we should remember that in this case I am advocating governmental action, in the form of regulations. Even where individuals don't have obligations to care about the welfare of future people, we tend to believe that the state does. If we look at the justification for government, we see that the reason for government isn't merely that it should protect those citizens who are now alive. Many of government's actions are designed for the security of the state both now *and* in the future: environmental laws to be sure, but others as well: the idea is to set up lasting institutions, so as to create a lasting state, to benefit those who are alive now and those who will be alive in the future. The Preamble to the Constitution of the United States says:

> We the People of the United States, in Order to form a more perfect Union, establish Justice, insure domestic Tranquility, provide for the common defense, promote the general Welfare, and secure the Blessings of Liberty to ourselves and our Posterity, do ordain and establish this Constitution for the United States of America.

Similarly, the Norwegian constitution states that

> Every person has a right to an environment that is conducive to health and to a natural environment whose productivity and diversity are maintained. Natural resources should be managed on the basis of comprehensive long-term considerations whereby this right will be safeguarded for future use as well.[9]

And again, the Japanese constitution, in enumerating rights, says, "These fundamental human rights guaranteed to the people by this Constitution shall be conferred upon the people of this and future generations as eternal and inviolate rights."[10]

Even if we didn't accept the claims made above that future generations have rights, the sentiment that is expressed here should have some weight in determining policy: generally citizens want their nation to continue beyond one generation, and the accomplishment of whatever is necessary to this end is entrusted to the government. The state can and should take on responsibilities that might not be seen as the provenance of individual citizens. After all, we don't expect individuals to make sure that restaurants are sanitary, or that bridges are in good repair, or to go around educating children other than their own, but we do want these things done. Once we have formed a government, it takes on responsibilities that don't attach to individuals, responsibilities for procuring social goods that will be enjoyed in common. One of these responsibilities is to ensure, so far as that is possible, a stable future. We expect the government to take steps for the orderly continuance of services, so that we keep records of, say, bridge maintenance that can be referred to by those in the future so that bridges won't collapse under their futuristic cars. It has a responsibility for taking steps for its own stable continuance, even as individual members of the government come and go—we consider rules for orderly changes of administration essential to good government. So government actions are generally taken with a long view as to future effects. Naturally, this doesn't always happen, but when shortsighted measures turn out to have temporary benefits that are outweighed by much more lasting harms, we decry them as ill-considered, and often as selfish—we think people in government should be watching out for future interests as well as for our own.

Just as we want safe bridges and attractive national parks for future citizens, we want basic goods to be available—basic resources and basic security. One job the government has is taking the steps that make that possible. What might be supererogatory for a private person becomes obligatory in terms of state action. Again a government with the motto "Après nous, le déluge" would be a supremely irresponsible government. A good government recognizes the obligation to balance the interests of those now alive and those who are to come, even when some actions may frustrate those who are alive now, and who lose sight of the interests of future people when respecting those interests conflicts with something they want. In the case of population reduction, individual restraint probably won't be effective enough—we need the government to coordinate efforts toward population control for those to succeed. Given this, government intervention on behalf of those who don't yet exist is not only permissible, it is a duty.

THE NONIDENTITY PROBLEM

This last objection may be the most controversial. To some, it's very obviously right, and to others, it's very obviously so wrong as to be downright silly. It is this: we don't do anything wrong when we create a really disagreeable, overpopulated future environment because we don't harm anyone when we do that. We won't harm anyone by overpopulating, because if we didn't have overpopulation, these particular people wouldn't exist. If living in an overcrowded, unpleasant world is a condition of their very existence, they can't complain, because they could not have been born into a better world. After all, the whole point of limiting births is not to bring some people into existence, and you can't (usually) benefit them by not bringing them into existence, nor (usually) harm them by bringing them into existence. To harm someone is to make him worse off than he otherwise would have been, and that's not what you do in creating a person who is himself part of the overpopulation problem. If we cut back on the number of children we have, we may bring *other* people into existence, and *their* lives will have a better quality than the lives of the people who would have existed amid overpopulation, but that doesn't mean you've made anyone better off than they otherwise would have been.

This problem was raised by Derek Parfit in 1984, and has received a lot of attention from philosophers, although, as I say, many other people dismiss it as wrongheaded. Parfit raises it in the following example:

> The 14-year-old girl: This girl chooses to have a child. Because she is so young, she gives her child a bad start in life. Though this will have bad effects throughout this child's life, his life will, predictably, be worth living. If this girl had waited for several years, she would have had a different child, to whom she would have given a better start in life. . . . Suppose that we tried to persuade this girl that she ought to wait. ". . . It will be worse for [your child] if you have him now. If you have him later, you will give him a better start in life." We failed to persuade this girl. She had a child when she was 14, and, as we predicted, she gave him a bad start in life. Were we right to claim her decision was worse for her child? If she had waited, this particular child would never have existed. And, despite its bad start, its life is worth living.[11]

On Parfit's account, it *is* possible to harm someone by bringing him into existence *if* his life is so bad that he'd be better off dead. In that case, the person would be better off unborn, so *not* giving birth to him would in fact be doing him a favor. Short of this, though, people are better off being born than not being born, or, at the least, they are not harmed by being born. Producing a better world with fewer people cannot be said to help those who don't reap that world's advantages. And you don't harm them by bringing them into the only world that's an option for them. To harm someone is to make him worse off than he otherwise would have been, and in this case, he wouldn't otherwise have been at all. So, according to Parfit, you don't do anything wrong if you bring someone into a painfully overpopulated world, until that world is so bad that he's truly better off unborn or dead.

Parfit realizes that this view has a number of interesting, if not startling, implications. Say that a woman is thinking of becoming pregnant. She has an infection so that if she becomes pregnant now, her child will be physically and mentally handicapped, and will need painful surgeries to keep living. If she waits a month until the infection passes, she will have a child who is completely normal, and able to live a full and happy life.[12] Opinion is pretty much universal that she should wait a month. If we accept the conclusion Parfit reaches in the nonidentity case, though, there is no reason for her to wait and give birth to a healthy and happy child, rather than conceiving now and giving birth to a child who will suffer pain and severe disability. As long as the life of the disabled child is not absolutely unbearable, it is no worse off alive than not having been born, and so she has done nothing wrong.

This is, to say the least, contrary to any number of beliefs we hold about what constitutes responsible moral behavior. Typically, we say that people should wait until they can provide, if not optimal conditions for having a child, at least those that are relatively good: good relative to what most children get, or, if that is not possible because of, say, unavoidable poverty, at least good circumstances relative to their own potential. For that reason, we advise young people that they should be able to support a child adequately before they conceive; they should wait until they are emotionally mature, until they have finished school, wait until they can, basically, provide the basics for a child. This is why we give a great deal of money for abstinence education in schools, and why having a high rate of teen pregnancy is generally reckoned a bad thing. This is not to say that people who are disabled, or poor, or born to a very young parent can't have happy and useful lives. It is simply to say that where we do see a greater likelihood of a child's having the richest panoply of human experience if the parent waits to conceive, we think it is better to wait. On Parfit's account, though, all of this is mistaken. The child a woman has if she waits until she is ready, as we normally think of that, will be a different child, so no one will be harmed if she gives birth when she is not yet ready to be a decent parent. What we generally regard as irresponsible behavior would no longer be blameworthy.

Similarly, many of the legal constraints we now have in place in order to safeguard the welfare of children would, on this account, be inappropriate. Laws that require that sperm and egg donors meet certain health standards would be wrongheaded, insofar as the standards are put in place for the sake of the resulting baby: if these sperm/eggs, with whatever problems, aren't used, some other child will be born—it's not that this one will be born but in a healthier state.[13] Screening embryos for implantation in order to exclude those that have genetic malformations would be pointless, at least as far as the children those embryos might become are concerned. (One might still care about these things for the sake of the parents who will do the caretaking, but the welfare of the children themselves is no longer relevant.) Those who worry about cloning on the grounds that a cloned offspring might be deformed, given our lack of experience in human cloning, would be wrong to think this is a problem—as long as the offspring's life is not so bad that its life is not worth living, there is no reason not to have it, since life in its deformed state is the only life it can have. We don't have to take steps to make sure that certain offspring have as good a chance as anyone of living a happy life, if the only way they can be born is to live a less happy life than others. The fact that instead of these unhappy, unhealthy children we could have produced happy, healthy children is irrelevant.

This strikes most of us as peculiar. It is true, on the one hand, that those who have sued for wrongful birth—who have sued on the grounds that their very birth was, in terms of law, a tort, a wrong to them that they have the right to collect damages for—have generally failed, since courts have shown themselves unwilling to rule that life itself can be a harm to the person who is born. Courts are willing to grant damages to the parents who would have gotten an abortion if they had been properly informed of their child's diagnosis, but not to the sons and daughters who count their birth as injuries to themselves: rewarding such a plaintiff would, as one judge said, "require this court to find [the child] had an interest in avoiding his own birth, e.g. that there is a fundamental legal right not to be born when birth would necessarily entail a life of hardship."[14]

Courts, though, labor under special burdens when considering who can sue, and the idea that the unborn are bearers of rights not to be born, for whose violation they can later sue, brings the threat of all sorts of lawsuits, by children when they are eventually born or by others on their behalf, and courts don't like to make decisions that will result in a proliferation of cases. And, of course, one can imagine the claim that some lives aren't worth living being used as a foundation for the further claim that there is a right to die, something the courts have been unwilling to recognize. Legal reasoning, though, is not the same as moral reasoning, and the legal standards used to make such a determination don't show what is morally required of us. The fact that a child is not so unhappy that it is better off dead doesn't seem enough, doesn't seem the appropriate standard of when to have a child. It's just not the measure of responsible procreation.

While these are all cases where we are deciding whether it is okay to intend to have a child, or not have a child, based on the circumstances it will live in, the nonidentity problem is really much more pervasive. After all, which child we have isn't just a matter of intention: lots of accidents of timing, physical condition, and so forth affect which particular zygote is formed. It's been pointed out that a policy of avoiding dangerous radioactive waste will, as a side effect, make a difference in which children are born, so if we take steps to avoid producing waste, we may have different children from those who would have been born under another policy. If we fail to have the very children who would have been born into the radioactive world, we haven't benefited them by our cleanup plan.[15] Even apparently praiseworthy personal choices—biking instead of taking the car—may affect which particular child is conceived when the man comes home (later, more tired, or whatever). His hopes for behaving in a way that creates a better world for his child won't be met—the child that would have been born into the polluted world won't be born into the cleaner world, so he hasn't helped anyone.[16]

This all seems very hard to accept, and this is because the argument does not, in the end, work.

First, we should note that future overpopulation isn't exactly a nonidentity case. In the original case, there was one scenario where a particular child was born, and an alternative scenario where a distinct child was born: two possible futures, each with a different child. When we look at overpopulation, it doesn't work like that. Some of the people who live in the overpopulated future (Grayworld) would have lived in the less populated world (Greenworld). The fact that Grayworld has more people doesn't mean it has entirely distinct people.[17] Granted, some of the people born into Greenworld would not be born into Grayworld—if people are planning to limit their pregnancies, that may change the timing of the one child they do have, so it's a different child than would have been born into Grayworld. But some people won't do that—they may have their only child just when they would otherwise have had one of the numerous children they would have had in Grayworld. So we can, even if we accept Parfit's reasoning, say that at least these people have actually been harmed: we could have had them into either Greenworld or Grayworld, and we chose Grayworld, and thereby caused them a very severe harm we could have avoided. They are, then, wronged by our behavior.

Second, if we do indeed continue with parallel population growth and consumption growth, we will reach a point at which we have so harmed the planet that there is a good chance that a fair number of those who come will actually have lives not worth living. Even if we accept the nonidentity problem, it is wrong to produce a child whose life is so full of travail that it would be better off never having been born. Of course, there is a big question as to what would make a life not worth living.[18] We do know that in a severely overpopulated future there will be material want. There will also be a lack of solitude, and of natural beauty, and of security. Want increases violence, whether individual or in the form of wars, and violence and insecurity make the enjoyment of the amenities of life extremely difficult to come by. Constant warfare can itself make a life not worth living, and with war there is often general civil disruption; poverty is made worse, and suffering is compounded. Eventually, it would become miserable indeed.

However, there are other reasons to reject the nonidentity thesis. The reason we find it hard to accept its peculiar conclusions (that it's okay to have created a severely disabled child now rather than waiting a month to conceive a healthy child, etc.) is that most of us think the reasoning it uses is wrong.

On that theory, the only way we can count harms or benefits is if we have a specific person of whom we can say he would have been better off, or worse off, if his circumstances had been different. For many of us, this is not a correct description of the way we think about better and worse lives. If I choose to become pregnant when I am in a good situation to have a child economically and emotionally, when I have conquered whatever drug/alcohol/disease problem that endangers the child's physical health, I feel I have done the right thing; I have created a child with a better life than the child that otherwise would have come into existence. When I think of the future, I think that I should have a happy child, whoever that child may be. When we think generally of the future, we don't think so much that we want a determined set of people to have lives that are as good as they can be given the very dire circumstances they are born into. Instead, we would like to bring about circumstances in which there will be truly happy people, whoever they are.

Dan Brock has described this as our acceptance of a "non person-affecting" principle: it is morally good to act in a way that results in less suffering and more opportunity in the world.[19] (The phrase "non person-affecting" is unfortunate, I think, in that it might suggest he is saying that how persons feel—how they are affected—doesn't matter. On the contrary, we are trying to promote a good life precisely because there will be people who experience it.) The point is that it is a better world in which there are happy people rather than miserable people, even if no particular person's position is improved in the better world over what it would have been in the miserable world. My potentially miserable child will not be made better by my having a healthy and happy child instead, but it is still better that I have a healthy and happy child instead—there will be more good human experience in this world.

The relevant question is not whether there is some person who could justly complain about how I've treated him if I bring him into the overpopulated world. The question is whether I could have created a better world with happier people. To most of us, this seems obvious. Philip Peters has suggested that the model of wrongness where we only do wrong if we make an identifiable person worse off comes from the legal system, where someone can only sue if he has standing—if he can show that he personally is affected by whatever was done.[20] In the court system, we can't sue on behalf of future generations, or on behalf of anyone who happens to have been harmed but who doesn't himself sue: I can't go to court on the grounds that I think my unsuspecting neighbor was gypped by her contractor. The person suing has to have suffered the harm in question, or must be the designated representative of the person who suffered harm. This has been a problem in environmental law—we need to show that there is a person who is affected by, say, the failure to respect the Clean Water Act before we can go to court. Merely saying a case of water pollution is bad for the environment, or that it will make the world an uglier and less healthy place for those to come, doesn't cut it.

This hardly exhausts the realm of morality, though. Courts have practical problems—as mentioned above, they don't want to be inundated with suits, given the limits to the time and resources available to them, and if they start to allow suits by third parties, that is just what might happen. For most of us, whether or not a lawsuit is appropriate is not the best criterion for morally right action.

WHY DON'T WE CARE?

Even if we are not yet at the point where population numbers augur imminent disaster, we are at least close enough, given our increasing consumption, that you would think more people would be concerned about this. It's not the kind of thing you can easily fix—or fix at all—if you wait until huge amounts of damage are actually occurring. Why don't we focus on it? One reason is presumably political: at least in the United States, the religious Right has tried to prevent any discussion of anything that might suggest that the use of contraception should be encouraged. Some of them are actively opposed to contraception, and others think that promoting it will "send a message" that having sex while wishing to avoid procreation is morally acceptable. Insofar as the religious right wing has managed to impose its religious views on public policy by controlling those who need to formulate such policy, it's been hard to get any discussion of population to be had at all, much less promulgated, in government circles.

Failure to Appreciate Facts

Individuals, though, are not as dependent on funding from lobbying groups as politicians are, and it is still true that most people don't worry about this. They consider their own time and their own finances when they think of having a second or third (or fourth or fifth) child, but that is seen as the end of their moral responsibility. There are probably several reasons for this indifference. First, of course, is ignorance. A lot of people—maybe most people—don't realize how much population has grown in the last two hundred years, and haven't taken the time to look at population projections for the future. Of course, some of this ignorance may be due to the religious Right, insofar as, again, public discussion of such possibilities is frowned upon, but there are other reasons, too. We just aren't as interested in future events if they seem sufficiently distant.

Identified versus Statistical Victims

We care less about people who are more distant from us, whether they are distant in space or distant in time. The further away they are, the less we are motivated to help them: we tend to rouse ourselves greatly to help a family in the same town whose house has burned down, and much less strongly to help hurricane victims in another part of the country. People in distant countries have even less appeal to our sympathy. Part of this is the difficulty we have in responding to people who look different or speak different languages and live in very different ways. While in theory we recognize that such people have as much importance as we do, we don't seem to vividly appreciate harm that comes to them in the way that we see the badness of more local harms. We recognize that a fire in a house in Beijing is just as painful to the occupants as a fire in the neighboring town, but the effect on our emotions just isn't the same.

In particular, we know we don't respond as readily to victims who aren't identified. The neighbors whose house burns down are people I can put a face and name to, even if I don't know them well. Being told that thousands (or worse, millions) of people are suffering leaves us with no focus for our empathy. This is why charities try to focus on a single, identifiable child when they are soliciting money, rather than focusing on thousands of people who are in danger of starvation. It's not that we don't believe the suffering of thousands matters as much, or even more, than that of one person. We just don't feel it in the same way. This distinction between identified and statistical victims, as it is called, is one that matters when it comes to getting people to feel the significance of others' pain.[21] Obviously, though, it doesn't make any difference to what is right and what is wrong. People's value is the same if they are here or there, and our inability to assess that properly is just our shortcoming, not an accurate insight that only those who are near to us really matter.

The future, to us, is a very faraway country full of people with whom we have no direct acquaintance. We know that some future people, somewhere, sometime, will suffer because of our choices, but we don't find that as motivating as we would if I knew that something I'm thinking of doing today would immediately cause a family of identifiable people next door in my town to suffer pain, injury, and premature death. If I were contemplating a second child and knew that this would be the result, I would think better of it. I would think I didn't have that right. If we have reason to believe our assessment of future harm is accurate, we need to act on that assessment, whether the harm is near or far.

False Induction

Another reason we don't worry about procreation arises from our general inability to believe that anything we've always done in the past could be harmful in the future. This plays a role in people's own prudential decisions: it's part of why it's hard to give up our unhealthy food for a better diet, and part of what weakens our motivations to give up dangerous practices like smoking. There are reasons for this: induction, generally, is a good tool. It tells us not to start each day as if we hadn't learned anything over the course of our lives. If hitting the cue ball into the seven ball has always resulted in the seven rolling forward, I don't really need to pause and wonder if this time it will cause the seven ball to explode into a million particles. We rely on induction, and we should rely on induction. However, we also need to realize that induction doesn't work when the circumstances are different. If I know that someone *has* loaded the seven ball with nitroglycerin, I can't reasonably say to myself, "So far, so good, no reason to change my ways just because someone has done a little tampering." Reproduction in a past time didn't do foreseeable harm. Now things have changed. What was once a blessing is now much closer to becoming a curse, and we need to deal with that.

Passing the Buck

Yet another reason we tend not to take the possibility of overpopulation seriously is that when it comes to helping others, we generally hope someone else will do it for us. We discussed incremental harms—harms in which each of us only plays a small role—in Chapter 3. This is related. Here, each generation can conceivably pass the problem down to the next generation, hoping that that generation will cut back in reproduction enough to avoid any possible problems. Life is not yet unbearable, or even very bad, for most of us, they will argue, so why take on hardships now when someone else can do it later?

This "pass the buck" thinking, while tempting, has obvious problems. Basically, it's too costly, which is presumably why passing the buck generally has a bad name. If you fail to act, you have no reason to think those who come after will act. Indeed, your inaction may even make it less likely that they will act—we are influenced, obviously, by the culture we are in, and if we grow up with a sense of fin de siècle fatalism, or simply with an acceptance of selfishness, it may be harder to see it as our duty to help where we can. And the longer a society faced with overpopulation puts off dealing with it, the worse the situation that is passed on to the next generation will be: more damage will have occurred, some of it irreparable. And the population will be larger, so that (barring plagues, devastating warfare, and such, which we can hardly look to with satisfaction to solve our problems for us) it will take much longer to bring it down to a sustainable size. The likelihood that even one child per family would be unsustainable becomes greater. By waiting, we would pass on a problem that is even more difficult to fix than the one we failed to fix. The fact that it would be possible, in theory, for those who come later to take on hardships worse than those we faced doesn't mean it's okay for us to put them in that situation. We hold you responsible for the fire you set, even if others could possibly intervene and put it out after you've let it grow.

NOTES

1. This was first referred to as 'the nonidentity problem' in Derek Parfit's *Reasons and Persons*, Oxford University Press (New York) 1984.
2. Justin Gillis, "U.S. Climate Has Already Changed, Study Finds, Citing Heat and Floods," *New York Times*, May 6, 2014.
3. Editorial Board, "Running Out of Time," *New York Times*, April 20, 2014.
4. Ibid.
5. An argument made and refined through several editions of *An Essay on the Principle of Population*, various editions, 1798–1826.
6. Paul Ehrlich, *The Population Bomb*, Sierra Club / Ballantine Books (New York) 1968.
7. *Risky Business: The Economic Risks of Climate Change in the United States*, June 2014, riskybusiness.org/uploads/files/RiskyBusiness_PrintedReport_FINAL_WEB_OPTIMIZED.pdf.

8. Both the bomb example and the baby who can't yet walk come from Joel Feinberg's "A Child's Right to an Open Future," in *Freedom and Fulfillment,* ed. Joel Feinberg, Princeton University Press (Princeton, NJ) 1992.
9. Norwegian Constitution, Article 110 b.
10. Japanese Constitution 1946, Chapter 3, Article 11.
11. Parfit, *Reasons and Persons,* 358–359.
12. I don't want to suggest that the lives of the disabled are always worse than the lives of the abled. The example turns on a case where the life of a specifically affected disabled person is worse than the life of an average abled person.
13. These and other cases are discussed in I. Glenn Cohen, "Regulating Reproduction: The Problem with Best Interests," *Minnesota Law Review,* vol. 96, 2011, 423–519.
14. *Siemeniec v. Lutheran General Hospital,* 117 Ill. 2d 230 (1987), at 243. See also *Nelson v. Krusen,* 678 S.W. 2d 918 (Tex. 1984).
15. Elizabeth Harman, "Can We Harm and Benefit in Creating?" *Philosophical Perspectives,* vol. 18, 2004, 89–113.
16. Example from Axel Gosseries, "On Future Generations' Future Rights," *Journal of Political Philosophy,* vol. 16, #4, 2008, 446–474.
17. I owe this point to I. Glenn Cohen, "Regulating Reproduction," 457ff.
18. Some people will presumably argue that life is always worth living, even if the person whose life it is actually hates it, not just for a moment but continuously. These are some of the people who oppose the right to die, and the legality of physician-assisted suicide—not just because they are afraid the practice might be abused, but because they think even the most rational person, who is experiencing excruciating pain, who knows it will continue with no hope of cure, and who makes a decision to die now rather than later, shouldn't be allowed to do that. Such people believe that whether the person living it likes it or not, his life is worth living and he must live it. This, though, is a sufficiently dogmatic and irrational position that I don't think it stands in need or refutation: for most of us, life is valuable for the wonderful experiences it brings, and if it is no longer possible for the life to have whatever the person considers valuable experiences, it's not worth living. More rationally, though, there is a question as to *when* a life is not worth living, and that is more difficult to assess.
19. Dan Brock, "The Non-identity Problem and Genetic Harms—The Case of Wrongful Handicaps," *Bioethics,* vol. 9, #3, 1995, 273.
20. Philip G. Peters, "Implications of the Nonidentity Problem for State Regulation of Reproductive Liberty," in *Harming Future Persons: Ethics, Genetics, and the Nonidentity Problem,* ed. Melinda A. Roberts and David T. Wasserman, Springer (Dordrecht) 2009.

21. The distinction between identified and statistical victims was introduced, as far as I know, by Thomas Schelling, in "The Life You Can Save May Be Your Own," in *Problems in Public Expenditure Analysis*, ed. S. B. Chase, Brookings Institution (Washington, DC) 1968, 127–162.

[6]

UNWANTED CONSEQUENCES

A population may be too crowded, though all be amply supplied with food and raiment. It is not good for man to be kept perforce at all times in the presence of his species. A world from which solitude is extirpated is a very poor ideal. Solitude, in the sense of being often alone, is essential to any depth of meditation or of character; and solitude in the presence of natural beauty and grandeur, is the cradle of thoughts and aspirations which are not only good for the individual, but which society could ill do without.

—John Stuart Mill, *Principles of Political Economy*

When we talk about public policy, we want to know more than whether our rights are being violated. We want to know what the costs are of implementing such a policy, to see if the policy is beneficial on the whole. We may think that if the costs are great enough, the claim that is being made on us isn't justified. I've argued in Chapter 3, after all, that autonomy rights are contextual, that the claims one can make are bounded by their costs to others. I said that since having more than one child is not something one has a basic interest in, the only argument for its being a right would depend on its simply being an exercise of autonomy. But, you can't exercise your autonomy in ways that are too harmful to others, so it isn't a right. Someone might respond that protecting others from overpopulation is itself too costly, that it will have bad side effects whose cost is so great that we can't be asked to bear them.

There are a couple of answers a person might make to this. One is that what is at stake here is others' basic welfare, the very ability to live a decent life. When the value of someone's life is at stake, she is allowed to make much greater claims on us than she would be for lesser things. The expression of autonomy in the particular choice of how one wants to live is important, but not as important as the very ability to live a human life itself. If we see ourselves as depriving others of basic goods that are essential to what we consider a truly human life, we may well concede that we owe it to others to bear even very great costs if those are inextricably attached to changing our destructive behaviors.

It would be nicer all around, though, to discover that the costs we have to pay are not so high. Nicer, because pain is bad. And nicer, because the more costly we see a policy as being to ourselves, the less likely we are to pursue it, even when we admit that it is morally justified. We aren't perfect people, and we don't always do what we think is right (and we often change our opinions about what is right to suit what is most convenient to us). So we want to look at the undesirable side effects that people worry about when they consider limiting population growth and see how bad these side effects are. What I will discuss in this chapter are the fears that reducing population growth will (1) be ruinous to the economy, including in particular the maintenance of retirees; (2) result in the numbers of girls and women growing disproportionately small, through sex-selective IVF, sex-selective abortions, or even sex-selective infanticide; (3) lead to the loss of certain cultures altogether, as the number of practitioners falls below what is sustainable for a unique culture and they are subsumed into the culture of the majority; and (4) be unfair to those children who will be born, insofar as they will be deprived of siblings. Obviously, in the space I have here, I will not give each of these topics the exhaustive discussion it may merit. Some of them deserve a book, at least—and fortunately there are indeed books devoted to them. What I will do is present reasons for thinking that the worst outcomes envisaged in these areas can be avoided, and in those cases where painful costs are foreseeable, even worse costs may arise from not limiting population.

THE ECONOMY

This is one that worries many people. The basic premises are that (1) economic growth is necessary for the economy to be healthy, and (2) population growth is necessary for economic growth. While reducing the number of children we have to one will not lead to an immediate end to population growth, given demographic momentum, it would eventually do so, and indeed would eventually lead to a drop in population. While the goal would be to bring us to a population level at which we could sustain ourselves at a replacement level, that would take a while. So in the short run, we would have a population that is, at first, not growing as much as it might and, eventually, not growing at all, but rather shrinking, until we are at a sustainable number.[1] And, the claim is, our thriving economy, the source of the comfortable lives we lead, the leisure we enjoy, our very longevity, would be destroyed. We can't ask of ourselves that we be reduced to lives that are poor, miserable, and short, just so that other people can avoid lives that are poor, miserable, and short.

This is a powerful argument, in that some of what it says is true. If an economy is based on growth, and then there is no more growth, that economy will fail. And if our lives will be as bad as all that, and certainly if they will be as bad as the lives we're trying to help other people avoid, sacrificing our happiness for theirs makes no sense: why embrace our misery to avoid the misery of others?

However, the pretty obvious problem is that growth as we know it can't continue forever. Even our present rate of consumption is too much: as stated in a 2005 report by the United Nations Environment Program, "Human actions are depleting Earth's natural capital, putting such strain on the environment that the ability of the planet's ecosystems to sustain future generations can no longer be taken for granted."[2] Barring an unlikely scenario of immediate (and never-ending!) planetary colonization, if we continue to grow as we have, we will sooner or later just run out of stuff. Whatever we want for life, we need to recognize that we can only get it from a system of resources that unfortunately just isn't infinite. As Tim Jackson writes, even the fulfillment of our most basic needs must be based on an acknowledgment of

> the finite nature of the ecological resources within which life on earth is possible. These resources include the obvious material ones: fossil fuels, minerals, timber, water, land and so on. They also include the regenerative capacity of ecosystems, the diversity of species and the integrity of the atmosphere, the soils and the oceans. None of these resources is infinite. . . . We may not yet know exactly where all the limits lie. But we know enough to be absolutely sure that, in most cases, even the current level of economic activity is destroying ecological integrity and threatening ecosystem functioning, perhaps irreversibly.[3]

A growing population makes this worse:

> The second limiting factor on our capability to live well is the scale of the global population. This is simple arithmetic. With a finite pie and any given level of technology, there is only so much in the way of resources and environmental space to go around. The bigger the global population the faster we hit the ecological buffers, the smaller the population the lower the pressure on ecological resources. This basic tenet of systems ecology is the reality of life for every other species on the planet.[4]

This isn't a surprise, because, as Jackson argues, it is inevitable and obvious. The recent report from the Royal Society of Great Britain, *People and the Planet*, articulates the same concern: "One of the major obstacles to achieving human wellbeing in a sustainable way is that the conventional model assumes that consumption growth is the key to improved wellbeing,"[5] and again,

> Material consumption is currently closely related to economic consumption. Economic consumption is a key component of the GDP. Thus, growth in the GDP tends to drive increasing material throughput. There is a clear need to address the underlying economic model and go beyond the GDP in the measurement of economic progress. This task may be challenging in the short term—for political and structural reasons. But there are some powerful reasons for beginning to tackle it now. Irrespective of this need, immediate attention has to be focused on dematerializing economics—decoupling economic activity from material consumption.[6]

It's because growth based on material consumption just can't continue indefinitely that many have advocated the need for a new model for the economy. In particular, some, like Jackson, have argued for a steady-state economy—one that remains healthy without growth. This isn't a new idea—John Stuart Mill advocated it in his *Principles of Political Economy* in 1848, where he referred to it as the "stationary state." In surprisingly contemporary terms, he wrote: "I know not why it should be a matter of congratulation that persons who are already richer than anyone needs to be, should have doubled their means of consuming things which give little or no pleasure except as representative of wealth."[7] In relation to the combination of material consumption and population in particular, he went on,

> If the earth must lose that great portion of its pleasantness which it owes to things that the unlimited increase of wealth and population would extirpate from it, for the mere purpose of enabling it to support a larger, but not a better or a happier population, I sincerely hope, for the sake of posterity, that they will be content to be stationary, long before necessity compels them to it.[8]

Mill was certainly not an environmentalist as we would understand that, but here he hits on two themes that environmentalists and ecological economists have since developed at great length: first, that unending growth will do harm in "extirpating" many things necessary to our enjoyment (including, we would now say, the survival of ecosystems, species, and many of the means to our own welfare) and second, that we aren't really getting anything valuable from this compulsive consumption.

This is significant. While we can all agree that it will be extremely difficult to change the way we conceive of, and engage in, economic activity, many people also agree that, environmental problems aside, the modern economy is in many ways unsatisfactory as it is.

For one thing, it follows from the discussion above that the success of our economy is, to some extent, illusory. As these and others critics have argued, we appear to succeed to the extent we do because we don't "count" the costs of natural resources. We are, as they say, borrowing against time, borrowing something we can't pay back. It may look good on the books, but of course, like any bad accounting method, it catches up with us. Our success is based on the habit of not measuring externalities, even when those are necessary to economic production and, as argued here, are finite.

> Today's market system is distorted by failure to price environmental and social impacts, leading to perverse incentives for unsustainable activities. GDP is a poor measure of social wellbeing and does not account for natural capital. In the past it has proven an attractive measure for policy makers because it reduces many complex issues into a single figure that can be compared between countries. It is also a strategic weapon in a world where nations compete for economic and political significance—often at the expense of future well being.[9]

For another thing, we know that, for example, the American economy is productive of very great inequality. While we are foremost in the consumption of resources, this has, notoriously, not been spread even close to equally among the citizenry. In 2012, the top 10% of earners received 48.2% of the earnings pie, and the gap between the top 1% and the remaining 99% was the largest it's been since the 1920s;[10] the ratio of pay between CEOs and workers was on the average 350 to 1 in 2012.[11] Nobel Prize–winning economist Robert J. Shiller has widely been quoted in saying that income inequality is "the most important problem that we are facing today."[12]

This is not the place for an exhaustive discussion of the perils of inequality, and such discussions are easy to come across elsewhere. In brief, we may agree to this: while inequality is not always a bad thing, in the case of the modern economy, it has had unacceptable consequences. Part of the problem is that inequality of wealth leads to inequality of political and social power in a way that is inimical to democracy. And, while there can be unequal situations in which everyone has what is needed for a decent life, that's not the inequality we've got. We have too many people without the basics for life: too many in the United States, where, rich as we are, 15% live at or below the poverty level—some 45.3 million people.[13] And of course, in the wider world there are many more who live in dire conditions—according to the World Bank, in 2011 2.5 billion lived (or failed to live) on $2 a day—only a slight decrease from the 2.59 billion who lived on the same income in 1981.[14] And even if our economic system were capable of generating equality by bringing everyone up to the highest contemporary standards of living (which it shows no signs of), that isn't physically possible—the planet just can't provide that much stuff.

The situation as it stands is untenable and in many ways simply unsatisfactory. We may note, too, that even the benefits of our consumption are not as great as we might think. Of course, it is a wonderful thing to have our material needs met, whether these are the needs for food, for housing, for medical care. There are, without doubt, some things a healthy economy has brought us that have truly made us better off. To maintain our unending economic growth, though, we have gone beyond this. While some people remain without the basic goods needed for a decent life, others have been encouraged to buy products that really have no earthly (or for that matter, spiritual) use. Satisfying basic needs doesn't produce enough profit. Thus, anyone who watches commercials on television can see that we are urged to buy things that we can't possibly need, and that don't make us better off. We are aware now of the dangers of junk food—food that not only doesn't provide nutrition, but that loads us with fat, sugar, and salt that are positively harmful. Food, though, is not the only area where we are encouraged to spend money on things that not only don't make us happier but are positively harmful—sometimes to us, and sometimes to the planet. We are urged, for example, to buy cars whose top speed is faster than anyone can safely go, and for which (at an average price of $31,252 in 2013)[15] we must necessarily get in debt—and then a few years later we are encouraged to get the newer, slightly different model. We are pushed to buy clothes that will be out of fashion in a season, to put down carpets that will only require more purchases to keep them clean, and (!!) bottled water, in a country where tap water is entirely safe to drink, and plastic bottles "pile up as a mountain of waste."[16] In addition to our addiction to junk food, we've developed—with similar encouragement—an addiction to junk stuff.

Why? Studies show that while we have more possessions than we did in 1950, and in terms of growth, have a much larger economy, we are no happier. In fact, we may be less happy, as we work longer hours and become more and more stressed.[17] The fact that we want something and then satisfy that desire by buying it doesn't turn into actual contentment. Tim Jackson has argued persuasively that for many of us in the developed world, continuing purchases are fueled by the desire for status and the pleasure of novelty. No one needs a 6,000-square-foot house, much less a 12,000-square-foot mansion. (After a brief decline during the recession, American house sizes are once again setting new records.)[18] Yet these are becoming increasingly common, despite the obvious costs of purchasing and maintaining them—or perhaps because of this obvious cost. Insofar as we peg status to money, as we tend to do, obvious expenditures show that we are rich, and thus higher in status than (at least some) others. No one needs gold faucets just in order to get water. We are exquisitely attuned to earmarks of status, and when status attaches to what we have, and what we have is valued at how much it costs, we embark on a quest to buy things for their symbolic value.

And we like novelty. The idea of a new model of car, or a new season's fashion, or, of course, new electronics, makes us want to buy. The reasons for this may be evolutionary—perhaps the remainder of a useful form of curiosity and fascination with experimentation. Like the taste for salt, though, not everything that was useful in the course of evolution is good when it can be indulged to the extent it now can. And, whereas once our interest in newness may have been channeled into useful innovation, too often now it is simply the pursuit of novelty for novelty's sake.

So the pursuit both of status and of novelty can have harmful consequences. The more important thing to see here, though, is that neither of them yields lasting satisfaction. Novelty, obviously, is temporary. If we focus on it as the object of desire, we are inexorably moved from one object to the next. Rather than leading us to a state of contentment, our appetite is continually unsatisfied. It is (and I know I've been relying on the analogy to salt a lot here, but it's apt) like eating a potato chip, when that just makes us want the next one. Status is similar: insofar as we achieve status through showing more wealth than others, we are led into a never-ending escalation where keeping up with the Joneses becomes an unending pursuit of unfathomable salaries, dwellings so palatial as to suggest parody, and other spirals of increase. This is often given as the reason some CEOs earn such bizarre amounts of money, beyond what anyone would really know how to enjoy. You don't have to be the Dalai Lama to perceive that the endless pursuit of status and novelty will lead to restlessness and stress rather than to happiness.

Yet, while the needs for status and novelty can't be lastingly fulfilled by any given purchase and thus can't lead to lasting satisfaction, we are overwhelmed by the push to buy things in order to augment our status or because they are new. We are encouraged to do this, of course, through advertising and a general social norm that suggests we need to do this to be successful. There is a sense in which the roles have been reversed: rather than a healthy economy being one that serves our needs, we act so as to fulfill the needs of the economy. In 1954, one of the masters of science fiction, Frederick Pohl, published a story called "The Midas Plague."[19] It depicts a society of overwhelming material wealth, but the depiction is decidedly dystopian: people are oppressed by the duty to consume far more than they want, just for the sake of maintaining the health of the economy. Product quotas are issued by the government, and citizens must consume as much as they are told to consume. Status is indicated by the privilege of not having to consume so much—of being allowed to live simply, in a small house, with only one car, where the highly ranked person can dig his own potatoes in the morning. Those lower down the social scale are forced to live in huge mansions, stuffed with carpets, furniture, bric-a-brac, and useless gadgets, and the major activity of each day is using up unwanted clothes, lotions, sports equipment, and so much food that they can't help but get fat. We, of course, are not forced by the government to consume as much as we do: Pohl's pessimistic story may actually have been optimistic in its psychology, in that he didn't seem to realize that advertising and peer pressure alone would be enough to get us to buy things we don't need.

Sometimes inversions of support are okay. Having gotten a dog to keep me company, I find myself with the unexpected duty of scheduling myself so that she is not alone too often. That's all right—it's rewarding in the long run. But sometimes such inversions are truly oppressive. When we find ourselves compelled to buy stuff that we don't need, and often can't afford, and which yields us no great satisfaction, and which furthermore wreaks havoc on the environment and, eventually, those who rely on a healthy environment, we should all agree that things just haven't worked out. In his book *The Politics of Happiness*, Derek Bok seems to think that ending growth would make us better off, but that it is simply too difficult to implement—the government would have to promulgate cumbersome, unworkable regulations to prevent the economy from growing.[20] If the population were falling, however, reduction in economic activity would come naturally. Once we get to a sustainable population, keeping it at a sustainable level wouldn't stop all growth, but might well curb the fevered growth we have seen of late. Instead, we've got the sorcerer's apprentice, only worse. A change in the way we run the economy is inevitable because our resources are finite, but it should furthermore be seen as welcome.

What about people on government pensions? One specific corner of the economy is often cited as requiring that there be at least as many workers in the new generation as there are retirees: the retirees need to be supported by the earnings of the younger workers, who in turn will be supported by the next generation, ad infinitum. In the United States this government-supplied subsidy is known as Social Security. The government requires automatic deductions from a worker's paycheck that then go in to the Social Security system, which in turn pays out the money to retired workers in ways related to age and their own lifetime earnings. It is feared by some that, not surprisingly, if there are fewer workers, less money will go into the system, and thus less money will be available for those who've retired, having been misled into regarding these payments as a reliable source of income in their older years.

Again, this is a big question, and deserves detailed debate it will not receive here. It is good to note, though, that even as it is at current fertility rates, many fear that the Social Security system is failing. CNN reports:

> The government's official position is that there is enough money saved to pay benefits at the currently scheduled amounts until 2041. The Social Security Administration admits on its Web site that benefits will likely be reduced after that, barring changes that improve the financial strength of the system.
>
> Some critics say that benefits could be at risk as early as 2016 or 2017, when Social Security cash flow turns negative. They claim that since the money paid in over the last few decades is part of the government's overall budget, it is available only on paper; other branches of the government have spent it and left IOUs. In order to pay benefits through 2041, the government would have to borrow.[21]

Of course, to say that things are already bad doesn't entail that they couldn't be worse. With fewer people earning wages, and an economy that doesn't grow, the amount of money the government takes in will be much less, and there will be proportionately less to pay out to retirees—*if* we continue to use the same retirement system. The conclusion we should draw is that we need to change the system. Again, if benefits are maintained only by a growing population of younger people, that in itself could involve impositions on people's actions, if the fertility rate continues to drop through people's individual choice. We can imagine having to push people to have more children than they want, just to maintain the Social Security system. No one wants to promote mandatory childbearing, though, even if that would bolster our pension system. It's arguably much more of an imposition than limiting people to only one child, given that the natural trend in developed countries has been for fertility to drop. And here is the trifling fact that having more children, even if it supported our pension system in the short run, would be generally a disaster:

> Before we get to what we might do, though, let me repeat once again what won't work: having more babies. To stabilize the ratio of retirees to workers, US fertility would have to surge to a rate of three births per woman or higher. Not only is that unlikely to happen, it also would produce a population the size of China's within a few generations. It's not realistic.[22]

Or more bluntly:

> [T]he case for increased fertility or higher immigration derived from more mechanistic models is overstated and . . . the implicit assumption sometimes made that policy should aim to stabilize the old-age dependency ratio is wrong.[23]

So, what should we do? I'd love to say I know, but obviously I don't. What we do know, though, is that increasing the population is not the way to approach the problem. Most people realize this, and many of them are trying to think of better answers to this dilemma. Since many people agree that pension funds have too often been regarded as a handy source of cash for other branches of government (as mentioned in the CNN summary, above) we could at least stop doing that. Yet another idea is that government pension payments should be needs-based—people who have enough to live on without them wouldn't receive them, which would leave more for those who don't. As it is, people receive money according to how much they paid into the system, even if they are billionaires. A means test could channel benefits to those who don't have large private assets to rely on. Yet another suggestion is that older people should simply work longer before receiving payments, which would help. Part of the pressure on government retirement funds is that people are living much longer than they were when such payments were first envisioned (in the United States, in 1935). Some feel that government support of, say, 20 years of retirement is simply too much. In 1935, the average life expectancy (for all races and sexes) for those who reached adulthood was 65, which was the age at which benefits began.[24] In contemporary times, an American can start to receive benefits at 62. The average American man who reaches the age of 65 can expect to live to 84, and the average life expectancy in the United States for women who reach 65 is 86. One out of four persons who reaches 65 will live past 90.[25] This is great news, except that it is a lot of people receiving government funding for 20 or 30 years.

All of these ideas face opposition. Those in government like the ability to dip into Social Security to fund other projects. Rich people like getting a little extra whether or not they need it, and furthermore feel they are entitled to money from the system since they paid into it. Some have argued that older people are too often not in sufficiently good health to work longer. None of these seem to me to be definitive arguments against change, however, especially since change is clearly needed. Pension funds could be placed off limits to other branches of government. The rich could come to regard this as like a tax, something they have to pay for the good of the country whether or not they personally benefit from it, or perhaps as a form of insurance—a system they pay into before they know if they will end up wealthy, which they can rely on if it becomes necessary, but not if it does not. As to age, others argue that part of the reason for greater longevity is precisely that we are quite healthy. Not all of us, and not for all the years in which we now receive retirement benefits, but most of us for much later than the present eligibility age of 62. And, of course, people who aren't healthy can apply for something like the disability payments that now exist.

For many people this is not, of course, an attractive picture: it is natural to prefer retiring and being supported by the government (in however meager a form) to remaining at work, at least for most people. And because they are used to this system, and because they paid into it with the expectation that their benefits would begin at a certain age, they feel they deserve that outcome; the system should work, at least for them, without any changes that add to their burdens. However, neither the fact that retirement is attractive, nor the sense of entitlement we now have toward the present Social Security system, makes such benefits a right (as, apparently, the government agrees, since the age at which we can receive full benefits has in fact been pushed back a year, and not through a popular referendum). If change is needed to make a system workable, that change can be made. If 20 years of retirement can only be maintained by passing the environmental burden of overpopulation on to those who come after us, it's not something we can demand.

SEX SELECTION

We now have technology that allows us to know the sex of a child long before it is born. While this isn't readily available in every part of the world, it's available enough for fairly common use in many, including the nations with the largest populations, India and China. And it is true that some people use this technology to choose not to have a child whose sex is not what the parents want. This doesn't have to be something that results in more children born of one sex than another—in the United States, while there are cases where people do manipulate pregnancies for the sake of the sex of the future child, this apparently arises from a desire for "balance" within a family: those with girls sometimes want a boy, and those with boys may want a girl. The ratio of girls to boys in the overall population hasn't been affected. In other places, though, the motivation, and the results, are very different: sex selection is used more generally to avoid having female children. This is a very different sort of issue than that of economic progress—it's not a question of relative comfort, as the economic question may be seen to be, but one of gender discrimination.

This is a difficult issue. We can all agree that gender discrimination is wrong: it is unfounded, since women are in no way inferior to men, and it is oppressive, in that it makes women's lives worse than they should be, and sometimes very bad indeed. Any measures that would increase such discrimination could be taken only with the greatest hesitation. And, some argue that this is just what will happen if we introduce a one-child policy, even if we sanction it in the relatively mild ways I have argued for. If people are allowed to have only one child, they will favor boys. They will select for sex—those who do in vitro fertilization will choose male embryos for implantation; more commonly, since IVF is expensive, those who discover they are pregnant with girls will abort them; in the worst-case analysis, some parents will commit infanticide of unwanted girls.

This is no mere speculation. In some parts of the world the tendency to favor boys over girls is clear. As reported by the Indian census, there were 1,000 boys born to every 943 girls, an unnatural disproportion.[26] (There are naturally 105 boys born to every 100 girls, for reasons that may relate to evolutionary pressure. Eventually, given women's greater life expectancy, the disparity disappears, so that in the world population as a whole there are 101 women for every 100 men.) According to a World Bank report in 2011, in China there were 118 male births to 100 female births. In Azerbaijan, it's 116 boys to 100 girls, and Armenia has 114 male births to every 100 females.[27] While some variations in the birth ratio are natural, and others may be caused by environmental factors the parents don't control, the reasonable conclusion that most have drawn is that where there is an extreme and continuing disproportion between boys and girls, it's intentional.

If a one-child policy contributes to more sex-selective abortions, or to more sex selection in IVF, and this in turn results in the birth of a disproportionate number of males compared to females, what does that say about the viability of such a policy?

Consider abortion, since at present this is the more common way of selecting for sex in most places. We don't like the idea of parents choosing to abort a fetus just because it is female. However, this is a complicated issue, to say the least. Some reasons for abortions will strike us as bad reasons, reasons that aren't justifiable, and simply believing that girls are inferior creatures is wrong. On the other hand, it is also true that women who choose to have an abortion have a right to do so. And saying the woman has a right to have an abortion means that she can do that even when she has what we would consider bad reasons for doing that. We might blame her motivations, but we can still agree that she has a right to what she is doing. Some people may choose whom to vote for for reasons we would deplore, but they still have the right to vote. So, whatever the underlying purpose, if these women choose to have abortions, it is their right.

Furthermore, in some of these cases, women actually have good reasons to choose against having girls. If having a girl truly costs more than one can afford, and boys don't, that could be a good reason not to want a girl. Girls shouldn't cost more than boys—they shouldn't require expensive dowries, they should be able to get good jobs and bring home as much pay as boys, but, as we know, that isn't true. It's an unjust situation, but if a women finds herself in an unjust situation, it may be quite reasonable to respond to the pressure that others have placed on her by not wanting a daughter. Given the situation, choosing not to have a girl doesn't mean the individual woman making the decision is making a bad decision. Aside from the cost to her family, a woman might foresee a life of hardship for her female child, and decide to try instead for a child who will have better chances in her society. Such inequitable situations shouldn't exist, but they do, and choosing with that in mind isn't crazy or despicable.

The issue here, then, isn't whether women have a right to get an abortion in order to select the sex of their child. Still, we don't want to bring about more situations where women are pressured to abort female children. Even when someone has a right, you can arrange society in ways that force them to avail themselves of that right in situations we and perhaps they regret. Or, you can try to arrange society so that women don't feel pressure to have abortions simply because of their external circumstances. If a one-child policy would encourage women to select boys rather than girls, some people will feel that that is such a bad thing that the one-child policy wouldn't be worth it, even for the sake of preventing environmental degradation. They will argue that we can't distribute burdens unfairly, and if a good consequence can be brought about only by creating or exacerbating social inequality, it would be wrong to do this. No matter how praiseworthy the outcome, they argue, benefits and burdens of the policy have to be distributed fairly.

However, even if we take fairness to women as so significant as to override our concerns about the future, we need to consider whether a one-child policy would in fact cause such unfairness. We need to consider (a) whether sex selection would make women worse off, (b) whether a one-child policy is actually likely to significantly increase the number of sex-selective abortions, and (c) whether preventing (or removing) population controls is the best way to prevent sex-selective abortions.

What Are the Effects of Sex Selection?

This is largely speculative. While we are beginning to see some effects in China, that is only one place, one culture, and for only a recent period of time. Still, theories abound.

The cause of sex selection, as discussed below, is almost always sexism, directly or indirectly: an unfounded discrimination against women. To say that it is caused by sexism doesn't entail that it will necessarily bring about more oppression of women, though. Economist Gary Becker has argued that, in accordance with general economic theory, scarcity will make women more valuable: "As children become adult in cohorts with a high ratio of boys, the advantage of girls and women increases since they are scarcer."[28] And, he argues, by the same token, the change will be temporary: as parents see the value of girls rise, they will be motivated to have more of them. In the meantime, those girls who are born will be born to parents who wanted them (since if they hadn't, they could have avoided them), so we can expect the average treatment of girls in the home to be better.

Others argue that a gender imbalance will have very bad effects. Rarity might increase the value of women as a commodity, rather than increasing respect for them as individuals. Insofar as there is a shortage of women, there may be an increase in sex trafficking, with women forced into marriage or prostitution. The problem of sex trafficking is already huge, and while it is clearly not caused by any shortage of women, we certainly don't want to make it worse. While in theory increased policing could have a substantial effect here, in many places the trafficking of women isn't seen as a priority, and, with fewer women, this comparative neglect might become worse as, with fewer women voters, there might be less political pressure brought to bear.

Of course, one big question is how many fewer women we might expect—it is not the case, even in China, that women have been reduced to an insignificant minority. There are certainly enough of them that numbers alone wouldn't prevent them from being a powerful political faction, if China were more open to popular pressure in determining policy. And of course in states where women are half or more than half of the population, we still don't see them having proportionate power. The problem of disproportionate political power is not a function merely of numbers.

In this regard, we should note that a one-child scenario should provide some compensating advantages to women. If women gained economically under such a scenario, this would presumably be reflected in greater political and social power. We know that having fewer children in the home tends to correlate with the mother in the home being better off economically, in part because she is able to earn more money. Even in the developed world, most women find that having more children means more work in the home, and this is often exacerbated in economically less developed ares. When fertility is low, marriage and the family need no longer dominate women's lives, and they can work outside the home. Many have noticed that women in societies with greater economic development generally have fewer children, and while it is presumably true that economic development makes it possible for them to have fewer children, it also make some sense to think that having fewer children makes an individual woman's economic improvement possible. The fewer children at home, the less costly it is for the woman to leave the home and work where she will receive actual wages for her labor, which can then lead to increased standing and ultimately more political power.[29]

At the same time, we know that growing population will result in a shortage of resources, and thus greater poverty, and typically, in civil unrest and war. This bodes ill for women. When things go badly, it's the worst off who do worst. As it stands, women are among the poorest, so as the world gets poorer, they will be, if nothing changes, even worse off. Women's fate in conditions of internal unrest and war, too, tends to be horrific: consider the incidence of rape during the Bosnian conflict, and in the Congo. Even if a one-child policy does result in a sex imbalance, it is not at all clear this is worse than the alternatives overpopulation would create.

Will a One-Child Policy Increase Sex Selection?

As we've seen, the effects of a one-child policy may not be worse on the whole than the alternatives, even if it did result in an increased ratio of men to women. For purposes of argument, though, let's assume that a continuing sex imbalance would have net bad effects. Should we think of one-child policies as the primary cause of sex selection? Should this be our focus if we want to eliminate sex selection? No. One obvious fact, of course, is that this predominance of male births isn't confined to places that have a one-child policy. Of the countries mentioned above as having clear sex imbalances, China, Azerbaijan, India, and Armenia, only China has any policy in place intended to limit children. The difference in the other countries is a function of parents wanting more boys and fewer girls. So while a one-child policy might exacerbate sex-selective abortions, it isn't the primary cause. The primary cause is social: the preference for boys. As I mentioned, in the immediate sense this may be because of boys' greater earning power and the associated preference for the greater earner, but the ultimate reason for this is simply sex preference itself. Or, as we say in brief, sexism. Sexism is a tradition whose origins are unknown, but it has been the prevailing tradition in most of the world, and it remains a strong tradition in many places. Males have more money, power, and prestige, and many families prefer male children. The ultimate source of the difference in boy-girl birth ratios is not a one-child policy, but the preference for boys arising from the superior position of men in society.

This doesn't mean that a one-child policy can't increase the selection of boys over girls. Indeed, we have evidence in China that it has. But it does suggest that homing in on the one-child policy as the villain is shortsighted. The one-child policy isn't the primary source of the boy-girl imbalance, and the boy-girl imbalance certainly isn't the major source of women's secondary position in the world. The position of women is bad in many, many ways even where women predominate in terms of numbers. What we need is an improvement in the position of women, generally, rather than a narrow focus on the boy-girl birth ratio. I'm inclined to think that Americans who deplore the Chinese one-child policy because of its effect on the boy-girl birth ratio might do better to focus their efforts on the pay discrimination that still exists in the United States, where the boy-girl birth ratio is 105 to 100; that is, the natural one. If there were no preference for boys, one-child policies wouldn't generate more boys than girls.

After all, as we know, the fertility rate in the United States and western Europe has dropped, and in some part of Europe is considerably less than 2 children per women. Among the lowest are Germany, Hungary, and Romania, at 1.36, 1.30, and 1.25, respectively.[30] Yet, while a number of families are presumably having fewer than two children, we don't see that there has been a preference for boys—their boy-girl sex ratio is the natural one, 105 to 100 for Germany, 105.7 to 100 for Hungary, and 106 to 100 for Romania. The fact that people have fewer than two children doesn't entail that they will prefer boys over girls in the child they do have. So having only one child doesn't in itself mean there will be an imbalance of boys over girls, and there may be an imbalance of boys over girls where there is no one-child policy. Again, it is true that this doesn't mean that a one-child policy wouldn't, in some places, encourage sex-selective abortions. But it does mean that it is not the primary cause, and it means that overemphasis on such a policy is misplaced, because changing the policy wouldn't eliminate the problem. It also means that there are ways of preventing boy-girl imbalances other than avoiding one-child policies, to which we will now turn.

Are There Better Ways to Prevent Sex Selection?

It has been suggested that we might simply forbid physicians and fertility clinics from telling whether an embryo or fetus was male or female. While this might work in some contexts, however, there is certainly evidence that it doesn't always work. India adopted a similar act prohibiting the use of prenatal tests for sex determination in 1994, and when it was later argued that governments were not in fact doing enough to prevent this, the Indian parliament (in 2003) increased the penalties and other regulations. However, India's high boy-girl birth ratio suggests that this hasn't been effective, apparently because the law is still not enforced.[31] For such a law to be effective, it may require a more general change in the structure of institutions.

Some changes in law can be useful. If the ultimate cause of sex selection is sex discrimination, then we best address it by addressing the cause of sex discrimination. Even in societies with traditional gender roles such change is possible, especially if it is actively pursued. A modern success story, in terms of sex ratios at birth, is South Korea. In 1990, the ratio was 116.5 boys to 100 girls, due at least in part to sex-selective abortions. In 2012, the ratio was 105.7 to 100, in line with the natural ratio that occurs when no sort of sex selection is used.[32] This change was not an accident.

How did this happen? In 1988, South Korea, like India, passed a law making it illegal for doctors to reveal the sex of an embryo or fetus to the parents. (The law was later amended so that the parents can learn the sex of the baby at 32 weeks.) As seen in India, though, such a law by itself is not sufficient. Korea also experienced great economic development, and there is often correlation between economic development and a decline in preference for boys. Woojin Chung and Monica Das Gupta argue, though, that economic development alone was not responsible for this particular change, because Korea continued to have a strong predominance of male births even after it had become a member of the Organization for Economic Cooperation and Development in the mid-1990s, a formal acknowledgment of its developed status.[33] Rather, the change was due to more general changes in values.

Chng and Das Gupta argue that much of South Korea's former preference for boys was itself due to a historical cultural shift—a religious reorientation from Buddhism to Confucianism. Confucianism traditionally promoted a patriarchal system, where the family obeyed the father and this obedience was mirrored in the father's obedience to the state. Lineage and inheritance both went through the male line, with the first-born son having greater power than other siblings of either sex.[34] Much later, the development of an authoritarian regime in South Korea continued to promote the same structure. In the 1980s, though, a number of significant changes occurred. One big factor was the move from country to city, from the culture of a rural society to an urban culture, from the society of extended family to the society of strangers. Sometimes the loss of tradition such a move tends to cause is destructive, but other times it can be liberating. Then, when democracy was established in 1987, modernization meant that many of the legal rules that had promoted male dominance, including requirements for inheritance and the legal status of males as the heads of family, were altered or done away with, so that women could fill many of these traditional powerful and prestigious roles.[35]

Perhaps not surprisingly, the strength of preference for sons has declined radically. While in 1985, 47.70% of women reported that they felt they "must have a son," by 2003 only 17% reported the same.[36] The difference here is not just in the number of women who would prefer a boy, but how much those who prefer boys prefer them. A decrease in strength of preference is significant, since it means that even of those people who still prefer boys do not prefer them to the degree that they once did. This in turn means that it is easier to defeat the preference that remains, by introducing other factors that will outweigh the relatively weak preference. Making acting on that preference illegal, of course, is one such disincentive, although other, less coercive measures can also be effective when the preference becomes weak enough.

All of this suggests, not surprisingly, that preferences can evolve, even ones that have survived for many of hundreds of years. And, in the right conditions, they can change with astounding speed. In the United States, we have recently seen an acceptance of homosexuality that is astounding to those over 30—those who would never have dreamed of a future where gay marriage could even be taken seriously, much less actually enacted. And prejudice against homosexuality has been around for a long time, and very widespread, even considering the occasional times and cultures in which it was acceptable. (This change may stem in part from declining fertility—as the number of people who marry but do not intend to have children increases, we conceive of marriage as less for the sake of procreation, and more for the sake of love and companionship. If marriage is for companionship, the idea of people of the same sex wanting marriage no longer seems peculiar.)[37] Change can occur when we reconceptualize institutions and the role people play in them.

Sex selection, when it shows a bias against women, is a symptom of beliefs that are both false and harmful. These beliefs, though, are themselves the source of the problem. As long as sexist beliefs persist, women will retain a secondary position in the world, whatever their numbers may be. And if women receive rightful recognition and equal treatment, sex selection against women will end. To attack restrictions on childbearing for the sake of helping women is misguided: one-child policies don't cause the bias against women, and their elimination will not leave women better off. What we need is a reconceptualizing of women's role in the world, which can be wrought by a number of factors, including, perhaps, having fewer children in the home.

CULTURAL SURVIVAL

What about those who are worried specifically about the strength of their own ethnic group? A number of countries already have falling birth rates, and some of them are worried about this, so worried that they provide citizens with incentives to have more children. In Russia, for example, women now are paid to have more children, and Vladimir Putin has held up having three children as the ideal.[38] The worry is not that the world will run out of people, which is obviously not a danger, but that there will be fewer (or at least, somehow not enough) of their specific kind of people. Is this important?

This concern has its roots in several distinct beliefs. First, people may worry about the economic strength of their country going into the future, for the reasons discussed earlier. Insofar as they believe an increasing population is necessary for a successful economy, they will naturally want an increasing population. As argued above, though, we already have reasons for thinking that the economy needs revamping. In the short run, too, immigration can provide sufficient citizenry for most countries to sustain their population size, if that is what they choose to do. So the economic question, while a serious one, does not provide a reason to produce more children.

For a lot of people, though, the concern isn't so much that they won't have enough people in their country, but that they won't be the right *sort* of people. For these people, increased immigration is not only not an acceptable solution, but something that aggravates the problem. Nationalists who oppose immigration don't want, for example, for Hungary to have more people, but for there to be more Hungarians, as they conceive that; as some want more Russians in Russia, more Danes in Denmark, and so on. The desire is for greater numbers of a particular ethnic group, the one they conceive of as being "true" Hungarians, Russians, Americans, and so forth. This argument is used not only against immigration, but against the presence of minority groups who may have been around for hundreds of years, or who may even have predated the now-dominant group. We have seen increasing attacks on the Roma, for example, whose long presence in eastern Europe has not prevented them from being the object of attack of by those who feel their own welfare is somehow endangered by the presence of a minority. One complaint that is commonly made by those who resent immigrants and resident minority groups is that they have "too many" children, where the concern is not a degradation of the environment that will be harmful to all, but rather the idea that these people will have more power than the majority deems appropriate.

This worry about ethnic dominance is a function of two things. One of these, I think, is purely racist, even though it is not always couched explicitly in racist terms. (Sometimes, of course, it is.) There are those (perhaps in every country) who desire the specific survival and dominance of their own group. We are familiar with white racists who desire the dominance of white people and who therefore deplore the growth of the nonwhite population, but there are equally those who desire the specific continuance of ethnically pure Russians, Danes, Anglo-Americans, and so forth, and who then worry when their fertility rate drops, especially relative to that of other groups. For this reason, they promote more births among their own group (as well as deploring births among those they think of as not belonging).

This, as I say, is racism: that is, the idea that there could be too many of one racial/ethnic group because we want better DNA and not inferior DNA embodies both false factual claims and false values: that some groups are smarter, harder working, more sober, and so on, merely because of their shared genotype, and that it is a superior world in which we have more "pure" people of their particular sort. Such beliefs are just racist—false and harmful—and as such, worth consideration only insofar as we might want to oppose them.

There is another concern that is not so despicable, however. The focus here is not on physical "race" or ethnicity. Instead, people worry that their own culture is disappearing, and they want to save their own culture. Insofar as they see their culture depending on a robust population, they support more births—sometimes for the sake of more births than some other group is having, but sometimes just more births, to make sure there is a population large enough to sustain a culture.

I don't think there is anything morally suspect in wanting one's culture to continue. Insofar as we are all the product of our culture, it's where we feel at home. It is part of us, and we are part of it. Even when there are parts of your culture you positively despise, you are apt to prefer its food, its music, its holidays, its sports, the way its rooms are arranged, the way its people greet one another. American politics has driven me crazy ever since I became aware of it, but I can't imagine living contentedly anywhere else, even in the places whose politics I believe to be far superior. Of course, preferring a culture and feeling at home in it doesn't entail that you actually believe it is superior, but it does tend to mean you would miss it if it were to disappear.

This is fair enough. It isn't an argument for keeping the birth rate up, though. For one thing, a culture can survive immigration. Those whose origin is a different country with a different culture are very commonly absorbed into the culture of the adopted country. This may not happen to the actual immigrants themselves, but it is famously the case that the children of immigrants declare their allegiance to the norms of the new country, rather than to the one their parents left (which they've often never seen). This is a source of conflict between parents and children, but it's not a problem for the culture of the receiving country.

This isn't always the case. Some immigrant cultures can retain very much of their own way of doing things (say, the Amish in the United States) and some can object publicly to aspects of the host culture, and this can cause friction. In the Netherlands, there is controversy as I write over the use of Zwarte Piet (Black Pete) in Christmas celebrations. Zwarte Piet is a companion (or possibly servant) of Santa Claus and appears to be a stereotypical African, depicted with very black skin, very red lips, and gold earrings. (I am aware that some Dutch argue that Zwarte Piet is black because of ash in the chimney, rather than because of race. I'm just saying it appears to many people to be a depiction of an African.) A number of Dutch people have written that objections to Black Pete are an attack on traditional Dutch culture, by people who have come from some other culture and who don't understand Black Pete's meaning in traditional Christmas celebrations; and who, worse, are indifferent to, or even intent on, the destruction of harmless aspects of Dutch culture.

I don't know how Black Pete will end up. While I am not Dutch, however, and therefore must admit that I don't entirely feel the significance of Black Pete in the culture of Christmas, I do think Dutch culture will survive if Black Pete does not. The truth is that cultures are always changing. I love Christmas trees! But while my idea of Christmas is very largely centered on decorating the tree, and I would greatly miss that, I also know that Christmas trees were introduced into English-speaking cultures in the 19th century. Good King Wenceslas didn't decorate one. The American Santa Claus, the focus of every American child, is apparently also a product of the 19th century. There was Christmas before Santa and before the tree, and there were traditions that presumably made people just as happy. I don't have a yule log, given the lack of huge logs and a huge fireplace to burn one in, but I don't feel deprived by that, even though back in the day they might have thought being deprived of a yule log was tantamount to losing Christmas itself.

It is the nature of cultures to change. It is keeping a culture the same, rather than its changing, that is artificial, and efforts to do this are doomed to failure. Immigration can have some impact on a culture, but even without immigration the influences that affect a "native" culture are pervasive. Sometimes the origin of cultural change is technological—look at the impact of electronics in our lives, whether it's social media or video games or, one we're now more used to, television. Look at the impact on sexual, social, and familial relations of the birth control pill. Sometimes the source of change is economic—women being in the workforce has had more impact on all of our cultures than the demise of any Christmas symbol could have on the Dutch, I'd guess. Sometimes the impetus for cultural change comes from law—the possibility of divorce and the rise of the single parent, again, has more effect on children than Santa Claus. Some cultural changes are positive, in that they seem to make people better off, and some are no doubt bad. They are, though, ubiquitous. Russian (or American, or Dutch, or Hungarian) culture won't survive in the same way even if the (native-born, ethnically "pure") population increases. So having particular sorts of children in order to ensure that a particular culture will survive just isn't a reasonable course of action.

Indeed, given that information can be shared almost universally today, cultures that are based on actual ethnic membership or located in one exclusive geographic location may become a thing of the past. American women practice sumo, and coffee-houses abound in China. We learn about other cultures and adopt some of their customs, and local microcultures grow up around these, which may share connections to aficionados in many other places. Instead of seeing it as a loss of culture when one traditional pastime is replaced by another, we tend to attach ourselves to the new manifestation and build a culture around it. What seems to matter to our psychological well-being is not so much where a culture comes from as whether one has a culture to feel at home in, whether one has customs that are shared with others and that produce a sense of solidarity.

Cultural survival, then, is a complex thing. Cultures evolve, as some aspects are lost and others are gained, and it's true that after a number of changes the dominant culture in a particular location might become so different as to be a truly different culture from the one that was dominant a hundred years before. None of this means that there is no culture left, only that it is different. Sometimes this is an improvement and other times it is not. The resolution of this question—when cultural change is good, and when it is bad, and when change is so thorough that we may say there is truly one culture that was lost and a distinct one that developed—does not, however, depend on the DNA of babies that are born in a particular location.

SIBLINGS

Typically, under a one-child policy children wouldn't have siblings. I say typically because there would be nothing wrong with adopting second (or third, or fourth, etc.) children where those are available. The environmental issue concerns the number of children produced, not the number of children being raised in any one household. However, the assumption is that most households would have only one child per set of parents. How would that be for the child? Would it be bad? Would it be so bad that we could say the child's rights are violated?

A perusal of the vast literature on only children leads to one definite conclusion, which is that there is no consensus on whether only children are better off, worse off, or no different from children raised with siblings. In much of the 20th century there were general stereotypes about only children, and they were negative: only children were spoiled by too much attention, or oppressed by too much attention, or spoiled and oppressed by too much attention. More recent studies are more nuanced, and don't dwell on the claim that such children are "spoiled," so much as on the learning of social skills, and whether such learning is impeded when there aren't siblings around with whom one has to interact on a daily basis. Researcher Toni Falbo has become well known for her exploration of only children and her attempt to overturn the negative stereotypes attached to being an only child, but naturally her own views have drawn criticism as well.[39] One common-sense conclusion seems to be that there are pros and cons to being an only child, just as there are pros and cons to being one of several children. Another common-sense conclusion is that much depends on the parents: they may spoil their child or not, smother their child or not, allow their child to be lonely or not. The parents' attitude toward the child, and toward the fact that the child is an only child, will, obviously, play a big role in how the child conceives of him- or herself, and ultimately in how he or she interacts with others. Another common-sense conclusion is that whatever it may be like to be an only child in a society where most children have siblings, it is likely to be rather different to be an only child when almost everyone else is an only child as well. Insofar as only children may once have felt that they were in some sense deviant, lacking a normal home life, that would obviously change, when having one child is the norm. Furthermore, when there are no siblings, parents and children won't depend on siblings to be companions, but can arrange more socializing for their child with others. (Of course, an increase in socializing outside the home is already happening without a one-child policy—when both parents work, most children are in day care, where socializing with others is constant.)

What it's like to be an only child, then, will depend on a lot of things other than the mere fact that one is an only child. It is true that the only good example of a one-child society we have is that of China, and it is often said that Chinese only children have suffered from pressure placed on them to succeed at school and in their subsequent careers, and the understanding is that the weight of this pressure would be less heavy if there were siblings to bear the burden. However, some of this is peculiar to China's particular situation at the start of the one-child policy. While there is no doubt that the policy is one factor contributing to the greatly increased expectations placed by parents, this is due in large part to the particular demographic and cultural context. Vanessa Fong writes of her research into "singletons" in China that "what mattered most was not their singleton status per se, but rather that they were singletons in a society used to large families."[40]

In 1970 the fertility rate was 5.8 per woman; in 1980, a mere 10 years later, and just two years after the start of the one-child policy, it had dropped to 2.3. So, the drop in fertility was radical. China was a country with a tradition of large families, and this changed quite suddenly, and before other aspects of culture had accommodated to the demographic shift. A long tradition of filial duty had taught that older people would be supported by their children, and no government social security system had developed to supplant or supplement this. Meanwhile, mandatory retirement ages meant that there would be many parents with many years of dependence on their children's earnings.[41] If a system that relies primarily on children for support of the parents suddenly loses on average 3 children or more per family, the resulting pressure on the remaining child will naturally be great. (Furthermore, a 1979 law made failure to support parents a criminal offense punishable by up to five years in prison.)[42]

At the same time, the economy was shifting from an agrarian basis to an industrialized one, and people were moving from a village culture to an urban, relatively anonymous, society. Aspirations to First World lifestyles were widespread, while opportunities were relatively few, creating great competition within the younger generation, and often, dissatisfaction when parents could not provide the luxuries to which children aspired. Educated for economic success, "singletons' ambitions often clashed with the limitations of their Third World parents and societies."[43] Such a general cultural upheaval, combined with the prospect of poverty, can be expected to create an atmosphere of anxiety, to say the least.

None of this is inevitable, though. The Chinese situation may not be unique when it comes to adopting a one-child policy, but it is relatively rare, and most notably, it is temporary: the transition from a high fertility rate to a much, much lower one in a very short period of time is one whose repercussions may take a while to recover from—say, a generation—but which isn't ongoing.

And, of course, while we naturally want to consider what is good for children, there is a general question as to what children may claim as rights. Even if it were normally better for children to have siblings, for which, as I say, there is no strong evidence, most people don't think that children have the right to siblings. They have a right to be treated well, to receive love, to get attention, to receive an education, to have time to play—but this doesn't entail that they have the right that their parents send them to the best private school, or that they have a right to the most expensive toys, or even as much attention as their parents can possibly give. Their justified claims are balanced against the needs of others, including the needs of their parents to take some time for themselves, for example. There is a level of adequacy to which we may well say they have a right, but that doesn't entail the right to the most nearly perfect childhood that society can provide. If there is no reason not to give a child something that makes him better off, then it would be very strange not to give the child whatever it may be, but in this case there is a good reason not to provide siblings.

CONCLUSION

These are all serious and complicated issues, and the discussion I have given here is brief. The suggestion, though, is that while these are all issues to consider, none of them constitutes an argument against instituting a one-child policy. Some of them, I think, are not very serious problems, such as the life a child will have without siblings. Some of them—how to create an economy that will be generally beneficial, both now and in the future, or how to end sexual discrimination—are huge problems, but their solution does not hang on the question of how many children we have. And, in the long run, while these are all problems that must be faced, I think they pale in significance when compared to the problem of environmental degradation, which the one-child policy addresses.

NOTES

1. As discussed in the first chapter, once we get to a sustainable population level there would be no need to have a one-child policy, so in that context there would be no justification for requiring it.

2. As quoted by Shankar Vedantam, "Report on Global Ecosystems Calls for Radical Changes," *Washington Post*, March 30, 2005.

3. Tim Jackson, *Prosperity without Growth*, Earthscan (Washington, DC) 2011, 45.

4. Ibid.

5. Royal Society, *People and the Planet*, The Royal Society (London) 2012, 84.

6. Ibid., 87.

7. John Stuart Mill, *Principles of Political Economy* (abridged), ed. Stephen Nathanson, Hackett (Indianapolis) 2004, 190.

8. Ibid., 191.

9. Royal Society, *People and the Planet*, 104.

10. Paul Wiseman, "Richest 1 Per Cent Earn Biggest Share since '20's," *AP News*, September 2013.

11. Michael Hiltzik, "CEO to Worker Pay Is Obscene; Want to Know How Obscene?" *Los Angeles Times*, October 20, 2013.

12. Robert Reich, "Income Inequality Is the Enemy of Economic Growth," World News.com, October 17, 2013.

13. www.census.gov/hhes/www/poverty/about/overview.

14. www.worldbank.org/en/topic/poverty/overview.

15. www.usatoday.com/story/money/cars/2013/09/04/record-price-new-car-August/276134. In 2012 Forbes had recorded the average price to be $30,303, which was itself a record. www.forbes.com/sites/moneybuilder/2012/05/10/average-price-of-a-new-car.

16. Miguel Llanos, "Plastic Bottles Pile Up as a Mountain of Waste: Americans Thirst for Portable Water Is Behind Drop in Recycling Rate," March 3, 2005, www.nbcnews.com/id/5279230/ns/US_news-environmental/t/plastic-bottles-pile-Mountains-waste/#U1WD59Qo7L8.

17. Richard Easterlin, "Does Economic Growth Improve the Human Lot? Some Empirical Evidence," in *Nations and Households in Economic Growth: Essays in Honor of Moses Abramowitz*, ed. Paul A. David and Melvin W. Reder, Academic Press (New York) 1974, 89–125; Juliet B. Schor, *The Overspent American*-Basic Books (New York) 1998.

18. Les Christie, "McMansions Are Making a Comeback," *CNN*, June 4, 2013, http://money.cnn.com/2013/06/04/real_estate/home-size.

19. First published in *Galaxy* magazine, 1954; later reprinted in *Midas World*, St. Martin's Press (New York) 1983.

20.. Derek Bok, *The Politics of Happiness*, Princeton University Press (Princeton, NJ) 2010, 70-74.

21. http://money.cnn.com/retirement/guide/SocialSecurity_basics.money-mag/index18.htm?

22. Bill McKibben, *Maybe One: A Personal and Environmental Argument for Single-Child Families*, Plume (New York) 1998, 146.

23. Adair Turner, "Population Ageing: What Should We Worry About?" *Philosophical Transactions of the Royal Society B*, vol. 364, October 2009, 3016–3017.

24. Social Security Administration, "Social Security History: Life Expectancy for Social Security," http://www.ssa.gov/history/lifeexpect.html.

25. Social Security Administration, Calculators: Life Expectancy, http://www.ssa.gov/planners/lifeexpectancy.htm.

26. Census Organization of India, "Sex Ratio of India," http://www.census2011.co.in/sexratio.php.

27. Gretchen Livingston, "Will the End of China's One-Child Policy Shift Its Boy-Girl Ratio?" Pew Research Center, November 15, 2013, http://www.pewresearch.org/fact-tank/2013/11/15/will-the-end-of-chinas-one-child-policy-shift-its-boy-girl-ratio/.

28. Gary Becker, "Is Sex Selection of Births Undesirable?" Becker-Posner Blog, February 12, 2007.

29. Kristin Mammen and Christina Paxson, "Women's Work and Economic Development," *Journal of Economic Perspectives*, vol. 14, #4, 2000, 141–164.

30. These numbers are reported for 2011 by Eurostat, the statistical office of the European Union. http://epp.eurostat.ec.europa.ed/statistics_explained/index,php/File:Total_fertility_rate-1960-2011_(live_births_per_woman).png.

31. Sital Kalantry, "Sex Selection in the United States and India," *UCLA Journal of International Law and Foreign Affairs*, vol. 18, Fall 2013, 61–85.

32. In-Soo Nam, "South Korean Women Get Even, at Least in Number," *Wall Street Journal*, July 1, 2013.

33. Woojin Chung and Monica Das Gupta, "Why Is Son Preference Declining in South Korea? The Role of Development and Public Policy, and the Implications for China and India," World Bank, Development Research Group, Policy Research Working Paper 4373, October 2007.

34. Martina Deuchler, *The Confucian Transformation of Korea: A Study of Society and Ideology*, Harvard University Press (Cambridge, MA) 1992.

35. Chung and Das Gupta, "Son Preference Declining," 2–6.

36. Ibid., 20.

37. I owe this point to Jesse Prinz.

38. Tom Parfitt, "Vladimir Putin Calls on Russian Families to Have Three Children," *Telegraph*, December 12, 2012; C. J. Chivers, "Putin Urges Plan to Reverse Slide in Birth Rate," *New York Times*, May 11, 2006.

39. Toni Falbo, "The One-Child Family in the United States: Research Issues and Results," *Studies in Family Planning*, vol. 13, 1982, 212–215; Denise Polit and Toni Falbo, "The Intellectual Achievement of Only Children," *Journal of Biosocial Science*, vol. 20, 1988, 275–286.
40. Vanessa Fong, *Only Hope: Coming of Age under China's One-Child Policy*, Stanford University Press (Stanford, CA) 2004, 2.
41. Ibid., 128–129.
42. Ibid., 129.
43. Ibid., 3.

[7]

CONCLUSION
When?

That God had a plan, I do not doubt.
But what if His plan was, that we would do better?
—Mary Oliver, "Watching a Documentary about
Polar Bears Trying to Survive on the Melting Ice Floes"

WHEN?

How dire is this situation? When do we need to begin to work? And what exactly are we working toward—what is a sustainable population?

Of course, it depends in part on what we are talking about. When should we realize that in today's world procreation is not a private act? Now. When should we work to make contraceptives available to everyone who wants them? Now. When should we voluntarily refrain from having more than one child—for those of us for whom that is possible? Again, I would say now. It is true, of course, that we would be acting without full knowledge, and without knowing if our sacrifice is entirely needed. But given what we do know both about the harm we are now doing to the natural world, and given what we do know about population numbers, the likelihood is that we do need to do this, and as I've argued earlier, if great harm is likely to arise from something we do, and we can avoid that action without great harm to ourselves, we don't have a right to do it. It is almost always the case that we have to act without full knowledge. That harm is overwhelmingly likely in this case, though, we know: in its most recent report, the Intergovernmental Panel on Climate Change confirms what we believe, that "continued emission of greenhouse gases will cause further warming and long-lasting changes in all components of the climate system, increasing the likelihood of severe, pervasive and irreversible impacts for people and ecosystems."[1] And when it comes to population growth, the effect of restraint is always delayed: demographic momentum—the fact that the huge number of people now living will produce children who will again during their lifetimes produce children—means that even at one child each, the population will continue to grow for a while, at least, probably, until 2050.[2] Some estimate that the effects of climate change in particular will last longer than we have so far predicted—a recent article in the *Proceedings of the National Academy of Science* postulates that earlier studies haven't included all the relevant information, and that in fact "future warming could be more intense and longer lasting than previously thought."[3] So we can't wait until we reach some population tipping point and then expect that a one-child policy will immediately save us. If we wait until that time, either we are doomed, or, perhaps, we may take a much more draconian approach to population growth—lotteries where only one in three, or four, or five people can have a child.[4] It's better for all concerned if we introduce milder self-regulation now, however we have to. As mentioned in Chapter 4, it's estimated that if everyone had access to contraception and used it to avoid unwanted conception, the population in 2100 would be 3 billion less than it would otherwise be, all things being equal. According to the most recent figures as of this writing, dropping the fertility rate to 1 per woman by 2100 would result

> in a peak population size of 8.9 billion by 2056, followed by a decline of approximately 7 billion by 2100 (i.e. a return to the 2013 population size). Enforcing a one child per female policy world-wide by 2045 . . . [would result] in a peak population size of 7.95 billion by 2037, 7.59 billion by 2050, and a rapid reduction to 3.45 billion by 2100.[5]

A one-child policy sooner would make a huge difference; later would make a difference later; and not at all is probably unsustainable. At our present pace, a 2013 French study says we will reach a population of 9.7 billion by 2050, and a recent report in *Science* says the peak by 2100 might be as high as 12.3 billion.[6] Again, the status quo appears to be untenable, and the later we wait the more difficult it will presumably be to reverse our course. Now, these are obviously predictions, and predictions can be false. And, as said, I am a philosopher, not a statistician, a demographer, or an environmental scientist. I haven't tried to make my own predictions about population and its effect on the world. However, while there is certainly some disagreement about the specific numbers we can expect, and some disagreement on what exactly the effect of these numbers will be, there is a consensus that we are in trouble. The conclusion to be drawn is that the likelihood of harm is enough to warrant action. We need to change our ways, and we don't want to wait to do it.

Of course, another big question is when we can stop limiting births, and as we see above, what we do now may determine that. I've argued that we should limit ourselves to one child until overpopulation is no longer a danger, at which point we can allow ourselves replacement value—two children per couple. One question is what the optimal population actually is—at what point we could relax efforts to reduce population. That is one of many questions to which I don't know the answer. We want to use the earth sustainably, but how many of us can do that depends, of course, on at least a couple of things, including both facts and values. Relevant facts are what sort of lives future people will be living. What resources will they be using, and how quickly can those be replaced? This will depend in part on technology—how good we get at creating energy-saving, conservation-friendly devices. Part of it will depend on how much people will choose to consume: will individuals still be driving themselves wherever they want to go? Will houses be the mansions many aspire to today, or simple cottages, or perhaps energy-efficient apartment houses? Will as large a percentage live in poverty as we see now, or will the aim be relative economic equality? If we seek equality, at what level of subsistence? There are suggestions as to optimum population numbers, but all of these are subject to (at least) these variables.[7] It is probably impossible for us, at this stage of history, to foresee what exactly circumstances will be.

Still, it seems likely that we should prepare for the long haul. Things are looking bad at least until 2050, and how long they look bad after that depends on what exactly we do. If voluntary efforts fail, there will be an even worse situation to address when legislation finally addresses growth, and it will take much longer to bring the population down to sustainable numbers, and there will perhaps be fewer resources left to sustain people, meaning the population that can be sustained will be smaller than it could otherwise have been. So, how long this self-restraint would have to last depends in part on when we institute it, and that's something we don't yet know. We're unlikely to reach sustainable numbers during the lifetime of those of us alive now, though, even the lifetime of people now young. We can't look at this as a quick fix but as an enduring change in culture.

VALUES

Nature's Value to Humans

In addition to the facts of the matter—how large the population becomes before it starts to drop, what technologies we may have, and what remaining resources—our policy will be determined by the values we hold. Obviously, on my account, we have an obligation to spare present and future people greatly depleted lives when we can do that without sacrificing any substantial interest of our own. I think this justifies restraints on our actions according to any common reckoning of what duties we have to others. I think myself, though, that there are other reasons we have a moral obligation to make sure we do not produce too many people, and these considerations can affect what actually counts as too many people. These are not reasons that everyone will accept as compelling, but since I and at least some others feel they have some force, I will mention them.

For one thing, many people believe that nature contributes more to human life than just the means to basic wherewithal. One area in which we have been hugely enriched by the experience of the natural world is that of art, both in its inspiration to artists and the experience they pass on to those who rejoice in the artists' work. The poem by Mary Oliver at the beginning of this chapter is one of many examples of art largely inspired by nature: by its aesthetic qualities, and perhaps more generally by what different artists have perceived by its meaning (or meanings). Oliver, who has won both a Pulitzer Prize and a National Book Award, has been described by the *New York Times* as the United State's best selling poet.[8] These things indicate at the least that her poetry has reached many people and made a significant difference to their experience. Oliver is, of course, just one of a long tradition of artists who have been inspired either occasionally or primarily by their experience of nature, and who turned that experience into works that others have found peculiarly poignant. Whether it is the Emperor Huizong's 12th century *Finches and Bamboo* or Durer's 1502 watercolor of the *Young Hare* or Charlotte Brontë's description of Yorkshire moors, our artistic experience has been enriched in immeasurable ways by the experience of nature. It is not that we haven't plenty of great works of art that are set in, say, urban landscapes, entirely dominated by humans. It is just that by losing the experience of nature, we would lose one deeply valuable kind of artistic experience, one that has spoken to us, and continues to speak to us, in a unique way.

And then, there is the immediate effect that being in the natural world can have on our mood, our outlook, our dispositions. Many have talked about the value of solitude, the reward of spending some time entirely outside the human environment. Thoreau is famous, of course, for praise of his relatively simple life on Walden Pond. Aristotle, while no advocate of solitude, advises us to study nature because "every realm of nature is marvelous,"[9] and many believe that this appreciation of the natural, in all its intricacy and strangeness, increases our well-being in substantial ways. John Muir, the founder of the environmentally conscious Sierra Club, wrote that when spending time in the wilderness, "Nature's peace will flow into you as sunshine flows into trees. The winds will blow their own freshness into you, and the storms their energy, while cares will drop off like autumn leaves."[10]

Again, not everyone accepts this: some of us may feel nothing but fear at finding ourselves in a truly natural habitat, or may at best be bored. I am inclined to think, though, that taking away the possibility of experiencing the world of natural habitats threatens to be such a loss to happiness that we can't accept it, even without regard to the material losses we will suffer from resource depletion and climate change.

And there are other unexpected practical benefits nature may yet provide. There are any number of uses we make of other species, and as has often been pointed out, we have discovered more than once that a species we thought had no particular human use to us can in fact play a vital role in our welfare: consider taxol, which has proven a tremendously effective anticancer drug, and which was discovered as a naturally occurring compound in the Pacific yew.[11] As contemporary biologist E. O. Wilson in his March 2007 Ted talk points out,

> Human-forced climate change alone—again, if unabated—could eliminate a quarter of surviving species during the next five decades. What will we and all future generations lose if much of the living environment is thus degraded? Huge potential sources of scientific information yet to be gathered, much of our environmental stability and new kinds of pharmaceuticals and new products of unimaginable strength and value—all thrown away.[12]

Preservation of nature can enrich us in both psychological and material ways, and if we care about this, it provides a reason to limit environmental degradation even before such degradation posts a threat to the basic quality of life.

Nature's Intrinsic Value

The value things have through their usefulness to a certain human purpose is not the end of the story. Such instrumental value can sometimes be negated. That is, if we value a plant only because it is useful for us, but then we discover a synthetic compound that does the same thing and that we can produce just as easily, the plant loses its usefulness. Of course, the same plant might be able to yield some further useful product, but if that seems doubtful enough, we may think its preservation is not important. The more profound question when it comes to species preservation is whether animals and plants have any intrinsic value: whether it's a good thing to preserve different beings and their natural ways of living just because they are valuable in themselves, regardless of their usefulness to humans. If they are valuable in themselves, then we should treat them differently than we now do.

We know, after all, that we are wiping them out at a rapid rate. The present speed with which we are extirpating nonhumans is truly impressive, and merits its now-popular description as "the sixth extinction."[13] According to the World Wildlife Fund, we have less than half the population of vertebrates—mammals, birds, reptiles, amphibians, and fish—than we had forty years ago. "In other words, those populations around the globe have dropped by more than half in fewer than two human generations."[14] The primary causes are often exploitation (basically, we kill them) or loss of habitat. Consider the polar bears described in Oliver's poem above. This is art, but it is not a work of the imagination. Polar bear habitat has been literally melting away.

Without sufficient sea ice, polar bears lose the ability to capture their typical prey, ringed seals. Normally, polar bears eat an enormous number of seals on the ice to build up fat storage, and then as the ice melts in summer, the bears use this fat to get through the summers that they spend on land with less available to eat. As the period in which there is sea ice declines, the bears have to eat less. Scientists observing bears during the shorter ice seasons have observed that "Bears didn't grow as large, and some came ashore notably skinnier. Females gave birth less often and had fewer cubs. Fewer cubs survived."[15] Starvation is not the only danger. Naturally the bears try to find a habitat where they can eat, and that has its own heartbreaks. Bears may end up swimming enormous distances in the attempt to find the ice that will allow them to hunt: "in 2008 a radio-collared bear with a yearling cub swam an astounding 427 miles to reach ice off the northern Alaskan coast. The cub didn't make it."[16] If sea ice continues to melt at its current rate, scientists believe two-thirds of the world's 20,000 to 25,000 polar bears could be gone by 2050.[17] As Oliver says, we may well ask ourselves if we can't do better.

The polar bears' habitat loss is due to climate change. Other habitat loss is due to development, though agricultural expansion, residential development, and sometimes water diversion from wild(er) areas (like the Florida Everglades) to these residences and farms. We have a tendency to publicize the more dramatic causes of habitat loss (we condemn the bad guys who kill rhinos for their horns, and the perhaps badder guys who buy them) when the more significant causes get ignored. Think of forest elephants: we kill them for ivory, but we also have reduced their natural range to 6%–7% of what it was in 1900.[18] While we deplore the poaching of elephants for ivory, and reports on poaching appear regularly in the news, we give very little publicity to the equally significant fact that we have simply deprived them of a place to live a healthy and natural life.

As we lose individual animals, we inevitably lose entire species. Our burgeoning population has resulted in the loss of many natural species already, and threatens the loss of many, many more. While it is true species disappear through natural processes, without any interventions by humans, scientists estimate that we are losing species now at 1,000 to 10,000 times the natural rate, "with literally dozens going extinct every day."[19] With the continued growth of human population, there will be even more loss of habitat for animals who depend on them to live—animals who can't, as humans can, change their ways of living to accommodate to new circumstances. It is estimated that some of the greatest increases in population will occur in what are called biodiversity hotspots—places that have an unusually high number of species.[20] While we do have wildlife sanctuaries, many of these are under great pressure from population growth just beyond the borders of the protected territories.[21]

Does it matter if we lose a large percentage of the species that now inhabit the earth? Here again, intuitions vary. There are certainly those who think only humans have any intrinsic value, and that other things are valuable only insofar as they are useful to us. We are, after all, smarter than other animals, and capable of reflection, and capable of moral agency, and as far as we can tell, no other animals are. On the other hand, we do seem to value things other than intelligence, reflection, and agency. We value beauty, and we value the experience of pleasure, even when we ourselves are not experiencing it; we admire ingenuity, creativity, and complexity. Many species have unique beauty, and many are capable of many of the pleasures we ourselves enjoy. And the evolution of each species has many examples of what might be called ingenuity, complexity, and creativity—not, to be sure, on the part of any actual consciousness, but still, the result is ingenious, complex, and in some sense creative. Consider the way we value the proliferation of human cultures and their unique ways of being. Individuals might well thrive when a culture is lost, but we still value cultural variation—we value distinctive ways of being, even as they evolve into new varieties of distinctiveness. Some find these same values in animal species. Charles Darwin wrote in *The Origin of Species*,

> There is grandeur in this view of life, with its several powers, having been originally breathed into a few forms or into one; and that, whilst this planet has gone cycling on according to the fixed law of gravity, from so simple a beginning endless forms most beautiful and most wonderful have been, and are being, evolved.[22]

Of course, Darwin's saying it doesn't make it true—but we may not be surprised that those who actually study species are amazed at them. That individual plant and animal species have intrinsic value is hard to prove, and of course even something that has intrinsic value can sometimes justifiably be harmed, if other, greater values are at stake. But if we accept that they have such value, we would at least recognize that when animals and plants disappear from the earth, we have lost something irreplaceable and of great value, something "resplendent," to quote biologist Nathaniel Wheelwright, and that that is not a loss we can face with indifference.[23]

CONCLUSION

None of this discussion of overpopulation is intended to undercut the need many of us have to change other aspects of the way we live in radical ways. Changes in consumption and changes in emissions are vital, as many others have emphasized. We can each do something, and should bear in mind that everything makes a difference: diet, transportation, the way we build our houses, even the choices we make as to the clothes we wear.[24] On the bad side, this means we need to make a lot of changes. On the good side, this means there are many things we can actually do to bring about the preservation of our world in a flourishing state. So, the emphasis on consumption is certainly warranted. It still looks as if the single biggest thing people can do to preserve the environment is to limit themselves to one child, though. Even with very moderate consumption, the earth cannot sustain an increasing population.

Although I've argued for the permissibility of government regulations for reproduction, the point of this book is really to remind us of our personal responsibility, to remind us that the things we do determine other people's happiness. We don't want the fact that we are used to living a certain way to give us a sense of entitlement. We don't want to mistake what we want for what we have a right to. We don't want to be selfish. Sadly, even the desire to love can in fact be selfish; loving too many biologically related children at the cost of the rest of society's welfare isn't, it turns out, a manifestation of generosity. Further, love can be harmful even to those toward whom it is directed—one's descendants. It's true that it is hard for us to believe that something that people once had a right to can become something that we no longer have a right to when circumstances change and the practice becomes dangerous. It's hard to believe in "new" dangers, hard to believe that things we're used to doing can actually be bad for us, but of course they may. To live successfully we need to recognize when circumstances change and adapt our ways of living.

It's not easy. We have to be realistic, and this is really no fun at all when we are in a dangerous place. It is a natural human tendency to avoid focusing on problems, and especially to avoid focusing on big problems. We prefer to think about what we can easily fix, especially where the solution proves personally rewarding. There are things we can take care of without having to coordinate with others, and without, really, having to make profound changes in the way we are living. Unfortunately, the most serious problems often aren't like that. We have to see ourselves as part of a global pattern, difficult enough in any event and particularly when seeing ourselves that way will cause us to be uncomfortable. This is presumably the motivation behind denying climate change—if facing the truth is both difficult and disagreeable, why do it? The answer, of course, is that the consequences of inaction will be much worse than the disagreeable actions we're trying not to think about, and they will eventually be unavoidable. Since we're imperfectly rational agents, though, we find it hard to put that firmly into our minds. So this is work.

And we have to be prepared to be unpopular, because no one likes to be told what to do. Even attempts at persuasion can be resented when they run contrary to people's existing plans. If we do get to the point where we must actually make regulations that constrain people's choices, that will be, to say the least, controversial. We have a tendency to resent even the most insignificant restraints, at least initially—seat belt laws or cigarette taxes. The more substantial the interference, the more resentment it is likely to provoke, again, until the new mode of behavior becomes accepted as social norm.

Still, though, we need to think how to do this. How can we start? As I've emphasized in Chapter 4, education is important no matter what we choose to do. Granted, in some places the fertility rate has dropped without there being any particular attention paid to environmental impacts, simply because of the costs of having children or the desire of both parents to work outside the home, but we can't count on this. People need more generally to look at trends in population and consumption, and see the impact that family size has. This requires two sorts of education: scientific and political. We need to look at demographics and understand how our numbers increase. We need to learn about the impact each individual has on the planet, and the extent to which that varies—and the extent to which that doesn't vary—with the way we live. This is something we can do, through the educational institutions we have and through the focus of news media and other means of public outreach. It should be unproblematic that education about scientific facts is a good thing, however we go about doing that, because we need to make sure people know this stuff, the stuff that will shape our lives at present and in the future. Providing people with information is not an unwarranted intrusion into privacy but a duty toward our fellow humans.

And we need to educate ourselves about some political truths. We need to realize that having children is just not a private matter anymore. It is ironic that some of the people who oppose taking steps to reduce population growth do that on the grounds of privacy protection, when one of the things that reduces the possibility of privacy is the sheer number of people around. It's very hard now to do anything without having an impact on others. This is especially true when it comes to producing more people—our procreation practices will make a huge difference to those around us in a variety of ways. So protecting privacy in the long run will require recognizing the limits of privacy at present. If an action has a great and detrimental effect on others, it's empty rhetoric—but nonetheless harmful rhetoric—to insist that it is private. When we think we want to have children, we need to recognize that it is a decision that concerns everyone.

NOTES

1. Intergovernmental Panel on Climate Change, *Climate Change 2014: Synthesis Report: Summary for Policy Makers*, 8, http://www.ipcc.ch/pdf/assessment-report/ar5/syr/SYR_AR5_SPMcorr1.pdf.

2. Corey J. A. Bradshaw and Barry W. Brook, "Human Population Reduction Is Not a Quick Fix for Environmental Problems," *Proceedings of the National Academy of Science*, vol. 111, #46, November 18, 2014, 16610–16615.

3. R. E. Zeebe, "Time-Dependent Climate Sensitivity and the Legacy of Anthropogenic Greenhouse Gas Emissions," *Proceedings of the National Academy of Sciences*, vol. 110, #34, doi:10.1073/pnas.1222843110, August 20, 2013.

4. The idea of child lotteries was suggested to me by Brookes Brown.

5. Bradshaw and Brook, "Human Population Reduction," 16612.

6. Patrick Gerland, Adrian Raferty, et al., "World Population Stabilization Unlikely in This Century," *Science*, vol. 346, October 10, 2014, 234–237; Gilles Pison, "Tous les pays do monde," *Population et Sociétés*, #503, September 2013.

7. One 1994 estimate supports a population of 1 to 3 billion people, depending on the degree of prosperity in which they live. See David Pimentel, Rebecca Harman, et al., "Natural Resources and an Optimum Human Population," *Population and Environment*, vol. 15, #5, May 1994, 347–369.

8. Dwight Garner, "Inside the List," *New York Times Sunday Book Review*, February 18, 2007.

9. Aristotle, *Parts of Animals*, 645a16, trans. William Ogle, in *The Basic Works of Aristotle*, ed. Richard McKeon, Random House (New York) 1941.

10. John Muir, *Our National Parks*, Houghton Mifflin (Boston, New York) 1901, 56.

11. Taxol was discovered in the early 1970s as part of a National Cancer Institute screening of many species of higher plants for anticancer potential.

12. E. O. Wilson, "My Wish: Build the Encyclopedia of Life," March 2007, http://www.ted.com/talks/e_o_wilson_on_saving_life_on_earth?/language=en.

13. See Elizabeth Kolbert, *The Sixth Extinction: An Unnatural History*, Henry Holt (New York) 2014.

14. World Wildlife Fund, *Living Planet Report 2014*, http://www.worldwildlife.org/pages/living-planet-report-2014.

15. Susan McGrath, "On Thin Ice," *National Geographic Magazine*, July 2011.

16. Ibid.

17. Cheryl Lyn Dybas, "Life After Ice," *Defenders of Wildlife Magazine*, vol. 89, no. 4, Winter 2015.

18. World Wildlife Fund, *Living Planet Report 2014*.

19. Center for Biological Diversity, "The Extinction Crisis," http://www.bio-logicaldiversity.org/programs/biodiversity/elements_of_biodiversity/extinction_crisis/.
20. Bradshaw and Brook, "Human Population Reduction."
21. W. F. Laurance et al., "Averting Biodiversity Collapse in Tropical Forest Protected Areas," *Nature*, vol. 489, September 13, 2012, 290–294; R. P. Cincotta et al., "Human Population in the Biodiversity Hotspots," *Nature*, vol. 404, April 27, 2000, 990–992.
22. Charles Darwin, *The Origin of Species*, John Murray (London) 1859, 490.
23. Nathanial T. Wheelwright, "Enduring Reasons to Preserve Threatened Species," *Chronicle of Higher Education*, June 1, 1994.
24. Claudio Luz, "Waste Couture: Environmental Impact of the Clothing Industry," *Environmental Health Perspectives*, vol. 115, #9, September 2007, A449–A454.

BIBLIOGRAPHY

Ahmed, Nafeez. "The Coming Nuclear Energy Crunch," *Guardian*, July 2, 2013.

Archard, David. *Children: Rights and Childhood*. Routledge (New York) 1993.

Banister, Judith. *China's Changing Population*. Stanford University Press (Stanford, CA) 1987.

Barnwal, Ashok. "Success of the Indonesian Population Program: Lessons for India," *Journal of Development and Social Transformation*, vol. 1, 2004, 43–50.

Bayles, Michael D. "Limits to a Right to Procreate." In *Ethics and Population*, ed. Michael D. Bayles, Schenkman (Cambridge, MA) 1976, 41–55.

Becker, Gary. "Is Sex Selection of Births Undesirable?" Becker-Posner blog, February 12, 2007, http://becker-posner-blog.com/2007/02/is-s-s-of-b-u-becker.html.

Beitz, Charles. *The Idea of Human Rights*. Oxford University Press (New York) 2009.

Benatar, David. *Better Never to Have Been*. Oxford University Press (New York) 2006.

——. "The Limits of Reproductive Freedom." In *Procreation and Parenthood*, ed. David Archard and David Benatar. Oxford University Press (New York) 2010, 78–102.

Bentham, Jeremy."Nonsense upon Stilts," in *Rights, Representation, and Reform*, ed. Philip Schofield, Catherine Pease-Watkin, and Cyprian Blamires. Oxford University Press (Oxford) 2002.

Bok, Derek. *The Politics of Happiness*. Princeton University Press (Princeton, NJ) 2011.

Bradshaw, Corey J. A., and Barry W. Brook. "Human Population Reduction Is Not a Quick Fix for Environmental Problems." *Proceedings of the National Academy of Science*, vol. 111, #46, Nov. 18, 2014, 16610–16615.

Brock, Dan. "Funding New Reproductive Technologies." In *New Ways of Making Babies: The Case of Egg Donation*, ed. Cynthia Cohen. Indiana University Press (Bloomington) 1996, 213–230.

———. "The Moral Bases of a Right to Reproductive Freedom," in *Should Parents Be Licensed?*, ed. Peg Tittle. Prometheus Books (Amherst, NY) 2004.

———. "The Non-identity Problem and Genetic Harms: The Case of Wrongful Handicaps." *Bioethics*, vol. 9, #3, 1995, 269–275.

Brock, Dan. "Shaping Future Children: Parental Rights and Societal Interests." *Journal of Political Philosophy*, vol. 13, #4, 2005, 377–398.

Broome, John. "Should We Value Population?" *Journal of Political Philosophy*, vol. 13, #4, 2005, 399–413.

Brown, Elizabeth Nolan. "Over-the-Counter Birth Control Pills? Not in America," March 26, 2014, http://reason.com/archives/2014/03/26/over-the-counter-birth-control-pills-us.

Buchanan, Alan, Dan Brock, Norman Daniels, and Dan Wikler. *From Chance to Choice*. Cambridge University Press (Cambridge) 2000.

Buck v. Bell. 274 US 200 (1927).

Callahan, Daniel. "Ethics and Population Limitation: What Ethical Norms Should Be Brought to Bear in Controlling Population Growth?" *Science*, vol. 175, #4021, 1972, 487–394.

———. "What Obligations Do We Have to Future Generations?" In *Responsibilities to Future Generations: Environmental Ethics*, ed. Ernest Partridge. Prometheus Books (Buffalo, NY) 1981, 73–85.

Campbell, Flann. "Birth Control and the Christian Churches." *Population Studies* (Population Investigation Committee), vol. 14, no. 2, November 1960, 131–147.

Campbell, Martha. "Why the Silence on Population?" In *Life on the Brink*, ed. Philip Cafaro and Eileen Crist. University of Georgia Press (Athens, GA) 2012.

Campbell, Martha, Sahin-Hodoglugil Nuriye Nalan, and Malcolm Potts. "Barriers to Fertility Regulation: A Review of the Literature." *Studies in Family Planning*, vol. 37, #2, 2006, 87–98.

CBS News. "Heated Debate over NYC Big Sugary Drinks Ban Plan," July 25, 2012, http://www.cbsnews.com/heated-debate-over-nyc-big-sugary-drinks-ban-plan/.

Census Organization of India. "Sex Ratio of India," http://www.census2011.co.in/sexratio.php.

Center for Biological Diversity. " The Extinction Crisis," http://www.biologicaldiversity.org/programs/biodiversity/elements_of_biodiversity/extinction_crisis.

Christie, Les. "McMansions Are Making a Comeback," *CNN*, June 4, 2013, http://money.cnn.com/2013/06/04/real_estate/home-size.

Chung, Woojin, and Monica Das Gupta. "Why Is Son Preference Declining in South Korea? The Role of Development and Public Policy, and the Implications for China and India." World Bank, Development Research Group, Policy Research Working Paper 4373, October 2007.

Christman, John. "Self-Ownership, Equality, and the Structure of Property Rights." *Political Theory*, vol. 19, #1, February 1991, 28–46.

Cincotta, R. P., et al. "Human Population in the Biodiversity Hotspots." *Nature*, vol. 404, April 27, 2000, 990–992.

Cleland, J. G., R. P. Nudugwa, and E. M. Zulu. "Family Planning in Sub-Saharan Africa: Prognosis or Stagnation?" *Bulletin of the World Health Organization*, vol. 89, #2, February 2011, 137–143.

Cohen, I. Glenn. "Beyond Best Interests." *Minnesota Law Review*, vol. 96, April 2012, 1187–1274.

——. "Regulating Reproduction: The Problem of Best Interests." *Minnesota Law Review*, vol. 96, 2011, 423–519.

CNN. "Controversy Fizzing over Bloomberg's Soda Ban," June 4, 2012, http://news.blogs.cnn.com/2012/06/04/controversy-fizzing-over-bloombergs-soda-ban/.

CNN. "Ultimate Guide to Retirement: Will Social Security Still Exist When I Retire?" http://money.cnn.com/retirement/guide/SocialSecurity_basics.moneymag/index18.htm.

Committee on Gynecologic Practice. "Over-the-Counter Access to Oral Contraceptives," Committee Opinion, The American College of Obstetricians and Gynecologists, No. 544, December 2012.

Conly, Sarah. "The Right to Procreation: Merits and Limits." *American Philosophical Quarterly*, vol. 42, #2, April 2005, 105–115.

Cooter, Robert. "Expressive Law and Economics." *Journal of Legal Studies*, vol. 27, June 1998, 585–607.

Daniels, Norman. "Reasonable Disagreement about Identified vs. Statistical Victims." *Hastings Center Report*, vol. 42, #1, 2012, 35–45.

Delattre, Edwin. "Rights, Responsibilities, and Future Persons." *Ethics*, vol. 82, #3, April 1972, 254–258.

Deuchler, Martina. *The Confucian Transformation of Korea: A Study of Society and Ideology*. Harvard University Press (Cambridge, MA) 1992.

Dillard, Carter J. "Child Welfare and Future Persons." *Georgia Law Review*, vol. 43, 2008–2009, 367–445.

——. "Rethinking the Procreative Right." *Yale Human Rights and Development Law Journal*, vol. 10, 2007, 1–63.

——. "Valuing Having Children." *Journal of Law and Family Studies*, vol. 12, 2010, 151–98.

Dworkin, Gerald. *The Theory and Practice of Autonomy*. Cambridge University Press (Cambridge) 1988.

Dworkin, Ronald. "Right as Trumps," in *Theories of Right*, ed. Jeremy Waldron. Oxford University Press (New York) 1984, 153–167.

———. *Taking Rights Seriously*. Harvard University Press (Cambridge, MA) 1977.

Dybas, Cherly Lyn. "Life After Ice." *Defenders of Wildlife Magazine*, vol. 89, # 4, Winter, 2015.

Easterlin, Richard. "Does Economic Growth Improve the Human Lot? Some Empirical Evidence." In *Nations and Households in Economic Growth: Essays in Honor of Moses Abramowitz*, ed. Paul A. David and Melvin W. Reder. Academic Press (New York) 1974, 89–125.

Economist. "Falling Fertility: Astonishing Falls in the Fertility Rate Are Bringing with Them Big Benefits." October 29, 2009.

Ehrlich, Paul. *The Population Bomb*. Sierra Club/Ballantine Books (New York) 1968.

Engelman, Robert. "Trusting Women to End Population Growth," in *Life on the Brink*, ed. Philip Cafaro and Eileen Crist. University of Georgia Press (Athens, GA) 2012, 223–239.

Eurostat. "Total Fertility Rate, Selected Years (Live Births Per Woman)," October 23, 2012, http://ec.europa.eu/eurostat/statistics-explained/index. ph./File:Total_fertility_rate,_selected_years_(live_births_per_woman). png.

Fabre, Cecile. "Justice and the Compulsory Taking of Live Body Parts." *Utilitas*, vol. 15, #2, July 2003, 127–150.

———. *Whose Body Is It Anyway? Justice and the Integrity of the Person*. Oxford University Press (New York) 2006.

Falbo, Toni. "The One-Child Family in the United States: Research Issues and Results." *Studies in Family Planning*, vol. 13, 1982, 212–215.

Federal Research Division. *Singapore: A Country Study*, Library of Congress (Washington, DC) 1991.

Federal Research Division. *Indonesia: A Country Study*, Library of Congress (Washington, DC) 1993.

Feinberg, Joel. "A Child's Right to an Open Future." In *Freedom and Fulfillment: Philosophical Essays*. Princeton University Press (Princeton, NJ) 1994.

———. *Harm to Others*. Oxford University Press (New York) 1986.

———. *Harm to Self*. Oxford University Press (New York) 1986.

Floyd, S. L., and D. Pomerantz. "Is There a Natural Right to have Children?" In *Should Parents Be Licensed?* ed. Peg Tittle. Prometheus Books (Amherst, NY) 2004.

Fong, Vanessa L. *Only Hope: Coming of Age under China's One Child Policy*. Stanford University Press (Stanford, CA) 2006.

Food and Agriculture Organization of the United Nations. "Prospects for Food, Nutrition, Agriculture and Major Commodity Groups: World Agriculture towards 2030/2050." Interim Report. Global Perspectives Studies Unit, Food and Agriculture Organization of the United Nations, Rome, 2006.

Friedman, Thomas L. *Hot, Flat and Crowded*. Farrar, Straus and Giroux (New York) 2008.

Garner, Dwight. "Inside the List," *New York Times Sunday Book Review*, February 18, 2007.

Gerland, Patrick, Adrian Raferty, et al. "World Population Stabilization Unlikely This Century." *Science*, vol. 346, October 10, 2014, 234–237.

Gillis, Justin. "Heat-Trapping Gas Passes Milestone, Raising Fears." *New York Times*, May 10, 2013.

Gillis, Justin. "Climate Change Seen Posing Risks to Food Supplies," *New York Times*, November 1, 2013.

———. "U.S. Climate Has Already Changed, Study Finds, Citing Heat and Floods," *New York Times*, May 6, 2014.

Gold, Rachel Benson. "Going the Extra Mile: The Difference Title X Makes." *Guttmacher Policy Review*, Spring 2012, vol. 15, #2, www.guttmacher.org/pubs/gpr/15/2/gpr50213.html.

Gosseries, Axel. "On Future Generations' Future Rights." *Journal of Political Philosophy*, vol. 16, #4, 2008, 446–474.

Gribble, James N. "Fact Sheet: Unmet Need for Family Planning." *World Population Data Sheet* 2012, *Population Reference Bureau*, Washington, DC, 2012, www.prb.org/Publications/Datasheets/2012/world-population-date-sheet/fact-sheet-unmet-need.aspx.

Griffin, James. *On Human Rights*. Oxford University Press (New York) 2008.

———. "Rights in Conflict." In *Rights and Reason: Essays in Honor of Carl Wellman*, ed. Marilyn Friedman, Larry Mays, et al. Kluwer (Boston) 2000.

Hall, Charles A. S., et al. "The Environmental Consequences of Having a Baby in the United States." *Population and Environment*, vol. 15, #6, 1994, 505–524.

Harman, Elizabeth. "Can We Harm and Benefit in Creating?" *Philosophical. Perspectives*, vol. 18, 2004, 89–113.

Hiltzik, Michael. "CEO to Worker Pay Is Obscene; Want to Know How Obscene?" *Los Angeles Times*, October 20, 2013.

Intergovernmental Panel on Climate Change. *Climate Change 2014: Synthesis Report, Summary for Policy Makers*, http://www.ipcc.ch/pdf/assessment-report-ar5/syr/SYR_AR5_SPMcorrl.pdf.

Jackson, Tim. *Prosperity without Growth*. Earthscan (Washington, DC), 2011.

Kagan, Shelly. "Do I Make a Difference?' *Philosophy and Public Affairs*, vol. 39, #2, 2011, 105–141.

Kalantry, Sital. "Sex Selection in the United States and India." *UCLA Journal of International and Foreign Affairs*, vol. 18, Fall 2013, 61–85.

Kane, Penny, and Ching Y. Choi. "China's One Child Policy." *British Medical Journal*, vol. 319, 1999, 992–994.

Kates, Carol. "Reproductive Liberty and Overpopulation." *Environmental Values*, vol. 13, #1, 2004, 51–79.

Kevles, Daniel. *In the Name of Eugenics: Genetics and the Uses of Human Heredity*, Knopf (New York) 1985.

Klein, Naomi. *This Changes Everything: Capitalism vs. the Climate.* Simon and Schuster (New York) 2014.

Kolbert, Elizabeth. *The Sixth Extinction: An Unnatural History.* Henry Holt (New York) 2014.

Kraut, Richard. *What Is Good and Why: The Ethics of Well-Being.* Harvard University Press (Cambridge, MA) 2007.

Kristof, Nicholas. "Politicians, Teens, and Birth Control." *New York Times*, November 12, 2014.

LaFollette, Hugh. "Licensing Parents," *Philosophy & Public Affairs*, Winter 1980, 182–197.

Laurance, W. F., et al. "Averting Biodiversity Collapse in Tropical Forest Protected Areas." *Nature*, vol. 489, September 13, 2012, 290–294.

Lee, Luke T. "Law, Human Rights, and Population Policy." In *Population Policy*, ed. Godfrey Roberts. Praeger (New York) 1990, 1–20.

——. "Population: The Human Rights Approach." *Colorado Journal of International Environmental Law and Policy*, vol. 6, 1995, 327–339.

Lee, Ronald. "The Demographic Transition: Three Centuries of Fundamental Change." *Journal of Economic Perspectives*, vol. 17, #4, 2003, 167–190.

Livingston, Gretchen. "Will the End of China's One-Child Policy Shift Its Boy-Girl tank/2013/11/15.

Livingston, Gretchen, and D'Vera Cohn. "U.S. Birth Rate Decline Linked to Recession." April 6, 2010, Pew Research Center, Washington, DC.

Llanos, Miguel. "Plastic Bottles Pile Up as a Mountain of Waste: Americans' Thirst for Portable Water is Behind Drop in Recycling Rate," *NBC News*, March 3, 2015, www.nbcnews.com/id/5279230/ns/US_nes-environmental/t/plastic-bottles-pile-Mountains-waste/#U1WD59Qo7L8.

Locke, John. *The Second Treatise of Government and A Letter Concerning Toleration.* Basil Blackwell (Oxford) 1948.

Loving v. Virginia. 388 US 1 (1967).

Luz, Claudio. "Waste Couture: Environmental Impact of the Clothing Industry." *Environmental Health Perspectives*, vol. 115, #9, September 2007.

Malthus, Thomas. *An Essay on the Principle of Population.* Oxford University Press (New York) 2008.

Mammen, Kristen, and Christina Paxson. "Women's Work and Economic Development." *Journal of Economic Perspectives*, vol. 14, #4, 2000, 141–164.

Max Planck Institute for Demographic Research. "Economic Crisis Lowers Birth Rates." (Rostock) July 10, 2013.

McAdams, Richard. "The Attitudinal Theory of Expressive Law." *Oregon Law Review*, vol. 79, Summer 2000, 339–390.

———. "The Expressive Power of Adjudication." *University of Chicago Law Review*, 2005, 1043.

———. "Focal Point Theory of Expressive Law." *Virginia Law Review*, vol. 86, November 2000, 1649–1729.

McGrath, Susan. "On Thin Ice." *National Geographic Magazine*, July 2011.

McKibben, Bill. *Maybe One: A Case for Smaller Families*, Plume (New York) 1998.

———. "Worried? Us?" *Granta*, Spring 2003.

Mill, John Stuart. On Liberty. In *Utilitarianism and On Liberty*, ed. Mary Warnock. Blackwell (Malden, MA) 2003.

———. *Principles of Political Economy*, ed. Stephen Nathanson. Hackett (Indianapolis) 2004.

———. *A System of Logic*. Harper and Brothers (New York) 1891.

———. "Utilitarianism." In *Utilitarianism and On Liberty*, ed. Mary Warnock. Blackwell (Malden, MA) 2003.

Moreland, Scott, Ellen Smith, and Suneeta Sharma. *World Population Prospects and Unmet Need for Family Planning*. Futures Group (Washington, DC) 2010.

Muir, John. *Our National Parks*. Houghton Mifflin (Boston, New York) 1901.

Murtaugh Paul A., and Michael G. Shlax. "Reproduction and the Carbon Legacies of Individuals." *Global Environmental Change*, vol. 19, 2009, 14–20.

Nam, In-Soo. "South Korean Women Get Even, at Least in Number," *Wall Street Journal*, July 1, 2013.

Narveson, Jan. "Moral Problems of Population." In *Ethics and Population*, ed. Michael Bayles. Schenkman (Cambridge, MA) 1976.

Navarro, Mireya. "Breaking a Long Silence on Population Control," *New York Times*, October 31, 2011.

Newport, Frank. "Americans, Including Catholics, Say Birth Control Is Morally OK," *Gallup*, May 22, 2012.

New York Times Editorial Board. "Running Out of Time," *New York Times*, April 20, 2014.

New York Times Editorial Board. "Washing Away the Fields of Iowa," *New York Times*, May 4, 2011.

Nourse, Victoria F. *In Reckless Hands: Skinner v. Oklahoma and the Near Triumph of American Eugenics*. W. W. Norton (New York) 2008.

Nussbaum, Martha C. "Capabilities and Human Rights." In *Global Justice and Transnational Politics*. ed. Pablo De Greiff and Ciaran Cronin. MIT Press (Cambridge, MA) 2002, 117–149.

Nussbaum, Martha C. "Human Rights Theory: Capabilities and Human Rights." *Fordham Law Review*, vol. 66, 1997, 273–300.

Nussbaum, Martha C. *Woman and Human Development*. Cambridge University Press (Cambridge) 2000.

O'Neill, Brian C., and Lee Wexler. "The Greenhouse Externality to Childbearing: A Sensitivity Analysis." *Climactic Change*, vol. 47, 2000, 283–324.

O'Neill, Onora. "Begetting, Bearing, and Rearing." In *Having Children: Philosophical and Legal Reflections on Parenthood*, ed. Onora O'Neill and William Ruddick. Oxford University Press (New York) 1979, 25–38.

Overall, Christine. *Why Have Children?* MIT Press (Cambridge, MA) 2012.

Parfit, Derek. *Reason and Persons*. Oxford University Press (New York) 1984.

Penner, J. E. *The Idea of Property in Law*. Clarendon Press (Oxford) 1997.

Peralta, Eydar. "John Kerry to German Students: Americans Have 'Right to be Stupid,'" *NPR*, February 26, 2013.

Peterson, Peter G. *Will America Grow Up before It Grows Old?* Random House (New York) 1996.

Peters, Philip G. "Implications of the Nonidentity Problem for State Regulation of Reproductive Liberty." In *Harming Future Persons: Ethics, Genetics, and the Nonidentity Problem*, Melinda A. Roberts David T. Wasserman eds., Springer (Dordrecht) 2009.

Pimental, David. "Soil Erosion: A Food and Environmental Threat," Environment, Development and Sustainability, vol. 8, 2006, 119–137.

Pimental, David, Rebecca Harman, Matthew Pacenzi, Jason Pecarsky, and Marcia Pimental. "Natural Resources and an Optimum Human Population." *Population and Environment*, vol. 15, #5, May 1994, 347–369.

Pison, Gilles. "Tous les pays du monde," *Population et Sociétés*, #503, September 2013.

Pohl, Frederick. "The Midas Plague," in *Midas World*. St. Martin's Press (New York) 1983.

Polit, Denise, and Toni Falbo. "The Intellectual Achievement of Only Children." *Journal of Biosocial Science*, vol. 20, 1988, 275–286.

Potts, Malcolm, and Courtney E. Henderson. "Global Warming and Reproductive Health." *International Journal of Gynecology and Obstetrics*, October 2012, Suppl. 1, S64–S67.

Potts, Malcolm, Rachel Weinrib, and Martha Campbell. "Why Bold Policies for Family Planning Are Needed Now," *Contraception*, April 2013, http://www.arhp.org/publications-and-resources/contraception-journal/april-2013.

Powdthavee, Nattavudh. "Think Having Children Will Make You Happy?" *Psychologist*, vol. 22, #4, 2009, 308–310.

Purdy, Laura. "Can Having Children Be Immoral?" In *Should Parents Be Licensed?* ed. Peg Tittle. Prometheus Books (Amherst, NY) 2004, 143–156.

———. "Loving Future People." In *Reproduction, Ethics, and the Law*, ed. J. Callahan. Indiana University Press (Bloomington) 1995, 300–327.

Raz, Joseph. *The Morality of Freedom*. Oxford University Press (New York) 1986.

——. "Rights-Based Moralities." In *Theories of Rights*, ed. Jeremy Waldren. Oxford University Press (New York) 1984, 182–200.

Reich, Robert. "Income Inequality Is the Enemy of Economic Growth," *WorldNews.com*, October 17, 2013.

Risky Business: The Economic Risks of Climate Change in the United States, June 2014, riskybusiness.org/uploads/files/RiskyBusiness_PrintedReport_FINAL_WEB_OPTIMIZED.pdf.

Robertson, John. *Children of Choice*. Princeton University Press (Princeton, NJ) 1994.

——. "Procreative Liberty and the Control of Conception, Pregnancy, and Childbirth." *Virginia Law Review*, vol. 69, #3, April 1983, 405–464.

Royal Society. *People and the Planet*. The Royal Society (London) April 2012.

Schelling, Thomas. "The Life You Can Save May Be Your Own." In *Problems in Public Expenditure Analysis*, ed. S. B. Chase. Brookings Institution (Washington, DC), 1968, 127–162.

Schoeman, Ferdinand. "Rights of Children, Rights of Parents, and the Moral Basis of the Family." *Ethics*, vol. 91, #1, October 1980, 6–19.

Schor, Juliet B. *The Overspent American*. Basic Books (New York) 1998.

Sen, Amartya. "Elements of a Theory of Human Rights." *Philosophy and Public Affairs*, vol. 32, 2004, 315–356.

——. "Fertility and Coercion." *University of Chicago Law Review*, vol. 63, 1996, 1035–1061.

Senior, Jennifer. "All Joy and No Fun: Why Parents Hate Parenting," *New York Magazine*, July 4, 2010.

Sherif, Muzafer. *The Psychology of Moral Norms*. Harper (New York) 1936.

Shue, Henry. *Basic Rights: Subsistence, Affluence, and U.S. Foreign Policy*. Princeton University Press (Princeton, NJ) 1996.

Siemeniec v. Lutheran General Hospital. 177 Ill.2d 230 (1987).

Singer, Peter. "A Utilitarian Population Principle." In *Ethics and Population*, ed. Michael Bayles. Schenkman (Cambridge, MA) 1976.

Skinner v. Oklahoma. 316 US 535 (1942).

Social Security Administration. "Social Security History: Life Expectancy for Social Security," http://www.ssa.gov/lifeexpect.html.

Social Security Administration. "Calculators: Life Expectancy," http://www.ssa.gov/planners/lifeexpectancy.html.

Statman, Daniel. "The Right to Parenthood: An Argument for a Narrow View." *Ethical Perspectives*, vol. 10, 2003, 224–235.

Stone, Brian, Jr. *The City and the Coming Climate: Climate Change in the Places We Live*. Cambridge University Press (New York) 2012.

Sunstein, Cass R. "How Law Constructs Preferences." *Georgetown Law Journal*, vol. 86, 1998, 2637–2652.

Sunstein, Cass R. "Preferences and Politics," *Philosophy & Public Affairs*, vol. 20, #1, Winter 1991, 3–34.

———. "Social Norms and Social Roles." *Columbia Law Review*, vol. 96, 1996, 903–968.

Tavernise, Sabrina. "Fertility Rate Stabilizes as Economy Continues to Grow," *New York Times*, September 6, 2013.

Thomas, Judith Jarvis. "A Defense of Abortion," *Philosophy & Public Affairs*, vol. 1, #1, Autumn 1971, 47–66.

Tracy, Ben. "Carbon Dioxide Levels Highest in Recorded Human History." www. cbs.com/8301-18563_162_57883995/carbon-dioxide-levels-highest-in-recorded-human-history, May 10, 2013.

Tuck, Richard. *Natural Rights Theories*. Cambridge University Press (Cambridge) 1978.

Turner, Adair. "Population Ageing: What Should We Worry About?" *Philosophical Transactions of the Royal Society B*, vol. 364, October 2009, 3009–3021.

Trussell, James, Felicia Stewart, et al. "Should Oral Contraceptives Be Available without Prescription?" *American Journal of Public Health*, vol. 83, #8, 1993, 1094–1099.

United Nations, Department of Economics and Social Affairs, Population Division. *World Population Prospects: The 2010 Revision, Vol. II, Demographic Profiles*, 2011.

United Nations, Department of Economics and Social Affairs, Population Division. *World Population Prospects: The 2012 Revision, Vol. II, Demographic Profiles*, 2013.

United Nations Population Fund. *The State of the World Population, 2010–2011: People and Possibilities in a World of 7 Billion*. United Nations Population Fund (New York) 2011.

United Nations, UN-Habitat. *State of the World's Cities 2010-2011—Cities for All: Bridging the Urban Divide*, Earthscan (London) 2011.

United Nations Census Bureau. "Poverty: 2013 Highlights," http://www.census.gov/hhes/www/poverty/about/overview/.

USA Today. "Report: Average Price of a New Car Hits Record in August," August 2013, http://www.usatoday.com/story/money/cars/2013/09/04/record-price-new-car-august/2761341/.

Vedantam, Shankar. "Report on Global Ecosystems Calls for Radical Changes," *Washington Post*, March 30, 2005.

Wallace, Charles P. "Column One: Popular Population Control: Indonesia's Family Planning Program Has Become a Model for the World. A Mix of Moderation, Madison Avenue and Islamic Teachings Has Overcome Staggering Odds," *Los Angeles Times*, September 27, 1993.

Warner, Leif. "The Nature of Rights." *Philosophy and Public Affairs*, vol. 33, 2005, 223–252.

Warwick, Donald P. "The Ethics of Population Control." In *Population Policy*, ed. Godfrey Roberts. Praeger (New York) 1990.

Westman, Jack. *Licensing Parents: Can We Prevent Child Abuse and Neglect?* Insight Books/Plenum Press (New York) 1994.

Westoff, Charles F., and Akinrinola Bankole. "Mass Media and Reproductive Behavior in Africa." Demographic and Health Surveys: Analytical Reports No. 2, Macro International, Calverton, MD, 1997.

Wheelwright, Nathaniel T. "Enduring Reasons to Preserve Threatened Species," *Chronicle of Higher Education*, June 1, 1994.

Wilkinson, Richard, and Kate Pickett. *The Spirit Level: Why Greater Equality Makes Societies Stronger.* Bloomsbury Press (New York) 2010.

Wilson, E. O. "My Wish: Build the Encyclopedia of Life," March 2007, http://www.ted.com/talks/e_o_wilson_on_saving_life_on_earth/transcript?language=en.

Wiseman, Paul. "Richest 1 Per Cent Earn Biggest Share since '20's," *AP News*, September 2013.

World Bank. *Turn Down the Heat: Climate Extremes, Regional Impacts, and the Case for Resilience.* World Bank (Washington, DC) 2013.

World Bank. "Poverty Overview," http://www.worldbank.org/en/topic/poverty/overview.

World Bank. "World Bank Sees Progress against Extreme Poverty, but Flags Vulnerabilities." Press Release No. 2012/297/DEC. World Bank, Washington, DC, February 29, 2012.

World Wildlife Fund. *Living Planet Report 2014.*

Young, Thomas. "Overconsumption and Procreation: Are They Morally Equivalent?" *Journal of Applied Philosophy*, vol. 18, #2, 2001, 183–192.

Zabarenko, Deborah. "Human Warming Hobbles Ancient Climate Cycle," *Reuters*, April 27, 2008.

Zeebe, R. E. "Time-Dependent Climate Sensitivity and the Legacy of Anthropogenic Greenhouse Gas Emissions." *Proceedings of the National Academy of Sciences*, vol. 110, August 20, 2013, doi:10.1073/pnas.1222843110.

INDEX

abortion, 20, 24, 67–70, 80, 116–117, 132, 134–135, 165–178, 199, 210
    sex selective, 194–196, 200–201, 178. *See also* rights to abortion
Africa, 8, 12, 109
Amish, 85–86, 207
Aristotle, 222
autonomy, 5, 46, 65–66, 71–90, 91, 156, 177–178
    limits to, 87–90. *See also* rights to autonomy
aversion to change, 9–10, 11, 17, 86, 95, 172–173, 229

Becker, Gary, 196
Benatar, David, 116
Black Pete (Zwarte Piet), 207–208
Brock, Dan, 168
Brontë, Charlotte, 222

Callahan, Daniel, 92, 141
Catholic Church, 79, 86
China, 10, 20, 132, 148, 190, 193–194, 196–197, 211
Chung, Woojin, 201–202
climate change, 1, 5–8, 10, 26, 56, 106–109, 145–147, 218, 223, 225, 229
coercion. *See* laws, coercive

constitution
    Japan, 159
    Norway, 159
    United States, 33, 40, 46, 52, 83, 149
consumption, 5, 7–9, 14–18, 89, 147–148, 167, 170, 181–188, 227–228, 230
contraception, 3, 12, 20, 79–80, 84, 86–87, 109, 112–118, 122, 137, 149, 170, 218
    LARCs (long-lasting reversible contraception), 114
    over-the-counter, 114–115
    unmet need for, 115–116, 218–219
cultural survival, 24, 178–179, 204–209
    Netherlands, 207–208
    Russia, 204

Darwin, Charles, 227
Das Gupta, Monica, 201–202
Defense of Abortion, A, 67–70
demographic momentum, 11–12, 149, 179, 218
disincentives, 120
    tax penalty, 121–122, 129, 137
Douglas, William O., 40, 53
Dworkin, Gerald, 76
Dworkin, Ronald, 34

economy, 13–15, 23–24, 179–192, 204,
    212–213
  effects of population limits on, 23–24,
    131–132, 178, 179–192
education, 11, 20, 106–110, 137, 158,
    229–230
Ehrlich, Paul, 10, 149
Employment Division v. Smith, 82–84
environmental degradation, 1–2, 6, 7–9,
    11–16, 21–22, 96, 98, 106–107,
    146–151, 188, 210, 213, 224
equality. *See* inequality
eugenics, 45–46, 52–54
European Convention on Human Rights, 89

Falbo, Toni, 210
Feinberg, Joel, 107, 157
fertility rate, 3, 10–13, 17–18, 24, 112,
    115–116, 149, 190, 200, 205,
    219, 229
  Africa, 12, 109
  Asia, 138
  China, 148, 211–212
  Europe, 136, 148, 200
  Germany, 200
  Hungary, 200
  Indonesia, 112
  Romania, 200
  Uganda, 115
  United States, 11, 13, 136, 148–149,
    190, 200
Fong, Vanessa, 211–212
future people, 5, 21–23, 141–174. *See also*
    rights of future generations

grandma, killing, example, 96–97
Griffin, James, 72–73, 75
growth, 9
  economic, 23–24, 179–185, 188
  population, 190, 205–218, 226, 230
  slums, 22
gun on the playground, example, 151–152

habitat loss, 223–226
Haddix, Margaret Peterson, 131
Hobbes, Thomas, 8–9

hobby lobby, 85
Holmes, Oliver Wendell, 46, 93

identified vs. statistical victims, 171–172
immigration, 24, 190, 204–209
incentives, 110
  free contraception, 112–114, 116
  tax breaks, 20, 118–119
incremental harm, 96–98, 173
Indonesia, 112–113, 116
inequality, 16, 39, 39, 45–48, 52–57, 66, 86,
    90–92, 112, 183–184, 195–198, 220.
    See also rights to equal consideration
Intergovernmental Panel on Climate
    Change, 8, 146, 218

Jackson, Tim, 180–182, 185

Kant, Immanuel, 72–73
Klein, Naomi, 6

laws, 4, 19, 21, 41, 45–46, 50, 52–55, 61,
    67, 81, 88, 91, 97–98, 135–136, 159,
    164–165, 169
  coercive, 122–130
  necessity for, 123–127
  psychology of, 127–130, 229
  rationale for, 143–144
  religion and, 81–87
Locke, John, 66
  Letter Concerning Toleration, 80–84, 86
  Second Treatise, 67

Malthus, Thomas, 10, 11, 149–151
McAdams, Richard, 128
McKibben, Bill, 6, 65, 117, 122, 126
Mill, John Stuart, 88, 124
  Principles of Political Economy, 177, 182
Muir, John, 222

nature, value of, 26–27
  to humans, 221–224
  intrinsic, 224–227
negligence, 93–96
New York soda regulation, 91
nonidentity problem, 142, 161–170

Oliver, Mary, 217, 221–222, 225
only children, 179, 209–213
Overall, Christine, 6, 122
overpopulation, 148, 192

Paine, Thomas, 46
Panshin, Alexei, 131
Parfit, Derek, 162–164, 167
passing the buck, 173–174
Penner, J.E., 67
People and the Planet, 181
Peters, Philip, 169
Politics of Happiness, The, 188
pollution, 5, 96, 111, 147, 169
population, 2–3, 6–14, 16–18, 22, 28, 46,
    59, 108, 111, 122, 126, 132, 148–151,
    157, 161, 167–179, 193, 196, 206, 208,
    221, 226, 230
  growth, 5–11, 21, 23–24, 27, 103, 106,
    112, 138, 144, 148–149, 151–153, 167,
    179, 190, 198, 204–206, 218, 226
  limits, 6, 20, 27, 150
  over-, 2, 4, 26, 56, 86–89, 96, 97, 110,
    116–118, 132, 141–145, 149, 162, 166,
    174, 178, 192, 227
  sustainable, 18, 26, 149, 153, 174, 188,
    217, 220
  world, 7, 12, 107, 149, 181, 194, 218–219
privacy, 5, 28, 41, 89, 104–105, 114, 121,
    217, 230. *See also* rights to family life
propaganda, 109–110
property, 67–71, 77, 80, 133–134,
    142–143, 153
Putin, Vladimir, 24, 204

racism, 205–206
racist superscientist, example, 157
Raz, Joseph, 35
religion, 5, 19, 78–87, 117, 202
Religious Freedom Restoration Act, 84–85
retirement benefits, 178, 188–192
rights, 32–34
  to abortion, 67–70, 194–195
  to autonomy, 46, 56, 71–78, 177
  to basic welfare, 2, 34–36; criticisms
    of, 36–37

to control one's own body, 19, 65, 92
to equal consideration, 45–49,
    52–57, 89–92
to family life, 18, 41–45, 50–52
of future generations, 153–158
legal, 4, 33
property, 67–71
rationality-based, 35, 71–73, 75, 76, 110
to religious freedom, 79–90
Rite of Passage, 131
Robertson, John, 37–38
Royal Society of Great Britain, 181

sanctions, 20–21, 99, 130–137
  avoidance of, 105
  fines, 135–137
Sen, Amartya, 89
sex selection, 24–25, 178, 193–204
  Armenia, 194, 199
  Azerbaijan, 194, 199
  China, 194, 196–197, 199
  India, 194, 199, 201
  South Korea, 201–203
  United States, 193
sex trafficking, 197
sexism, 24–25, 196–203
Shadow Children, The, 131
Shiller, Robert J., 184
siblings, 25–26, 179, 209–213
Singapore, 109–111
Skinner, Jack T., 40, 53
Skinner v. Oklahoma, 40, 52–54
social security, 188–192
species
  diversity, 180
  extinction, 7, 26, 146, 182, 224–227
  preservation, 224–227
sterilization, 115–116
  China, 20, 132, 135
  Singapore, 111
  United States, 40, 56, 62–63

taxol, 223
Thomson, Judith Jarvis, 67–71
Thoreau, 222
trespasser, example, 133–134

United Nations, 7, 8, 12
United Nations Declaration of Human
    Rights, 18
United Nations Environment
    Program, 180
United States, 1, 10–13, 16, 33, 38, 45, 52,
    53, 79, 84, 85, 107, 114–116, 118, 128,
136, 146, 148, 170, 184, 188, 191,
    203, 207

Wheelwright, Nathaniel, 227
Wilson, E.O., 223
World Bank, 22, 184, 194
World Wildlife Fund, 224